Henri E. Bal   Boumediene Belkhouche
Luca Cardelli (Eds.)

# Internet
# Programming Languages

ICCL'98 Workshop
Chicago, IL, USA, May 13, 1998
Proceedings

T0223246

Springer

Series Editors

Gerhard Goos, Karlsruhe University, Germany
Juris Hartmanis, Cornell University, NY, USA
Jan van Leeuwen, Utrecht University, The Netherlands

Volume Editors

Henri E. Bal
Vrije Universiteit, Department of Mathematics and Computer Science
De Boelelaan 1081a, 1081 HV Amsterdam, The Netherlands
E-mail: bal@cs.vu.nl

Boumediene Belkhouche
Tulane University, EECS Department
New Orleans, LA 70118, USA
E-mail: bb@eecs.tulane.edu

Luca Cardelli
Microsoft Research
1 Guildhall St, Cambridge CB2 3NH, UK
E-mail: luca@luca.demon.co.uk

Cataloging-in-Publication data applied for

Die Deutsche Bibliothek - CIP-Einheitsaufnahme

Internet programming languages : proceedings ; workshop / ICCL'98, Chicago, IL,
USA, May 13, 1998. Henri E. Bal ... (ed.). - Berlin ; Heidelberg ; New York ;
Barcelona ; Hong Kong ; London ; Milan ; Paris ; Singapore ; Tokyo : Springer,
1999
(Lecture notes in computer science ; Vol. 1686)
ISBN 3-540-66673-7

CR Subject Classification (1998): D.3, F.3, C.2, D.1.3, D.4.6, F.1.2

ISSN 0302-9743
ISBN 3-540-66673-7 Springer-Verlag Berlin Heidelberg New York

© Springer-Verlag Berlin Heidelberg 1999
Printed in Germany

Typesetting: Camera-ready by author
SPIN: 10704410    06/3142 – 5 4 3 2 1 0    Printed on acid-free paper

# Preface

This book is a collection of articles about the influence that the recent greater scope and availability of wide area networks is having on the semantics, design, and implementation of programming languages. The Internet has long provided a global computing infrastructure but, for most of its history, there has not been much interest in programming languages tailored specifically to that infrastructure. More recently, the Web has produced a widespread interest in global resources and, as a consequence, in global programmability. It is now commonplace to discuss how programs can be made to run effectively and securely over the Internet.

The Internet has already revolutionized the distribution and access of information, and is in the process of transforming commerce and other areas of fundamental importance. In the field of programming languages, the Internet is having a deep revitalizing effect, by challenging many fundamental assumptions and requiring the development of new concepts, programming constructs, implementation techniques, and applications. This book is a snapshot of current research in this active area.

The articles in this book were presented at the Workshop on Internet Programming Languages, which was held on May 13, 1998 at Loyola University, Chicago, USA. The papers submitted to the workshop were screened by the editors. After the workshop, the presented papers were refereed by an external reviewer and one of the editors, resulting in the current selection.

This workshop provided a forum for the discussions of all aspects of computer languages for wide area systems, including specification languages, programming languages, semantics, implementation technologies, and application experience.

Together the papers give a good impression of active research topics in this area. Mobility is one theme that is touched by several of the papers, either in the form of mobile objects, mobile agents, computation migration, or Tuple Space migration. Also, agent technology, communication constructs, security, and fault tolerance are important issues addressed in many papers. Finally, the papers clearly show that Internet programming languages are a fruitful research area for theoretical and experimental, as well as application-driven work.

The paper *"Location-Independent Communication for Mobile Agents: A Two-Level Architecture"* by Peter Sewell, Paweł T. Wojciechowski, and Benjamin C. Pierce presents a two-level calculus for distributed computation. The low-level calculus can be fairly directly implemented on existing distributed infrastructures, while the high-level calculus, which includes location-independent communication primitives between mobile agents, is implemented on top of the low-level calculus. The critical high-level primitive is the reliable delivery of a message to an agent, wherever the agent is. Two infrastructure algorithms are described for the location-independent delivery of messages to mobile agents. The first algorithm uses a simple centralized database of agents and their current locations. The second algorithm has distributed site maps where each site maintains forwarding pointers for agents that have left. Both algorithms are described as formal translations from the high-level to the low-level calculus. The meaning of the calculi, and hence of the algorithms, is precisely given using the standard techniques of process semantics.

The paper *"A Lightweight Object Migration Protocol"* by Peter Van Roy, Per Brand, Seif Haridi, and Raphaël Collet describes a fault-tolerant protocol that supports lightweight mobile objects. The resulting model ensures that the two basic requirements, centralized semantics and predictable network behavior, are supported. To achieve this, issues of distributed execution, freely mobile objects, and fault-tolerant protocol are addressed. A distribution graph models the various language entities that are subject to distributed execution. Lightweight mobility is achieved by maintaining local copies of the code and by lazily copying the state. Finally, a distributed algorithm to implement the fault-tolerant protocol is described.

The paper *"Seal: A Framework for Secure Mobile Computations"* by Jan Vitek and Giuseppe Castagna presents the Seal calculus, a process calculus with hierarchical protection domains. The paper discusses the requirements for modeling Internet computation, including comparisons with other well-known concurrent formalisms. The Seal calculus is proposed as a foundation for computation over the Internet, and it includes, in particular, sophisticated mobility and security mechanisms. In this framework, communication may be local within a domain, or cross a domain boundary, in which case it is subject to policy controls. As a special case of communication, processes (and process hierarchies) may be moved from place to place. Seals have great control on interactions that happen within them; for example, communication and migration must be explicitly enabled and agreed upon by all parties.

The paper *"A Run-Time System for WCL"* by Antony Rowstron and Stuart Wray describes a coordination language (WCL) for Internet and Web-based agent systems. WCL is based on the Tuple Space model introduced by Linda and gives support for distributed (rather than parallel) applications. WCL supports several additional Tuple Space primitives, such as asynchronous communication and bulk data transfers. The paper describes an experimental run-time system for WCL, supporting tuple space migration. Also, it gives performance results on a distributed system running at three sites in the UK and Germany.

The paper *"PML: A Language Interface to Distributed Voice-Response Units"* by J. Christopher Ramming describes the design and implementation of a Phone Markup Language (PML). PML is used to program interfaces for Voice Response Units (VRU). PML is an imperative language that is based on HTML, but is intended for use in speech contexts. The paper introduces the basic constructs of PML and describes its abstract syntax. Issues, such as efficiency, static analysis, safety, and security are among the requirements that PML implements. An example that illustrates the use of PML is provided.

The paper *"Derivatives: A Construct for Internet Programming"* by Dominic Duggan describes a novel communication construct: a non-blocking receive operation that allows execution to continue speculatively, based on assumptions about the received value (such speculative value is called a derivative). A "case" construct, examining a derivative, introduces a rollback point that is activated if the value that eventually replaces the derivative is not the expected one. A "sendout" construct provides a non-rollbackable action. The paper describes the formal semantics of derivatives and, in particular, a semantics for rollback, which is a complex concept that is often useful in distributed algorithms.

The paper *"Network Programming Using PLAN"* by Michael Hicks, Pankaj Kakkar, Jonathan T. Moore, Carl A. Gunter and Scott Nettles discusses a programming language for active networks. An active network allows users to add functionality to network routers, but a key issue is how to do this in a secure way. PLAN (Packet Language for Active Networks) is a simple language that is limited enough to allow a secure implementation, yet flexible enough to support several interesting applications of active networks. The paper describes the language and several applications, including a tracerouter, multicast, and adaptive routing.

The referees that assisted us in the selection process were:

Cedric Fournet, Microsoft Research, UK
Andrew D. Gordon, Microsoft Research, UK
Wilhelm Hasselbring, Tilburg University, The Netherlands
James Jennings, Tulane University, USA
Orlando Karam, Tulane University, USA
Gilles Muller, INRIA/IRISA, France
John H. Reppy, Bell Laboratories, Lucent Technologies, USA
Nicole Terry, Tulane University, USA
Maarten van Steen, Vrije Universiteit Amsterdam, The Netherlands
Scott William, Tulane University, USA

July 1999

Henri Bal
Boumediene Belkhouche
Luca Cardelli

# Contents

Location-Independent Communication for Mobile Agents:
A Two-Level Architecture ................................................................................. 1
*Peter Sewell, Paweł T. Wojciechowski and Benjamin C. Pierce*

A Lightweight Object Migration Protocol ...................................................... 32
*Peter Van Roy, Per Brand, Seif Haridi and Raphaël Collet*

Seal: A Framework for Secure Mobile Computations ................................. 47
*Jan Vitek and Giuseppe Castagna*

A Run-Time System for WCL .......................................................................... 78
*Antony Rowstron and Stuart Wray*

PML: A Language Interface to Distributed Voice-Response Units ........... 97
*J. Christopher Ramming*

Derivatives: A Construct for Internet Programming ................................. 113
*Dominic Duggan*

Network Programming Using PLAN ............................................................. 127
*Michael Hicks, Pankaj Kakkar, Jonathan T. Moore, Carl A. Gunter and
Scott Nettles*

# Location-Independent Communication for Mobile Agents: A Two-Level Architecture

Peter Sewell[1]    Paweł T. Wojciechowski[1]

Benjamin C. Pierce[2]

**Abstract.** We study communication primitives for interaction between mobile agents. They can be classified into two groups. At a low level there are *location dependent* primitives that require a programmer to know the current site of a mobile agent in order to communicate with it. At a high level there are *location independent* primitives that allow communication with a mobile agent irrespective of its current site and of any migrations. Implementation of these requires delicate distributed infrastructure. We propose a simple calculus of agents that allows implementations of such distributed infrastructure algorithms to be expressed as encodings, or compilations, of the whole calculus into the fragment with only location dependent communication. These encodings give executable descriptions of the algorithms, providing a clean implementation strategy for prototype languages. The calculus is equipped with a precise semantics, providing a solid basis for understanding the algorithms and for reasoning about their correctness and robustness. Two sample infrastructure algorithms are presented as encodings.

## Table of Contents

1    Introduction
2    The Calculi
     2.1    Low-Level Calculus
     2.2    High-Level Calculus
     2.3    Examples and Idioms
3    A Simple Infrastructure Translation
4    A Forwarding-Pointers Infrastructure Translation
5    Reduction Semantics
6    Discussion
     6.1    Infrastructure Description
     6.2    Related Calculi
     6.3    Implementation
     6.4    Future Work

---

[1] Computer Laboratory, University of Cambridge.
{Peter.Sewell,Pawel.Wojciechowski}@cl.cam.ac.uk
[2] Dept. of Computer & Information Science, University of Pennsylvania.
bcpierce@cis.upenn.edu

# 1 Introduction

Recent years have seen an explosion of interest in wide-area distributed applications, executing on intranets or on the global internet. A key concept for structuring such applications is *mobile agents*, units of executing code that can migrate between sites [CHK97]. Mobile agent programming requires novel forms of language and runtime support—for interaction between agents, responding to network failures and reconfigurations, binding to resources, managing security, etc. In this paper we focus on the first of these, considering the design, semantic definition, and implementation of communication primitives by which mobile agents can interact.

Mobile agent communication primitives can be classified into two groups. At a low level, there are *location dependent* primitives that require a programmer to know the current site of a mobile agent in order to communicate with it. If a party to such communications migrates, then the communicating program must explicitly track its new location. At a high level, there are *location independent* primitives that allow communication with a mobile agent irrespective of its current site and of any migrations of sender or receiver. Location independent primitives may greatly simplify the development of mobile applications, since they allow movement and interaction to be treated as separate concerns. Their design and implementation, however, raise several difficult issues. A distributed infrastructure is required for tracking migrations and routing messages to migrating agents. This infrastructure must address fundamental network issues such as failures, network latency, locality, and concurrency; the algorithms involved are thus inherently rather delicate and cannot provide perfect location independence. Moreover, applications may be distributed on widely different scales (from local to wide-area networks), may exhibit different patterns of communication and migration, and may demand different levels of performance and robustness; these varying demands will lead to a multiplicity of infrastructures, based on a variety of algorithms. These *infrastructure algorithms* will be exposed, via their performance and behaviour under failure, to the application programmer — some detailed understanding of an algorithm will be required for the programmer to understand its robustness properties under, for example, failure of a site.

The need for clear understanding and easy experimentation with infrastructure algorithms, as well as the desire to simultaneously support multiple infrastructures on the same network, suggests a two-level architecture—a low-level consisting of a single set of well-understood, location-dependent primitives, in terms of which a variety of high-level, location-independent communication abstractions may be expressed. This two-level approach enables one to have a standardized low-level runtime that is common to many machines, with divergent high-level facilities chosen and installed at run time. It also facilitates simple implementation of the location-independent primitives (cf. protocol stacks).

For this approach to be realistic, it is essential that the low-level primitives should be directly implementable above standard network protocols. The Internet Protocol (IP) supports asynchronous, unordered, point-to-point, unreliable packet delivery; it abstracts from routing. We choose primitives that are directly implementable using asynchronous, unordered, point-to-point, reliable messages. This abstracts away from a multitude of additional details—error correction, retransmission, packet fragmentation, etc.—while still retaining a clear relationship to the well-understood IP level. It also well suited to the process calculus presentation that we use below. More controversially, we also include agent migration among the low-level primitives. This requires substantial runtime support in individual network sites, but not sophisticated distributed algorithms—only one message need be sent per migration. By treating it as a low-level primitive we focus attention more sharply on the distributed algorithms supporting location-independent communication. We also provide low-level primitives for agent creation, for sending messages between agents at the same site, for generating globally unique names, and for local computation.

Many forms of high-level communication can be implemented in terms of these low-level primitives, for example synchronous and asynchronous message passing, remote procedure calls, multicasting to agent groups, etc. For this paper we consider only a single representative form: an asynchronous message-passing primitive similar to the low-level primitive for communication between co-located agents but independent of their locations and transparent to migrations.

This two-level framework can be formulated very cleanly using techniques from the theory of process calculi. Such a formulation permits a precise definition of both low and high levels, and allows distributed infrastructure algorithms to be treated rigorously as translations between calculi. The operational semantics of the calculi provides a precise and clear understanding of the algorithms' behaviour, aiding design, and ultimately, one may hope, supporting proofs of correctness and robustness. Our presentation draws on ideas first developed in Milner, Parrow, and Walker's $\pi$-calculus [MPW92,Mil92] and extended in the distributed join-calculus of Fournet et al [FGL+96].

To facilitate experimentation, the *Nomadic Pict* project is implementing prototype mobile agent programming languages corresponding to our high- and low-level process calculi. The low-level language extends the compiler and run-time system of *Pict* [PT97,Tur96], a concurrent language based on the $\pi$-calculus, to support our primitives for agent creation, migration, and location-dependent communication. High-level languages, with particular infrastructures for location-independent communication, can then be obtained by applying user-supplied translations into the low-level language. In both cases, the full language available to the user remains very close to the process calculus presentation, and can be given rigorous semantics in a similar style. Analogous extensions could be given for other concurrent uniprocessor programming languages, such as Amber [Car86], Concurrent ML [Rep91], and Concurrent Haskell [JGF96].

In the next section we introduce the two calculi informally, discussing our primitives in detail and giving examples of common programming idioms. In §3 and §4 we then present two sample infrastructure algorithms — one using a centralised server and one using chains of forwarding pointers — as illustrations of the use of the calculi. The operational semantics of the calculi are defined precisely in §5, in terms of a reduction semantics. We conclude with some further discussion of related work, implementation, and future extensions. The paper develops ideas first presented in [SWP98] — that work introduced a slightly different calculus, using it to describe the forwarding-pointers infrastructure.

## 2 The Calculi

In this section our two levels of abstraction are made precise by giving two corresponding process calculi, the low- and high-level *Nomadic $\pi$-calculi*. Their design involves a delicate trade-off — the distributed infrastructure algorithms that we want to express involve non-trivial local computation within agents, yet for the theory to be tractable (particularly, for operational congruences to have tractable characterisations) the calculi must be kept as simple as possible. The primitives for agent creation, agent migration and inter-agent communication that we consider do not suffice to allow the required local computation to be expressed clearly, so we integrate them with those of an asynchronous $\pi$-calculus [HT91,Bou92]. The other computational constructs that will be needed, e.g. for finite maps, can then be regarded as lightweight syntactic sugar for $\pi$-processes.

The low- and high-level calculi are introduced in §2.1 and §2.2 respectively, followed by some examples and programming idioms in §2.3. In this section the operational semantics of the calculi are described informally — the precise reduction semantics will be given in §5. For simplicity, the calculi are presented without typing or basic values (such as integers and booleans). Type systems are briefly discussed in §6.3.

### 2.1 Low-Level Calculus

We begin with an example. Below is a term of the low-level calculus showing how an applet server can be expressed. It can receive (on the channel named *getApplet*) requests for an applet; the requests contain a pair (bound to $a$ and $s$) consisting of the name of the requesting agent and the name of its site.

$$
\begin{aligned}
&*getApplet?(a\ s) \rightarrow \\
&\quad \textbf{agent } b = \\
&\quad\quad \textbf{migrate to } s \rightarrow (\langle a@s \rangle ack!b \mid B) \\
&\quad \textbf{in} \\
&\quad\quad 0
\end{aligned}
$$

When a request is received the server creates an applet agent with a new name bound to $b$. This agent immediately migrates to site $s$. It then sends an acknowledgement to the requesting agent $a$ (which is assumed to also be on site $s$) containing its name. In parallel, the body $B$ of the applet commences execution.

The example illustrates the main entities represented in the calculus: sites, agents and channels. *Sites* should be thought of as physical machines or, more accurately, as instantiations of the Nomadic Pict runtime system on machines; each site has a unique name. This paper does not explicitly address questions of site failure, network failure and reconfiguration, or security. Sites are therefore unstructured; neither network topology nor administrative domains are represented in the formalism. *Agents* are units of executing code; an agent has a unique name and a body consisting of some term; at any moment it is located at a particular site. *Channels* support communication within agents, and also provide targets for inter-agent communication—an inter-agent message will be sent to a particular channel within the destination agent. Channels also have unique names.

The inter-agent message $\langle a@s \rangle ack!b$ is characteristic of the low-level calculus. It is location-dependent—if agent $a$ is in fact on site $s$ then the message $b$ will be delivered, to channel $ack$ in $a$; otherwise the message will be discarded. In an implementation at most one inter-site message is sent.

*Names* As in the $\pi$-calculus, names play a key rôle. We take an infinite set $\mathcal{N}$ of names, ranged over by $a, b, c, s$, and $x$. Formally, all names are treated identically; informally, $a$ and $b$ will be used for agent names, $c$ for a channel name, and $s$ for a site name. (A type system would allow these distinctions to be enforced.) The calculus allows new names (of agents and channels) to be created dynamically.

Names are *pure*, in the sense of Needham [Nee89]; they are not assumed to contain any information about their creation. They can therefore be implemented by any mechanism that allows globally-unique bit strings to be created locally, e.g. by appending sequence numbers to IP addresses, or by choosing large random numbers.

*Values* We allow the communication of first-order values, consisting of names and tuples.

$$u, v ::= x \qquad\qquad\qquad \text{name}$$
$$\phantom{u, v ::=} [v_1 .. v_n] \qquad\qquad \text{tuple } (n \geq 0)$$

*Patterns* As is the $\pi$-calculus, values are deconstructed by pattern matching on input. Patterns have the same form as values, with the addition of a wildcard.

$$p ::= \_ \qquad\qquad\qquad \text{wildcard}$$
$$\phantom{p ::=} x \qquad\qquad\qquad \text{name pattern}$$
$$\phantom{p ::=} (p_1 .. p_n) \qquad\qquad \text{tuple pattern } (n \geq 0, \text{ no repeated names})$$

*Process terms* The main syntactic category is that of *process terms*, ranged over by $P, Q$. We will introduce the low-level primitives in groups.

> **agent** $a = P$ **in** $Q$      agent creation
> **migrate to** $s \rightarrow P$      agent migration

The execution of the construct **agent** $a = P$ **in** $Q$ spawns a new agent on the current site, with body $P$. After the creation, $Q$ commences execution, in parallel with the rest of the body of the spawning agent. The new agent has a unique name which may be referred to both in its body and in the spawning agent (i.e.

$a$ is binding in $P$ and $Q$). Agents can migrate to named sites — the execution of **migrate to** $s \rightarrow P$ as part of an agent results in the whole agent migrating to site $s$. After the migration, $P$ commences execution in parallel with the rest of the body of the agent.

| | |
|---|---|
| $P \mid Q$ | parallel composition |
| $0$ | nil |

The body of an agent may consist of many process terms in parallel, i.e. essentially of many lightweight threads. They will interact only by message passing.

| | |
|---|---|
| **new** $c$ **in** $P$ | new channel name creation |
| $c!v$ | output $v$ on channel $c$ in the current agent |
| $c?p \rightarrow P$ | input from channel $c$ |
| $*c?p \rightarrow P$ | replicated input from channel $c$ |
| **if** $u = v$ **then** $P$ **else** $Q$ | value equality testing |

To express computation within an agent, while keeping a lightweight semantics, we include $\pi$-calculus-style interaction primitives. Execution of **new** $c$ **in** $P$ creates a new unique channel name; $c$ is binding in $P$. An output $c!v$ (of value $v$ on channel $c$) and an input $c?p \rightarrow P$ in the same agent may synchronise, resulting in $P$ with the names in the pattern $p$ replaced by corresponding parts of $v$. A replicated input $*c?p \rightarrow P$ behaves similarly except that it persists after the synchronisation, and so may receive another value. In both $c?p \rightarrow P$ and $*c?p \rightarrow P$ the names in $p$ are binding in $P$. The conditional allows any two values to be tested for equality.

**iflocal** $\langle a \rangle c!v \rightarrow P$ **else** $Q$     test-and-send to agent $a$ on current site

Finally, the low-level calculus includes a single primitive for interaction between agents. The execution of **iflocal** $\langle a \rangle c!v \rightarrow P$ **else** $Q$ in the body of an agent $b$ has two possible outcomes. If agent $a$ is on the same site as $b$, then the message $c!v$ will be delivered to $a$ (where it may later interact with an input) and $P$ will commence execution in parallel with the rest of the body of $b$; otherwise the message will be discarded, and $Q$ will execute as part of $b$. The construct is analogous to test-and-set operations in shared memory systems — delivering the message and starting $P$, or discarding it and starting $Q$, atomically. It can greatly simplify algorithms that involve communication with agents that may migrate away at any time, yet is still implementable locally, by the runtime system on each site.

As in the $\pi$-calculus, names can be *scope-extruded* — here channel and agent names can be sent outside the agent in which they were created. For example, if the body of agent $a$ is

$$
\begin{aligned}
&\textbf{agent } b = \\
&\quad \textbf{new } d \textbf{ in} \\
&\qquad \textbf{iflocal } \langle a \rangle c!d \rightarrow 0 \textbf{ else } 0 \\
&\quad \textbf{in} \\
&\qquad c?x \rightarrow x!
\end{aligned}
$$

then channel name $d$ is created in agent $b$. After the output message $c!d$ has been sent from $b$ to $a$ (by **iflocal**) and has interacted with the input $c?x \to x!$ there will be an output $d!$ in agent $a$.

We require a clear relationship between the semantics of the low-level calculus and the inter-machine messages that would be sent in an implementation. To achieve this we allow communication between outputs and inputs on a channel only if they are *in the same agent* — messages can be sent from one agent to another only by **iflocal**. Intuitively, there is a distinct $\pi$-calculus-style channel for each channel name in every agent. For example, if the body of agent $a$ is

$$
\begin{aligned}
&\textbf{agent } b = \\
&\quad \textbf{new } d \textbf{ in} \\
&\qquad d? \to 0 \\
&\qquad \mid \textbf{iflocal } \langle a \rangle c!d \to 0 \textbf{ else } 0 \\
&\quad \textbf{in} \\
&\qquad c?x \to x!
\end{aligned}
$$

then after some reduction steps $a$ contains an output on $d$ and $b$ contains an input on $d$, but these cannot react. At first sight this semantics may seem counter-intuitive, but it reconciles the conflicting requirements of expressiveness and simplicity of the calculus. An implementation would create the mailbox datastructure — a queue of pending outputs or inputs — required to implement a channel as required; it could be garbage collected when empty.

Summarizing, the terms of the low-level calculus are:

| $P, Q ::=$ | **agent** $a = P$ **in** $Q$ | agent creation |
|---|---|---|
| | **migrate to** $s \to P$ | agent migration |
| | $P \mid Q$ | parallel composition |
| | $0$ | nil |
| | **new** $c$ **in** $P$ | new channel name creation |
| | $c!v$ | output $v$ on channel $c$ in the current agent |
| | $c?p \to P$ | input from channel $c$ |
| | $*c?p \to P$ | replicated input from channel $c$ |
| | **if** $u = v$ **then** $P$ **else** $Q$ | value equality testing |
| | **iflocal** $\langle a \rangle c!v \to P$ **else** $Q$ | test-and-send to agent $a$ on current site |

Note that the only primitive which involves network communication is **migrate**, which requires only a single message to be sent, asynchronously, between machines. Distributed implementation of the low-level calculus is therefore straightforward, requiring no non-trivial distributed algorithms. It could be done either above a reliable datagram layer or above TCP, using a lightweight layer that opens and closes streams as required.

Two other forms of location-dependent output will be useful in writing encodings, and are expressible in the calculus given.

| $\langle a \rangle c!v$ | output to agent $a$ on the current site |
|---|---|
| $\langle a@s \rangle c!v$ | output to agent $a$ on site $s$ |

The execution of an output $\langle a \rangle c!v$ in the body of an agent $b$ will either deliver the message $c!v$ to agent $a$, if agent $b$ is on the same site as $a$, or will silently discard the message, if not. The execution of an output $\langle a@s \rangle c!v$ in the body of an agent will either deliver the message $c!v$ to agent $a$, if agent $a$ is on site $s$, or will silently discard the message, if not. We regard these as syntactic sugar for

**iflocal** $\langle a \rangle c!v \rightarrow 0$ **else** $0$

and

**agent** $b = (\textbf{migrate to } s \rightarrow (\textbf{iflocal } \langle a \rangle c!v \rightarrow 0 \textbf{ else } 0))$ **in** $0$

(where $b$ is fresh) respectively. In an implementation, the first is implementable locally; the second requires only one asynchronous network message. Note that one could optimize the case in which the second is used on site $s$ itself by trying **iflocal** first:

**iflocal** $\langle a \rangle c!v \rightarrow$
    $0$
**else**
    **agent** $b = (\textbf{migrate to } s \rightarrow (\textbf{iflocal } \langle a \rangle c!v \rightarrow 0 \textbf{ else } 0))$ **in** $0$

## 2.2 High-Level Calculus

The high-level calculus is obtained by extending the low-level calculus with a single location-independent communication primitive:

$\langle a@? \rangle c!v$                        location-independent output to agent $a$

The intended semantics of an output $\langle a@? \rangle c!v$ is that its execution will reliably deliver the message $c!v$ to agent $a$, irrespective of the current site of $a$ and of any migrations.

## 2.3 Examples and Idioms

We give some syntactic sugar and programming idioms that will be used in the translations. Most are standard $\pi$-calculus idioms; some involve distributed communication.

*Syntactic sugar* Empty tuples and tuple patterns will generally be elided, writing $c!$ and $c? \rightarrow P$ for $c![]$ and $c?() \rightarrow P$. Multiple new channel bindings will be coalesced, writing **new** $c, c'$ **in** $P$ for **new** $c$ **in new** $c'$ **in** $P$. Let-declarations will be used, writing **let** $p = v$ **in** $P$ for **new** $c$ **in** $c!v \,|\, c?p \rightarrow P$ (where $c$ is a name not occurring free in $v$ or $P$).

*Procedures* Within a single agent one can express 'procedures' as simple replicated inputs. Below is a first attempt at a pair-server, that receives values $x$ on channel *pair* and returns two copies of $x$ on channel *result*, together with a single invocation of the server.

$$\textbf{new } pair, result \textbf{ in}$$
$$*pair?x \rightarrow result![x\ x]$$
$$|\ pair!v$$
$$|\ result?z \rightarrow \ldots z \ldots$$

This pair-server can only be invoked sequentially—there is no association between multiple requests and their corresponding results. A better idiom is below, in which new result channels are used for each invocation.

$$\textbf{new } pair \textbf{ in}$$
$$*pair?(x\ r) \rightarrow r![x\ x]$$
$$|\ \textbf{new } result \textbf{ in } pair![v\ result]\,|\,result?z \rightarrow \ldots z \ldots$$
$$|\ \textbf{new } result \textbf{ in } pair![w\ result]\,|\,result?z \rightarrow \ldots z \ldots$$

The example can easily be lifted to remote procedure calls between agents. We show two versions, firstly for location-dependent RPC between static agents and secondly for location-independent RPC between agents that may be migrating. In the first, the server becomes

$$\textbf{new } pair \textbf{ in}$$
$$*pair?(x\ r\ b\ s) \rightarrow \langle b@s \rangle r![x\ x]$$

which returns the result using location-dependent communication to the agent $b$ on site $s$ received in the request. If the server is part of agent $a_1$ on site $s_1$ it would be invoked from agent $a_2$ on site $s_2$ by

$$\textbf{new } result \textbf{ in}$$
$$\langle a_1@s_1 \rangle pair![v\ result\ a_2\ s_2]$$
$$|\ result?z \rightarrow \ldots z \ldots$$

If agents $a_1$ or $a_2$ can migrate this can fail. A more robust idiom is easily expressible in the high-level calculus—the server becomes

$$\textbf{new } pair \textbf{ in}$$
$$*pair?(x\ r\ b) \rightarrow \langle b@? \rangle r![x\ x]$$

which returns the result using location-independent communication to the agent $b$. If the server is part of agent $a_1$ it would be invoked from agent $a_2$ by

$$\textbf{new } result \textbf{ in}$$
$$\langle a_1@? \rangle pair![v\ result\ a_2]$$
$$|\ result?z \rightarrow \ldots z \ldots$$

*Locks, methods and objects* An agent consisting of a parallel composition of replicated inputs, such as

$$*method1?arg \rightarrow \ldots$$
$$| \ *method2?arg \rightarrow \ldots$$

is analogous to an object with methods *method1* and *method2*. Mutual exclusion between the bodies of the methods can be enforced by using a lock channel:

> **new** *lock* **in**
>> *lock*!
>> | *method1?arg →
>>> *lock*? →
>>>> . . .
>>> *lock*!
>> | *method2?arg →
>>> *lock*? →
>>>> . . .
>>> *lock*!

Here the lock is free if there is an output on channel *lock* and not free otherwise. State that is shared between the methods can be conveniently kept as the value of the output on the lock channel:

> **new** *lock* **in**
>> *lock*!*initialState*
>> | *method1?arg →
>>> *lock*?*state* →
>>>> . . .
>>> *lock*!*state'*
>> | *method2?arg →
>>> *lock*?*state* →
>>>> . . .
>>> *lock*!*state''*

For more detailed discussion of object representations in process calculi, the reader is referred to [PT94].

*Finite maps* The algorithms given in the following two sections involve finite maps — in the first, there is a daemon maintaining a map from agent names to site names; in the second, there are daemons maintaining maps from agent names to lock channels. The translations make use of the following constructs:

| | |
|---|---|
| *c*!**emptymap** | output the empty map on channel *c* |
| **lookup** *a* **in** *m* **with**<br>   **found**(*p*) → *P*<br>   **notfound** → *Q* | look up *a* in map *m* |
| **let** *m'* = (*m* **with** *a* ↦ *v*) **in** *P* | add a new binding |

Our calculi are sufficiently expressive to allow these to be expressed directly, in a standard $\pi$-calculus style — we regard the constructs as syntactic sugar for the three process terms below. In the second and third the names $x$, *found*, and *notfound* are assumed not to occur free in $P$, $Q$, or $a$.

$$c!\text{emptymap} \;\stackrel{def}{=}\; \textbf{new } m \textbf{ in}$$
$$c!m$$
$$|\; *m?(x\,found\,notfound) \to notfound!$$

$$\textbf{lookup}\ldots \;\stackrel{def}{=}\; \textbf{new } found,\ notfound \textbf{ in}$$
$$m![a\,found\,notfound]$$
$$|\; found?p \to P$$
$$|\; notfound? \to Q$$

$$\textbf{let}\ldots \;\stackrel{def}{=}\; \textbf{new } m' \textbf{ in}$$
$$*m'?(x\,found\,notfound) \to$$
$$\textbf{if } x = a \textbf{ then}$$
$$found!v$$
$$\textbf{else}$$
$$m![x\,found\,notfound]$$
$$|\; P$$

These represent a finite map as a channel on which there is a process that receives lookup requests. Requests consist of a triple of a key and two result channels; the process returns a value on the first if the lookup succeeds, and otherwise signals on the second.

## 3   A Simple Infrastructure Translation

In this section and the following one we present two infrastructure algorithms, expressed as translations. The first is one of the simplest algorithms possible, highly sequential and with a centralized server daemon; the second is one step more sophisticated, with multiple daemons maintaining forwarding-pointer chains. The algorithms have been chosen to illustrate our approach, and the use of the calculi — algorithms that are widely applicable to actual mobile agent systems would have to be yet more delicate, both for efficiency and for robustness under partial failure. Even the simplest of our algorithms, however, requires delicate synchronization that (the authors can attest) is easy to get wrong; expressing them as translations between well-defined calculi provides a solid basis for discussion and algorithm design.

The algorithm presented in this section involves a central daemon that keeps track of the current sites of all agents and forwards any location-independent messages to them. The daemon is itself implemented as an agent which never migrates; the translation of a program then consists roughly of the daemon agent in parallel with a compositional translation of the program. For simplicity we consider only programs that are initiated as single agents, rather than many agents initiated separately on different sites. (Programs may, of course, begin by creating other agents that immediately migrate). The precise definition is given in Figures 1 and 2. Figure 2 defines a top-level translation $[\![\,]\!]$. For each term $P$ of the high-level calculus, considered as the body of an agent named $a$ and initiated at site $s$, the result $[\![P]\!]_{a,s}$ of the translation is a term of the low-level calculus. The definition of $[\![\,]\!]$ involves the body $Daemon$ of the daemon agent and an auxiliary compositional translation $[\![P]\!]_a$, defined phrase-by-phrase, of $P$ considered as part of the body of agent $a$. Both are given in Figure 1.

Let us look first at the daemon. It contains three replicated inputs, on the *register*, *migrating*, and *message* channels, for receiving messages from the encodings of agents. The daemon is essentially single-threaded — the channel *lock* is used to enforce mutual exclusion between the bodies of the replicated inputs, and the code preserves the invariant that at any time there is at most one output on *lock*. The *lock* channel is also used to maintain the site map — a finite map from agent names to site names, recording the current site of every agent. The body of each replicated input begins with an input on *lock*, thereby acquiring both the lock and the site map.

Turning to the compositional translation $[\![\_]\!]_a$, only three clauses are not trivial — for the location-independent output, agent creation, and agent migration primitives. We discuss each, together with their interactions with the daemon, in turn.

*Location-independent output*  A location-independent output in an agent $a$ is implemented simply by using a location-dependent output to send a request to the daemon $D$, at its site $SD$, on its channel *message*:

$$[\![\langle b@?\rangle c!v]\!]_a = \langle D@SD\rangle message![b\ c\ v]$$

The corresponding replicated input on channel *message* in the daemon

$$
\begin{aligned}
&|\ *message?(a\ c\ v) \rightarrow \\
&\quad lock?m \rightarrow \\
&\quad \textbf{lookup}\ a\ \textbf{in}\ m\ \textbf{with} \\
&\quad \textbf{found}(s) \rightarrow \\
&\qquad \langle a@s\rangle deliver![c\ v] \\
&\qquad |\ dack? \rightarrow lock!m \\
&\quad \textbf{notfound} \rightarrow 0
\end{aligned}
$$

first acquires the lock and current site map $m$, then looks up the target agent's site in the map and sends a location-dependent message to the *deliver* channel of that agent. It then waits to receive an acknowledgement (on the *dack* channel) from the agent before relinquishing the lock. This prevents the agent migrating before the *deliver* message arrives. Note that the **notfound** branch of the lookup will never be taken, as the algorithm ensures that all agents register before messages can be sent to them. The inter-agent communications involved

$$[\langle b@?\rangle c!v]_a = \langle D@SD\rangle\, message![b\ c\ v]$$

$$[\textbf{agent } b = P \textbf{ in } Q]_a = currentloc?s \rightarrow$$
$$\qquad \textbf{agent } b =$$
$$\qquad\qquad *deliver?(c\ v) \rightarrow (\langle D@SD\rangle\, dack!\,|\,c!v)$$
$$\qquad\qquad |\ \langle D@SD\rangle\, register![b\ s]$$
$$\qquad\qquad |\ ack? \rightarrow (\langle a\rangle ack!\,|\,currentloc!s\,|\,[P]_b)$$
$$\qquad \textbf{in}$$
$$\qquad\qquad ack? \rightarrow (currentloc!s\,|\,[Q]_a)$$

$$[\textbf{migrate to } s \rightarrow P]_a = currentloc?_- \rightarrow$$
$$\qquad \langle D@SD\rangle\, migrating!a$$
$$\qquad |\ ack? \rightarrow$$
$$\qquad\qquad \textbf{migrate to } s \rightarrow$$
$$\qquad\qquad\qquad \langle D@SD\rangle\, migrated!s$$
$$\qquad\qquad\qquad |\ ack? \rightarrow (currentloc!s\,|\,[P]_a)$$

$$[0]_a = 0$$
$$[P\,|\,Q]_a = [P]_a\,|\,[Q]_a$$
$$[c?p \rightarrow P]_a = c?p \rightarrow [P]_a$$
$$[*c?p \rightarrow P]_a = *c?p \rightarrow [P]_a$$
$$[\textbf{iflocal } \langle b\rangle c!v \rightarrow P \textbf{ else } Q]_a = \textbf{iflocal } \langle b\rangle c!v \rightarrow [P]_a \textbf{ else } [Q]_a$$
$$[\textbf{new } c \textbf{ in } P]_a = \textbf{new } c \textbf{ in } [P]_a$$
$$[\textbf{if } u = v \textbf{ then } P \textbf{ else } Q]_a = \textbf{if } u = v \textbf{ then } [P]_a \textbf{ else } [Q]_a$$

$$Daemon = \textbf{new } lock \textbf{ in}$$
$$\qquad lock!\textbf{emptymap}$$
$$\qquad |\ *register?(a\ s) \rightarrow$$
$$\qquad\qquad lock?m \rightarrow$$
$$\qquad\qquad \textbf{let } m' = (m \textbf{ with } a \mapsto s) \textbf{ in}$$
$$\qquad\qquad\qquad lock!m'\,|\,\langle a@s\rangle ack!$$
$$\qquad |\ *migrating?a \rightarrow$$
$$\qquad\qquad lock?m \rightarrow$$
$$\qquad\qquad \textbf{lookup } a \textbf{ in } m \textbf{ with}$$
$$\qquad\qquad\qquad \textbf{found}(s) \rightarrow$$
$$\qquad\qquad\qquad\qquad \langle a@s\rangle ack!$$
$$\qquad\qquad\qquad\qquad |\ migrated?s' \rightarrow$$
$$\qquad\qquad\qquad\qquad\qquad \textbf{let } m' = (m \textbf{ with } a \mapsto s') \textbf{ in}$$
$$\qquad\qquad\qquad\qquad\qquad lock!m'\,|\,\langle a@s'\rangle ack!$$
$$\qquad\qquad\qquad \textbf{notfound} \rightarrow 0$$
$$\qquad |\ *message?(a\ c\ v) \rightarrow$$
$$\qquad\qquad lock?m \rightarrow$$
$$\qquad\qquad \textbf{lookup } a \textbf{ in } m \textbf{ with}$$
$$\qquad\qquad\qquad \textbf{found}(s) \rightarrow$$
$$\qquad\qquad\qquad\qquad \langle a@s\rangle deliver![c\ v]$$
$$\qquad\qquad\qquad\qquad |\ dack? \rightarrow lock!m$$
$$\qquad\qquad\qquad \textbf{notfound} \rightarrow 0$$

**Fig. 1.** A Simple Translation: the compositional translation and the daemon

in delivery of a single location-independent output are illustrated below.

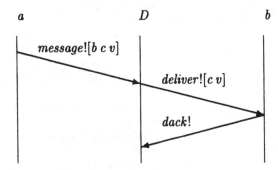

**Creation** In order for the daemon's site map to be kept up to date, agents must register with the daemon, telling it their site, both when they are created and after they migrate. Each agent records its current site internally as an output on its *currentloc* channel. This channel is also used as a lock, to enforce mutual exclusion between the encodings of all agent creation and migration commands within the body of the agent.

The encoding of an agent creation in an agent $a$

$$[\textbf{agent } b = P \textbf{ in } Q]_a = currentloc?s \rightarrow$$
$$\textbf{agent } b =$$
$$*deliver?(c\ v) \rightarrow (\langle D@SD \rangle dack! \,|\, c!v)$$
$$|\ \langle D@SD \rangle register![b\ s]$$
$$|\ ack? \rightarrow (\langle a \rangle ack! \,|\, currentloc!s \,|[P]_b)$$
$$\textbf{in}$$
$$ack? \rightarrow (currentloc!s \,|[Q]_a)$$

first acquires the lock and current site $s$ of $a$, and then creates the new agent $b$. The body of $b$ sends a *register* message to the daemon and waits for an acknowledgement. It then sends an acknowledgement to $a$, initializes the lock for $b$ and allows the encoding of the body $P$ of $b$ to proceed. Meanwhile, in $a$ the lock is kept until the acknowledgement from $b$ is received. The body of $b$ is put in parallel with the replicated input

$$*deliver?(c\ v) \rightarrow (\langle D@SD \rangle dack! \,|\, c!v)$$

which will receive forwarded messages for channels in $b$ from the daemon, send an acknowledgement back, and deliver the value locally to the appropriate channel.

The replicated input on *register* in the daemon

$$|\ *register?(a\ s) \rightarrow$$
$$lock?m \rightarrow$$
$$\textbf{let } m' = (m \textbf{ with } a \mapsto s) \textbf{ in}$$
$$lock!m' \,|\, \langle a@s \rangle ack!$$

first acquires the lock and current site map, replaces the site map with an updated map, thereby relinquishing the lock, and sends an acknowledgement to the registering agent. The inter-agent communications involved in a single agent creation are illustrated below. (Communications that are guaranteed to be between agents on the same site are drawn with thin arrows.)

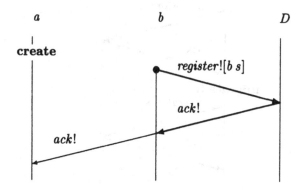

*Migration* The encoding of a **migrate** in agent $a$

$$[\text{migrate to } s \to P]_a = \mathit{currentloc?}_- \to$$
$$\langle D@SD\rangle \mathit{migrating!a}$$
$$\mid \mathit{ack?} \to$$
$$\text{migrate to } s \to$$
$$\langle D@SD\rangle \mathit{migrated!s}$$
$$\mid \mathit{ack?} \to (\mathit{currentloc!s} \mid [P]_a)$$

first acquires the lock for $a$ (discarding the current site data). It then sends a *migrating* message to the daemon, waits for an *ack*, migrates to its new site $s$, sends a *migrated* message to the daemon, waits again for an *ack*, and releases the lock (with the new site $s$). The replicated input on *migrating* in the daemon

$$\mid *\mathit{migrating?a} \to$$
$$\mathit{lock?m} \to$$
$$\textbf{lookup } a \textbf{ in } m \textbf{ with}$$
$$\textbf{found}(s) \to$$
$$\langle a@s\rangle \mathit{ack!}$$
$$\mid \mathit{migrated?s'} \to$$
$$\textbf{let } m' = (m \textbf{ with } a \mapsto s') \textbf{ in}$$
$$\mathit{lock!m'} \mid \langle a@s'\rangle \mathit{ack!}$$
$$\textbf{notfound} \to 0$$

first acquires the lock and current site map, looks up the current site of $a$ and sends an *ack* to $a$ at that site. It then waits to receive the new site, replaces the site map with an updated map, thereby relinquishing the lock, and sends an acknowledgement to $a$ at its new site. The inter-agent communications involved in a single migration are shown below.

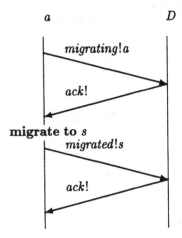

*The top level* Putting the daemon and the compositional encoding together, the top level translation, defined in Figure 2, creates the daemon agent, installs the

$[P]_{a,s} = $ **new** *register, migrating, migrated, message, dack, deliver, ack, currentloc* **in**
  **agent** $D = Daemon$ **in**
    **let** $SD = s$ **in**
      $*deliver?(c\ v) \rightarrow (\langle D@SD \rangle dack! \mid c!v)$
      $\mid \langle D@SD \rangle register![a\ s]$
      $\mid ack? \rightarrow (currentloc!s \mid [P]_a)$

where the **new**-bound names, $SD$, and $D$, do not occur in $P$.

**Fig. 2.** A Simple Translation: the top level

replicated input on *deliver* for $a$, registers agent $a$ to be at site $s$, initializes the lock for $a$, and starts the encoding of the body $[P]_a$.

## 4   A Forwarding-Pointers Infrastructure Translation

In this section we give a more distributed algorithm, in which daemons on each site maintain chains of forwarding pointers for agents that have migrated. It removes the single bottleneck of the centralised-server solution in the preceding section; it is thus a step closer to algorithms that may be of wide practical use. The algorithm is more delicate; expressing it as a translation provides a more rigorous test of the framework.

As before, the translation consists of a compositional encoding of the bodies of agents, given in Figure 3, daemons, defined in Figure 4, and a top-level translation putting them together, given in Figure 5. The top-level translation of a program, again initially a single agent, creates a daemon on each site mentioned by the agent. These will each maintain a collection of forwarding pointers for all agents that have migrated away from their site. To keep the pointers current, agents synchronize with their local daemons on creation and migration. Location independent communications are implemented via the daemons, using the forwarding pointers where possible. If a daemon has no pointer for the destination agent of a message then it will forward the message to the daemon on the site where the destination agent was created; to make this possible an agent name is encoded by a triple of an agent name and the site and daemon of its creation. Similarly, a site name is encoded by a pair of a site name and the daemon name for that site. A typed version of the encoding would involve a translation of types with clauses

$$[\textbf{Agent}] = [\textbf{Agent Site Agent}]$$
$$[\textbf{Site}] = [\textbf{Site Agent}]$$

We generally use lower case letters for site and agent names occurring in the source program and upper case letters for sites and agents introduced by its encoding.

Looking first at the compositional encoding, in Figure 3, each agent uses a *currentloc* channel as a lock, as before. It is now also used to store both the site where the agent is and the name of the daemon on that site. The three interesting clauses of the encoding, for location-independent output, creation, and migration, each begin with an input on *currentloc*. They are broadly similar to those of the simple translation.

Turning to the body of a daemon, defined in Figure 4, it is parametric in a pair $s$ of the name of the site $S$ where it is and the daemon's own name $DS$. It has four replicated inputs, on its *register*, *migrating*, *migrated*, and *message* channels. Some partial mutual exclusion between the bodies of these inputs is enforced by using the *lock* channel. The data stored on the *lock* channel now maps the name of each agent that has ever been on this site to a lock channel (e.g. *Bstate*) for that agent. These agent locks prevent the daemon from attempting to forward messages to agents that may be migrating. Each stores the site and daemon (of that site) where the agent was last seen by this daemon — i.e. either this site/daemon, or the site/daemon to which it migrated to from here. The use of agent locks makes this algorithm rather more concurrent than the previous one — rather than simply sequentialising the entire daemon, it allows daemons to process inputs while agents are migrating, so many agents can be migrating away from the same site, concurrently with each other and with delivery of messages to other agents at the site.

*Location-independent output* A location-independent output $\langle b@?\rangle c!v$ in agent $A$ is implemented by requesting the local daemon to deliver it. (Note that $A$ may migrate away before the request is sent to the daemon, so the request must be of the form $\langle DS@S\rangle message![b\ c\ v]$, not of the form $\langle DS\rangle message![b\ c\ v]$.)

The *message* replicated input of the daemon gets the map $m$ from agent names to agent lock channels. If the destination agent $B$ is not found, the message

$$
\begin{aligned}
&[\langle b @ ? \rangle c! v]_A && = \mathit{currentloc}?(S\ DS) \to \\
&&& \quad \langle DS @ S \rangle \mathit{message}![b\ c\ v] \\
&&& \quad |\ \mathit{currentloc}![S\ DS] \\
&[\mathbf{agent}\ b = P\ \mathbf{in}\ Q]_A && = \mathit{currentloc}?(S\ DS) \to \\
&&& \quad \mathbf{agent}\ B = \\
&&& \quad\quad \mathbf{let}\ b = [B\ S\ DS]\ \mathbf{in} \\
&&& \quad\quad\quad \mathit{currentloc}![S\ DS] \\
&&& \quad\quad\quad |\ \langle DS \rangle \mathit{register}! B \\
&&& \quad\quad\quad |\ \mathit{ack}? \to (\langle A \rangle \mathit{ack}!\ |[P]_B) \\
&&& \quad \mathbf{in} \\
&&& \quad\quad \mathbf{let}\ b = [B\ S\ DS]\ \mathbf{in} \\
&&& \quad\quad\quad \mathit{ack}? \to (\mathit{currentloc}![S\ DS]\ |[Q]_A) \\
&[\mathbf{migrate\ to}\ u \to P]_A && = \mathit{currentloc}?(S\ DS) \to \\
&&& \quad \mathbf{let}\ (U\ DU) = u\ \mathbf{in} \\
&&& \quad \mathbf{if}\ [S\ DS] = [U\ DU]\ \mathbf{then} \\
&&& \quad\quad \mathit{currentloc}![U\ DU] \\
&&& \quad \mathbf{else} \\
&&& \quad\quad \langle DS \rangle \mathit{migrating}! A \\
&&& \quad\quad |\ \mathit{ack}? \to \\
&&& \quad\quad\quad \mathbf{migrate\ to}\ U \to \\
&&& \quad\quad\quad\quad \langle DU \rangle \mathit{register}! A \\
&&& \quad\quad\quad\quad |\ \mathit{ack}? \to \\
&&& \quad\quad\quad\quad\quad \langle DS @ S \rangle \mathit{migrated}![A\ [U\ DU]] \\
&&& \quad\quad\quad\quad\quad |\ \mathit{ack}? \to (\mathit{currentloc}![U\ DU]\ |[P]_A) \\
&[\mathbf{iflocal}\ \langle b \rangle c! v \to P\ \mathbf{else}\ Q]_A && = \mathbf{let}\ (B\ \_\_) = b\ \mathbf{in} \\
&&& \quad \mathbf{iflocal}\ \langle B \rangle c! v \to [P]_A\ \mathbf{else}\ [Q]_A \\
&[0]_A && = 0 \\
&[P\ |\ Q]_A && = [P]_A\ |[Q]_A \\
&[c?p \to P]_A && = c?p \to [P]_A \\
&[*c?p \to P]_A && = *c?p \to [P]_A \\
&[\mathbf{new}\ c\ \mathbf{in}\ P]_A && = \mathbf{new}\ c\ \mathbf{in}\ [P]_A \\
&[\mathbf{if}\ u = v\ \mathbf{then}\ P\ \mathbf{else}\ Q]_A && = \mathbf{if}\ u = v\ \mathbf{then}\ [P]_a\ \mathbf{else}\ [Q]_A
\end{aligned}
$$

**Fig. 3.** A Forwarding-Pointers Translation: the compositional translation

$Daemon_s = $ **let** $(S\,DS) = s$ **in**
**new** *lock* **in**

    *lock*!**emptymap**

    | *∗register?B* → *lock?m* → **lookup** $B$ **in** $m$ **with**
        **found**⟨*Bstate*⟩ →
        *Bstate*?(_ _) →
         *Bstate*![$S\,DS$]
        | *lock*!*m*
        | ⟨$B$⟩*ack*!
        **notfound** →
        **new** *Bstate* **in**
         *Bstate*![$S\,DS$]
        | **let** $m' = (m$ **with** $B \mapsto Bstate)$ **in** *lock*!$m'$
        | ⟨$B$⟩*ack*!

    | *∗migrating?B* → *lock?m* → **lookup** $B$ **in** $m$ **with**
        **found**⟨*Bstate*⟩ →
        *Bstate*?(_ _) →
        *lock*!*m*
        | *B*!*ack*
        **notfound** → 0

    | *∗migrated?*($B\,(U\,DU)$) → *lock?m* → **lookup** $B$ **in** $m$ **with**
        **found**⟨*Bstate*⟩ →
        *lock*!*m*
        | *Bstate*![$U\,DU$]
        | ⟨$B$@$U$⟩*ack*!
        **notfound** → 0

    | *∗message?*(($B\,U\,DU$) $c\,v$) → *lock?m* → **lookup** $B$ **in** $m$ **with**
        **found**⟨*Bstate*⟩ →
        *lock*!*m*
      | *Bstate*?($R\,DR$) →
        **iflocal** ⟨$B$⟩*c*!*v* →
        *Bstate*![$R\,DR$]
        **else**
         ⟨$DR$@$R$⟩*message*![[$B\,U\,DU$] $c\,v$]
        | *Bstate*![$R\,DR$]
        **notfound** →
        *lock*!*m*
        | ⟨$DU$@$U$⟩*message*![[$B\,U\,DU$] $c\,v$]

**Fig. 4.** A Forwarding-Pointers Translation: the Daemon

is forwarded to the daemon $DU$ on the site $U$ where $B$ was created. Otherwise, if $B$ is found, the agent lock $Bstate$ is grabbed, obtaining the forwarding pointer $[R\,DR]$ for $B$. Using **iflocal**, the message is then either delivered to $B$, if it is here, or to the daemon $DR$, otherwise. Note that the *lock* is released before the agent lock is requested, so the daemon can process other inputs even if $B$ is currently migrating.

A single location-independent output, forwarded once between daemons, involves inter-agent messages as below.

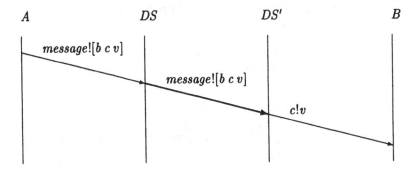

*Creation* The compositional encoding for **agent** is similar to that of the encoding in the previous section. It differs in two main ways. Firstly the source language name $b$ of the new agent must be replaced by the actual agent name $B$ tupled with the names $S$ of this site and $DS$ of the daemon on this site. Secondly, the internal forwarder, receiving on *deliver*, is no longer required: the final delivery of messages from daemons to agents is now always local to a site, and so can be done using **iflocal**. An explicit acknowledgement (on *dack* in the simple translation) is likewise unnecessary.

A single creation involves inter-agent messages as below. The agents are all guaranteed to be on the same site.

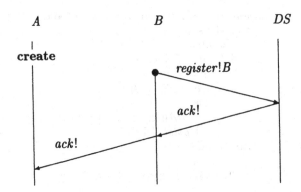

*Migration* Degenerate migrations, of an agent to the site it is currently on, must now be identified and treated specially; otherwise the Daemon can deadlock. An agent $A$ executing a non-degenerate migration now synchronises with the daemon $DS$ on its starting site $S$, then migrates, registers with the daemon $DU$ on its destination site $U$, then synchronises again with $DS$. In between the first and last synchronisations the agent lock for $A$ in daemon $DS$ is held, preventing $DS$ from attempting to deliver messages to $A$.

A single migration involves inter-agent messages as below.

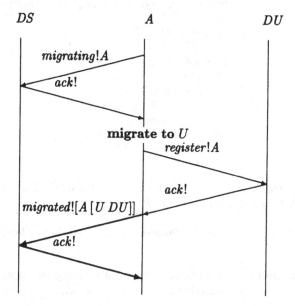

**Local communication** The translation of **iflocal** must now extract the real agent name $B$ from the triple $b$, but is otherwise trivial.

**The top level** The top-level translation of a program $P$, given in Figure 5, dynamically creates a daemon on each site mentioned in $P$. Each site name $si$ is re-bound to the pair $[si\ DSi]$ of the site name together with the respective daemon name. A top-level agent $A$ is created and initialised; the agent name $a$ is re-bound to the triple $[A\ S1\ DS1]$ of the low-level agent name $A$ together with the initial site and daemon names.

## 5  Reduction Semantics

The informal descriptions of the primitives in §2 can be made precise by giving them an operational semantics. We adopt a *reduction semantics*, defining the atomic state-changes that a system of agents can undergo by reduction axioms with a structural congruence, following the style of [BB92,Mil92].

The process terms of the calculi in §2.1,2.2 only allow the source code of the body of a single agent to be expressed. During computation, this agent may evolve into a system of many agents, distributed over many sites. The reduction relation must be between the possible states of these systems, not simply between terms of the source calculi; we express such states as *configurations* $\Gamma, P$. Here

$[P]_{a,s1..sn} = $ **new** $register, migrating, migrated, message, ack, currentloc, lock,$
  $daemondaemon, nd$ **in**
   $*daemondaemon?S \rightarrow$
    **agent** $D =$
     **migrate to** $S \rightarrow (Daemon_{[S \; D]} \,|\, \langle a@s1 \rangle nd![S \; D])$
    **in** 0
   $| \; daemondaemon!s1 \,|\, nd?s1 \rightarrow$
    $\cdots$
       $daemondaemon!sn \,|\, nd?sn \rightarrow$
       **let** $(S1 \; DS1) = s1$ **in**
        **agent** $A =$
         **let** $a = [A \; S1 \; DS1]$ **in**
          $currentloc!s1$
          $| \; \langle DS1 \rangle register!A$
          $| \; ack? \rightarrow [P]_A$
       **in** 0

where $P$ is initiated on site $s1$, the free site names in $P$ are $s1..sn$, and the new-bound names, $S1$, $DS1$, and $A$ do not occur in $P$.

**Fig. 5.** A Forwarding-Pointers Translation: the top level

$\Gamma$ is a *location context* that gives the current site of any free agent names; $P$ is a term of the (low- or high-level) calculus extended with two new forms.

$@_a P$                 $P$ as part of agent $a$
**new** $a@s$ **in** $P$      new agent name $a$, currently at site $s$

Configurations may involve many agents in parallel. The form $@_a P$ denotes the process term $P$ as part of the body of agent $a$, so for example $@_a P \,|\, @_b Q$ denotes $P$ as part of the body of $a$ in parallel with $Q$ as part of the body of $b$. It will be convenient to allow the parts of the body of an agent to be syntactically separated, so e.g. $@_a P_1 \,|\, @_b Q \,|\, @_a P_2$ denotes $P_1 \,|\, P_2$ as part of $a$ in parallel with $Q$ as part of $b$. Configurations must record the current sites of all agents. For free agent names this is done by the location context $\Gamma$; for the others, the form **new** $a@s$ **in** $P$ declares a new agent name $a$, which is binding in $P$, and records that agent $a$ is currently at site $s$.

We now give the detailed definitions. Process terms are taken up to alpha-conversion throughout. Structural congruence $\equiv$ includes the axiom

$$@_a (P \,|\, Q) \equiv @_a P \,|\, @_a Q$$

allowing the parts of an agent $a$ to be syntactically separated or brought together, and the axiom

$$@_a \; \textbf{new} \; c \; \textbf{in} \; P \equiv \textbf{new} \; c \; \textbf{in} \; @_a P \qquad \text{if } c \neq a$$

allowing channel binders to be extruded past $@_a$. It is otherwise similar to a standard structural congruence for an asynchronous $\pi$-calculus, with scope extrusion both for the new channel binder **new** $c$ **in** $P$ and for the new agent binder **new** $a@s$ **in** $P$. In full, it is the least congruence satisfying the following axioms.

$$P \equiv P \,|\, 0$$
$$P \,|\, Q \equiv Q \,|\, P$$
$$P \,|\, (Q \,|\, R) \equiv (P \,|\, Q) \,|\, R$$
$$P \,|\, \textbf{new } c \textbf{ in } Q \equiv \textbf{new } c \textbf{ in } P \,|\, Q \qquad \text{if } c \text{ not free in } P$$
$$P \,|\, \textbf{new } a@s \textbf{ in } Q \equiv \textbf{new } a@s \textbf{ in } P \,|\, Q \quad \text{if } a \text{ not free in } P$$
$$@_a \,(P \,|\, Q) \equiv @_a P \,|\, @_a Q$$
$$@_a \textbf{ new } c \textbf{ in } P \equiv \textbf{new } c \textbf{ in } @_a P \qquad \text{if } c \neq a$$

A configuration is a pair $\Gamma, P$, where the location context $\Gamma$ is a finite partial function from $\mathcal{N}$ to $\mathcal{N}$, intuitively giving the current site of any free agent names in $P$, and $P$ is a term of the (low- or high-level) extended calculus. The initial configuration, for a program $P$ of the (low- or high-level) unextended calculus, to be considered as the body of an agent $a$ created on site $s$, is:

$$\{a \mapsto s\},\, @_a P$$

We are concerned only with configurations that can arise by reduction of initial configurations for well-typed programs. In these, any particle (i.e., **agent**, **migrate**, output, input, **if**, or **iflocal**) will be under exactly one @ operator, specifying the agent that contains it. (In this paper we do not give a type system, and so leave this informal.) Other configurations have mathematically well-defined reductions but may not be easily implementable or desirable, for example

$$\Gamma,\, @_a \,(c?b \to @_b P)$$

receives an agent name and then adds $P$ to the body of that agent.

We define a partial function match, taking a value and a pattern and giving (where it is defined) a finite substitution from names to values.

$$\text{match}(v, \_) = \{\}$$
$$\text{match}(v, x) = \{x \mapsto v\}$$
$$\text{match}([v_1 \mathbin{..} v_m], (p_1 \mathbin{..} p_m)) = \text{match}(v_1, p_1) \cup \ldots \cup \text{match}(v_m, p_m)$$
$$\text{match}(v, (p_1 \mathbin{..} p_m)) \quad \text{undefined, if } v \text{ is not of the form } [v_1 \mathbin{..} v_m]$$

The natural definition of the application of a substitution from names to values to a process term $P$ is also a partial operation, as the syntax does not allow arbitrary values in all the places where free names can occur. We write $\{v/p\}P$ for the result of applying the substitution $\text{match}(v, p)$ to $P$. This may be undefined either because $\text{match}(v, p)$ is undefined, or because $\text{match}(v, p)$ is a substitution but the application of that substitution to $P$ is undefined.

The reduction axioms for the low-level calculus are as follows.

$$\Gamma, @_a \textbf{ agent } b = P \textbf{ in } Q \longrightarrow \Gamma, \textbf{new } b@\Gamma(a) \textbf{ in } (@_b P | @_a Q)$$
$$\Gamma, @_a \textbf{ migrate to } s \to P \longrightarrow (\Gamma \oplus a \mapsto s), @_a P$$
$$\Gamma, @_a \textbf{ iflocal } \langle b \rangle c!v \to P \textbf{ else } Q \longrightarrow \Gamma, @_b \, c!v | @_a P \qquad \text{if } \Gamma(a) = \Gamma(b)$$
$$\longrightarrow \Gamma, @_a \, Q \qquad \text{if } \Gamma(a) \neq \Gamma(b)$$
$$\Gamma, @_a \, (c!v | c?p \to P) \longrightarrow \Gamma, @_a \, \{v/p\}P$$
$$\Gamma, @_a \, (c!v | *c?p \to P) \longrightarrow \Gamma, @_a \, (\{v/p\}P | *c?p \to P)$$
$$\Gamma, @_a \textbf{ if } u = v \textbf{ then } P \textbf{ else } Q \longrightarrow \Gamma, @_a \, P \qquad \text{if } u = v$$
$$\longrightarrow \Gamma, @_a \, Q \qquad \text{if } u \neq v$$

The rules mentioning potentially-undefined expressions $\Gamma(x)$ or $\{v/p\}P$ in their side-condition or conclusion have an implicit additional premise that these are defined. Such premises should be automatically satisfied in derivations of reductions of well-typed programs.

Note that the only inter-site communication in an implementation will be for the **migrate** reduction, in which the body of the migrating agent $a$ must be sent from its current site to site $s$.

The high-level calculus has the additional axiom below, for delivering location-independent messages to their destination agent.

$$\Gamma, @_a \, \langle b@? \rangle c!v \longrightarrow \Gamma, @_b \, c!v$$

Reduction is closed under structural congruence, parallel, **new** $c$ **in** _ and **new** $a@s$ **in** _, as specified by the rules below.

$$\frac{Q \equiv P \quad \Gamma, P \longrightarrow \Gamma', P' \quad P' \equiv Q'}{\Gamma, Q \longrightarrow \Gamma', Q'} \qquad\qquad \frac{\Gamma, P \longrightarrow \Gamma', P'}{\Gamma, P | Q \longrightarrow \Gamma', P' | Q}$$

$$\frac{(\Gamma, a \mapsto s), P \longrightarrow (\Gamma, a \mapsto s'), P'}{\Gamma, \textbf{new } a@s \textbf{ in } P \longrightarrow \Gamma', \textbf{new } a@s' \textbf{ in } P'} \qquad \frac{\Gamma, P \longrightarrow \Gamma', P' \quad c \notin \text{dom}(\Gamma)}{\Gamma, \textbf{new } c \textbf{ in } P \longrightarrow \Gamma', \textbf{new } c \textbf{ in } P'}$$

# 6 Discussion

We conclude by discussing alternative approaches for the description of mobile agent infrastructures, related distributed process calculi, implementation, and future work.

## 6.1 Infrastructure Description

In this paper we have identified two levels of abstraction, precisely formulated them as process calculi, and argued that distributed infrastructure algorithms for mobile agents can usefully be expressed as translations between the calculi. Such translations should be compared with the many other possible ways of describing the algorithms — we briefly consider diagrammatic, pseudocode, and automata based approaches.

The *diagrams* used in §3,4 convey basic information about the algorithms — the messages involved in isolated transactions — but they are far from complete descriptions and can be misleading. The correctness of the algorithms depends on details of synchronisation and locking that are precisely defined by the translation but are hard to express visually.

For a *psuedocode* description to provide a clear (if necessarily informal) description of an algorithm the constructs of the psuedocode must themselves have clear intuitive semantics. This may hold for psuedocodes based on widespread procedural languages, such as Pascal. Infrastructure algorithms, however, involve constructs for agent creation, migration and communication. These do not have a widespread, accepted, semantics — a number of rather different semantic choices are possible — so more rigorous descriptions are required for clear understanding.

*Automata*-based descriptions have been widely used for precise specification of distributed algorithms, for example in the text of Lynch [Lyn96]. Automata do not allow agent creation and migration to be represented directly, so for working with a mobile agent algorithm one would either have to use a complex encoding or consider only an abstraction of the algorithm — a non-executable model, rather than an executable complete description.

The modelling approach has been followed by Amadio and Prasad in their work on IP mobility [AP98]. They consider idealizations of protocols from IPv6 proposals for mobile host support, expressed in a variant of CCS, and prove correctness results. There is a trade-off here: the idealizations can be expressed in a simpler formal framework, greatly simplifying correctness proofs, but they are further removed from implementation, inevitably increasing the likelihood that important details have been abstracted away.

Few current proposals for mobile agent systems support any form of location-independence. Those that do include the Distributed Join Language [FGL+96,Joi98], the MOA project of the Open Group Research Institute [MLC98], and the Voyager system of ObjectSpace [Obj97]. The distributed join language is at roughly the same level of abstraction as the high-level Nomadic $\pi$-calculus. It provides location-independent communication, with primitives similar to the outputs and replicated inputs used here. The MOA project associates a locating scheme to each agent; chosen from querying a particular site (updated on each migration), searching along a pre-defined itinerary, and following forwarding pointers. Voyager provides location-independent asynchronous and synchronous messages, and multicasts. Migrating objects leave trails of forwarders behind them; entities that communicate with these objects are sent updated addresses to be cached. Forwarders are garbage-collected; the garbage collection involves heartbeat messages. More precise descriptions of the algorithms used in these systems do not appear to have been published, making it difficult for the application programmer to predict their performance and robustness.

## 6.2 Related Calculi

In recent years a number of process calculi have been introduced in order to study some aspect of distributed and mobile agent computation. They include:

- The $\pi_l$ calculus of Amadio and Prasad [AP94], for modelling the failure semantics of Facile [TLK96].
- The Distributed Join Calculus of Fournet et al [FGL⁺96], intended as the basis for a mobile agent language.
- The language of located processes and the $D\pi$ calculus of Riely and Hennessy, used to study the semantics of failure [RH97,RH98] and typing for control of resource use by mobile agents [HR98b,HR98a].
- The calculus of Sekiguchi and Yonezawa [SY97], used to study various primitives for code and data movement.
- The dpi calculus of Sewell [Sew97a,Sew98], used to study a subtyping system for locality enforcement of capabilities.
- The Ambient calculus of Cardelli and Gordon [CG98], used for modelling security domains.
- The Seal calculus of Vitek and Castagna [VC98], focussing on protection mechanisms including revocable capabilities.

There is a large design space of such calculi, with very different primitives being appropriate for different purposes, and with many semantic choices. A thorough comparison and discussion of the design space is beyond the scope of this paper — a brief discussion can be found in [Sew99]; here we highlight only some of the main design choices:

*Hierarchy* We have adopted a two-level hierarchy, of agents located on sites. One might consider tree-structured mobile agents with migration of subtrees, e.g. as in [FGL⁺96]. The added expressiveness may be desirable from the programmer's point of view, but it requires somewhat more complex infrastructure algorithms — migrations of an agent can be caused by migrations of their parents — so we neglect it in the first instance.

*Unique Naming* The calculi of §2 ensure that agents have unique names, in contrast, for example, to the Ambients of [CG98]. Inter-agent messages are therefore guaranteed to have a unique destination.

*Communication* In earlier work [SWP98] the inter-agent communication primitives were separated from the channel primitives used for local computation. The inter-agent primitives were

| | |
|---|---|
| $\langle a@?\rangle!v$ | location-independent output of $v$ to agent $a$ |
| $\langle a@s\rangle!v$ | location-dependent output |
| $?p \to P$ | input at the current agent |

These give a conceptually simpler model, with messages sent to agents rather than to channels at agents, but to allow encodings to be expressed it was necessary to add variants and local channels. This led to a rather large calculus and somewhat awkward encodings.

## 6.3 Implementation

In order to experiment with infrastructure algorithms, and with applications that use location-independent communication, we have implemented an experimental programming language, *Nomadic Pict*. The Nomadic Pict implementation is based on the Pict compiler of Pierce and Turner [PT97]. It is a two-level language, corresponding to the calculi presented in this paper. The low level extends Pict by providing direct support for agent creation, migration and location-dependent communication. The high level supports location-independent communication by applying translations — the compiler takes as input a program in the high-level language together with an encoding of each high-level primitive into the low-level language. It type-checks and applies the encoding; the resulting low-level intermediate code can be executed on a relatively straightforward distributed run-time system. The two encodings given have both been successfully type-checked and executed.

*Typing* In this paper the calculi have been presented without typing. The Nomadic Pict implementation inherits from Pict its rather expressive type system. For reasoning about infrastructure encodings a simple type system for the calculi would be desirable, with types

$$T ::= Site \mid Agent \mid \updownarrow T \mid [T \mathinner{..} T] \mid X \mid \exists X.T$$

for site and agent names, channels carrying values of type $T$, tuples, and existential polymorphism.

The calculi allow a channel name to escape the agent in which it is declared and be used subsequently both for input and output within other agents. The global/local typing of [Sew97a,Sew98] could be used to impose tighter disciplines on channels that are intended to be used only locally, preventing certain programming errors.

*Input/Output and Traders* Up to this point we have considered only communications that are internal to a distributed computation. External input and output primitives can be cleanly provided in the form of special agent names, so that from within the calculus inputs and outputs are treated exactly as other communications. For example, for console I/O one might have a fictitious console agent on each site, together with globally-known channel names *getchar* and *putchar*. Messages sent to these would be treated specially by the local run-time system, leading to idioms such as

$$\textbf{new } a \textbf{ in } \langle console \rangle putchar![c\ a] \mid (a? \to P)$$

for synchronous output of a character $c$ to the local console, and

$$\textbf{new } a \textbf{ in } \langle console \rangle getchar!a \mid (a?x \to P)$$

for synchronous input of a character, to be bound to $x$, from the local console.

In realistic systems there will be a rich collection of input/output resources, differing from site to site, so agents may need to acquire resources dynamically. Moreover, in realistic systems agents will be initiated separately on many sites; if they are to interact some mechanism must be provided for them to acquire each other's names dynamically. To do this in a lexically-scoped manner we envisage each site maintaining a *trader*, a finite map from strings to values that supports registration and lookup of resources. Agents would typically obtain the trader name associated with a site at the same time as obtaining the site name. For traders to be type-sound a type Dynamic [ACPP91] is required.

## 6.4 Future Work

This paper provides only a starting point — much additional work is required on algorithms, semantics, and implementation.

- The choice of infrastructure algorithm(s) for a given application will depend strongly on many characteristics of the application and target network, especially on the expected statistical properties of communication and migration. In wide area applications, sophisticated distributed algorithms will be required, allowing for dynamic system reconfigurations such as adding new sites to the system, migrating parts of the distributed computation before shutting down some machines, tracing locations of different kinds of agents, and implementing tolerance of partial failures. The space of feasible algorithms and the trade-offs involved require detailed investigation.
- Turning to semantics, in order to state correctness properties (in the absence of failures) a theory of observational equivalence is required. Such a theory was developed for an idealised Pict in [Sew97b]; it must be generalized to the distributed setting and supported by coinductive proof techniques.
- Finally, to investigate the behaviour of infrastructure algorithms in practice, and to assess the usefulness of our high-level location-independent primitives in applications, the implementation must be developed to the point where it is possible to experiment with non-trivial applications.

The calculi of §2 make the unrealistic assumption that communications and sites are reliable. This is implausible, even for local area networks of moderate size, so usable infrastructure algorithms must be robust under some level of failure. To express such algorithms some notion of time must be introduced into the low-level calculus, to allow timeouts to be expressed, yet the semantics must be kept tractable, to allow robustness properties to be stated and proved.

One might also consider other high-level communication primitives, such as location-independent multicast, and agent primitives, such as tree-structured agents. More speculatively, the two levels of abstraction that we have identified may be a useful basis for work on security properties of mobile agent infrastructures — to consider whether a distributed infrastructure for mobile agents is secure one must first be able to define it precisely, and have a clear understanding of how it is distributed on actual machines.

**Acknowledgements** The authors would like to thank Ken Moody and Asis Unyapoth for discussions and comments. Sewell was supported by EPSRC grants GR/K 38403 and GR/L 62290, Wojciechowski by the Wolfson Foundation, and Pierce by Indiana University and by NSF grant CCR-9701826, *Principled Foundations for Programming with Objects*.

# References

[ACPP91] Martín Abadi, Luca Cardelli, Benjamin Pierce, and Gordon Plotkin. Dynamic typing in a statically typed language. *ACM Transactions on Programming Languages and Systems,*, 13(2):237–268, April 1991.

[AP94] R. M. Amadio and S. Prasad. Localities and failures. In P. S. Thiagarajan, editor, *Proceedings of $14^{th}$ FST and TCS Conference, FST-TCS'94. LNCS 880*, pages 205–216. Springer-Verlag, 1994.

[AP98] Roberto M. Amadio and Sanjiva Prasad. Modelling IP mobility. In *Proceedings of CONCUR '98: Concurrency Theory. LNCS 1466*, pages 301–316, September 1998.

[BB92] G. Berry and G. Boudol. The chemical abstract machine. *Theoretical Computer Science*, 96:217–248, 1992.

[Bou92] Gérard Boudol. Asynchrony and the $\pi$-calculus (note). Rapport de Recherche 1702, INRIA Sofia-Antipolis, May 1992.

[Car86] Luca Cardelli. Amber and the amber machine. In Guy Cousineau, Pierre-Louis Curien, and Bernard Robinet, editors, *Combinators and Functional Programming Languages, LNCS 242*, pages 21–70, 1986.

[CG98] Luca Cardelli and Andrew D. Gordon. Mobile ambients. In *Proc. of Foundations of Software Science and Computation Structures (FoSSaCS), ETAPS'98, LNCS 1378*, pages 140–155, March 1998.

[CHK97] D. Chess, C. Harrison, and A. Kershenbaum. Mobile agents: Are they a good idea? In *Mobile Object Systems – Towards the Programmable Internet. LNCS 1222*, pages 25–48, 1997.

[FGL$^{+}$96] Cédric Fournet, Georges Gonthier, Jean-Jacques Lévy, Luc Maranget, and Didier Rémy. A calculus of mobile agents. In *Proceedings of CONCUR '96. LNCS 1119*, pages 406–421. Springer-Verlag, August 1996.

[HR98a] Matthew Hennessy and James Riely. Resource access control in systems of mobile agents. In *Workshop on High-Level Concurrent Languages*, 1998. Full version as University of Sussex technical report CSTR 98/02.

[HR98b] Matthew Hennessy and James Riely. Type-safe execution of mobile agents in anonymous networks. In *Workshop on Mobile Object Systems, (satellite of ECOOP '98)*, 1998. Full version as University of Sussex technical report CSTR 98/03.

[HT91] Kohei Honda and Mario Tokoro. An object calculus for asynchronous communication. In Pierre America, editor, *Proceedings of ECOOP '91, LNCS 512*, pages 133–147, July 1991.

[JGF96] Simon Peyton Jones, Andrew Gordon, and Sigbjorn Finne. Concurrent Haskell. In *Conference Record of the $23^{rd}$ ACM Symposium on Principles of Programming Languages*, pages 295–308, St. Petersburg, Florida, January 21–24, 1996. ACM Press.

[Joi98]     The join calculus language, 1998.     Implementations available from
            http://pauillac.inria.fr/join/unix/eng.htm.

[Lyn96]     Nancy A. Lynch. *Distributed algorithms*. Morgan Kaufmann, 1996.

[Mil92]     Robin Milner. Functions as processes. *Journal of Mathematical Structures in Computer Science*, 2(2):119–141, 1992.

[MLC98]     D. S. Milojicic, W. LaForge, and D. Chauhan. Mobile Objects and Agents (MOA). In *USENIX COOTS '98, Santa Fe*, April 1998.

[MPW92]     R. Milner, J. Parrow, and D. Walker. A calculus of mobile processes, Parts I + II. *Information and Computation*, 100(1):1–77, 1992.

[Nee89]     R. M. Needham. Names. In S. Mullender, editor, *Distributed Systems*, pages 89–101. Addison-Wesley, 1989.

[Obj97]     ObjectSpace. Voyager core technology user guide, version 2.0 beta 1. Available from http://www.objectspace.com/, 1997.

[PT94]      Benjamin C. Pierce and David N. Turner. Concurrent objects in a process calculus. In *Theory and Practice of Parallel Programming (TPPP), Sendai, Japan*, November 1994.

[PT97]      Benjamin C. Pierce and David N. Turner. Pict: A programming language based on the pi-calculus. Technical Report CSCI 476, Computer Science Department, Indiana University, 1997. To appear in *Proof, Language and Interaction: Essays in Honour of Robin Milner*, Gordon Plotkin, Colin Stirling, and Mads Tofte, editors, MIT Press.

[Rep91]     John Reppy. CML: A higher-order concurrent language. In *Programming Language Design and Implementation*, pages 293–259. SIGPLAN, ACM, June 1991.

[RH97]      James Riely and Matthew Hennessy. Distributed processes and location failures. In *Proceedings of ICALP '97. LNCS 1256*, pages 471–481. Springer-Verlag, July 1997.

[RH98]      James Riely and Matthew Hennessy. A typed language for distributed mobile processes. In *Proceedings of the 25th POPL*, January 1998.

[Sew97a]    Peter Sewell. Global/local subtyping for a distributed π-calculus. Technical Report 435, University of Cambridge, August 1997. Available from http://www.cl.cam.ac.uk/users/pes20/.

[Sew97b]    Peter Sewell. On implementations and semantics of a concurrent programming language. In *Proceedings of CONCUR '97. LNCS 1243*, pages 391–405, 1997.

[Sew98]     Peter Sewell. Global/local subtyping and capability inference for a distributed π-calculus. In *Proceedings of ICALP '98, LNCS 1443*, pages 695–706, 1998.

[Sew99]     Peter Sewell. A brief introduction to applied π, January 1999. Lecture notes for the Mathfit Instructional Meeting on Recent Advances in Semantics and Types for Concurrency: Theory and Practice, July 1998. Available from http://www.cl.cam.ac.uk/users/pes20/.

[SWP98]     Peter Sewell, Paweł T. Wojciechowski, and Benjamin C. Pierce. Location independence for mobile agents. In *Workshop on Internet Programming Languages, Chicago*, May 1998.

[SY97]      Tatsurou Sekiguchi and Akinori Yonezawa. A calculus with code mobility. In Howard Bowman and John Derrick, editors, *Formal Methods for Open Object-based Distributed Systems (Proceedings of FMOODS '97)*, pages 21–36. IFIP, Chapman and Hall, July 1997.

[TLK96]  Bent Thomsen, Lone Leth, and Tsung-Min Kuo. A Facile tutorial. In *Proceedings of CONCUR '96. LNCS 1119*, pages 278–298. Springer-Verlag, August 1996.

[Tur96]  David N. Turner. *The Polymorphic Pi-calculus: Theory and Implementation.* PhD thesis, University of Edinburgh, 1996.

[VC98]  Jan Vitek and Guiseppe Castagna. Towards a calculus of mobile computations. In *Workshop on Internet Programming Languages, Chicago*, May 1998.

# A Lightweight Reliable
# Object Migration Protocol

Peter Van Roy[1,2], Per Brand[2], Seif Haridi[2], and Raphaël Collet[1]

[1] Université catholique de Louvain,
B-1348 Louvain-la-Neuve, Belgium
{pvr,raph}@info.ucl.ac.be
http://www.info.ucl.ac.be
[2] Swedish Institute of Computer Science,
S-164 28 Kista, Sweden
{perbrand,seif}@sics.se
http://www.sics.se

**Abstract.** This paper presents a lightweight reliable object migration protocol that preserves the centralized object semantics, allows for precise prediction of network behavior, and permits construction of fault tolerance abstractions in the language. Each object has a "home site" to which all migration requests are directed. Compared to the standard technique of creating and collapsing forwarding chains, this gives a better worst-case network behavior and it limits dependencies on third-party sites. The protocol defines "freely mobile" objects that have the interesting property of always executing locally, i.e., each method executes in the thread that invokes it. This makes them dual, in a precise sense, to stationary objects. The protocol is designed to be as efficient as a nonreliable protocol in the common case of no failure, and to provide sufficient hooks so that common fault tolerance algorithms can be programmed completely in the Oz language. The protocol is fully implemented in the network layer of the Mozart platform for distributed application development, which implements Oz (see http://www.mozart-oz.org). This paper defines the protocol in an intuitive yet precise way using the concept of *distribution graph* to model distributed execution of language entities. Formalization and proof of protocol properties are done elsewhere.

## 1 Introduction

What does it mean for an object to be mobile? Different systems interpret this notion in different ways [15]:

1. Only code is copied, not the state (e.g., Java applets [13]).
2. The original object is "frozen" and its code and state are both copied. The original is discarded before the copy is used. This is what is typically meant by "mobile agents" in programming books.
3. Concurrency control is added by freezing the original object, copying both its code and state, making it forward all messages, and then unfreezing it.

The copy maintains lexical scoping across the network by using network references for all of the original object's external references. This approach is taken by Emerald [10] and Obliq [5].

If the application programmer wants to control network behavior by placing objects on the appropriate sites and moving them as desired, then all three approaches have problems:

**Bad network behavior** If an alias is created from the old object to the new when it moves, then a sequence of moves creates a chain of aliases. There are various tricks to reduce the length of this chain, e.g., Emerald short-circuits it when a message is sent, but a basic unpredictability remains regarding third-party dependencies and number of network hops. Furthermore, if there is a site failure, Emerald uses a broadcast to recover the object, which is impractical on a WAN.

**Weak semantics** One way to get better network behavior is give up on the transparent semantics, i.e., to use one of the two first approaches above.

Is it possible to get both a predictable network behavior and a good semantics? A simple way to solve this problem is to make objects mobile by default, instead of stationary. We call these "freely mobile objects". Start with lightweight object mobility, in which a method always executes in the thread that invokes it. Implement this with a reliable distributed algorithm that guarantees predictable network behavior. Then control the mobility by *restricting* it. In this way, we achieve arbitrary mobility while keeping both predictable network behavior and good semantics. One purpose of this paper is to present a distributed algorithm that achieves these goals.

This paper consists of four parts. Section 2 introduces the graph model of distributed execution and its visual notation. Section 3 defines a home-based algorithm for freely mobile objects and discusses its properties and usefulness. Section 4 defines the basic mobile state protocol, which is the key algorithm at the heart of freely mobile objects [4, 19]. Section 5 extends the basic protocol to use precise failure detection, while maintaining the same performance as the basic protocol when there is no failure. This section also gives the state diagrams of both the basic and extended protocols. The extended protocol is part of the implementation of the Mozart programming system [11, 9], which implements the Oz language. Oz is a multiparadigm language with simple formal semantics that can be viewed as a concurrent object-oriented language with dataflow synchronization [8].

The extended protocol is being used to implement nontrivial fault tolerance abstractions in Oz [18, 17]. For example, we are currently testing an open distributed fault-tolerant transactional store [3, 7]. Clients to this store can come and go, and the store remains coherent as long as at least one working client exists at any given moment. A fuller explanation of the design of fault tolerance abstractions is beyond the scope of this paper.

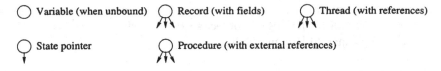

**Fig. 1.** Language entities as nodes in a graph

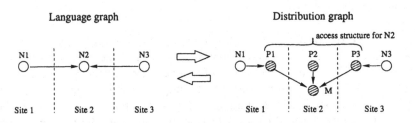

**Fig. 2.** Access structure in the distribution graph

## 2 Graph Notation for Distributed Executions

We depict distributed executions in a simple but precise manner using the concept of *distribution graph*. This section gives a self-contained explanation that suffices to understand the paper. We obtain the distribution graph in two steps from an arbitrary execution state of the system. The first step is independent of distribution. We model the execution state by a graph, called *language graph*, in which each language entity except for an object corresponds to one node (see Figure 1). A node can be considered as an active entity with internal state that can asynchronously send messages to other nodes and that can receive messages from other nodes. In terms of the language graph, Oz objects are compound entities, i.e., they consist of more than one node. Their structure is explained in Section 3.

In the second step, we introduce the notion of *site*. Assume a finite set of sites and annotate each node by its site (see Figure 2). If a node, e.g., N2, is referenced by at least one node on another site, then map it to a *set* of nodes, e.g., {P1,P2,P3,M}. This set is called the *access structure* of the original node. The map satisfies the following invariant. An access structure consists of at most one *proxy node* Pi on each site that referenced the original node and exactly one *manager node* M for the whole structure. The manager site is also called the *home site*. The resulting graph, containing both local nodes and access structures where necessary, is called the *distribution graph*. All example executions in the paper use this notation.

All distributed execution is modeled as distribution graph transformations. Nodes in the distribution graph are active entities with internal state that can send and receive messages. All graph transformations are atomic and initiated by the nodes. The two-level addressing mechanism by which a node identifies a send destination is beyond the scope of this paper (see [2]). We mention only that each access structure has a globally unique name, which is used to identify its nodes.

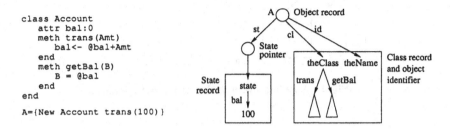

```
class Account
    attr bal:0
    meth trans(Amt)
        bal<- @bal+Amt
    end
    meth getBal(B)
        B = @bal
    end
end

A={New Account trans(100)}
```

**Fig. 3.** An object with one attribute and two methods

# 3 Freely Mobile Objects

In the distribution graph, an object shows up as a compound entity consisting of an object record, a class record containing procedures (the methods), a state pointer, and a record containing the object's state. The distributed behavior of the object is derived from the behavior of its parts. Figure 3 shows an object A that has one attribute, `bal`, and two methods, `trans` and `getBal`. The object is represented as an object record with three fields. The `st` field contains a state pointer, which points to the object's state record. The state pointer defines the site at which state updates can be done without network operations. The `cl` field contains the class record, which contains the procedures `trans` and `getBal` that implement the methods. The `id` field contains the object's unique identifier `theName`. The object record and the class record cannot be changed. However, by giving a new content to the state pointer, the object's state can be updated.

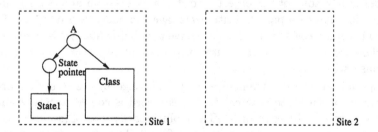

**Fig. 4.** A local object

Figure 4 shows an object A that is local to Site 1. There is no reference to A from any other site. Figure 5 shows an object A with one remote reference. The

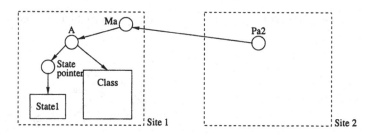

**Fig. 5.** A global object with one remote reference

object is now part of an access structure whose manager is on Site 1 and that has one proxy on Site 2. A local object A is transformed to a global (i.e., remotely-referenced) object when a message referencing A leaves Site 1. A manager node Ma is created on Site 1 when the message leaves. When the message arrives on Site 2, then a proxy node Pa2 is created there.

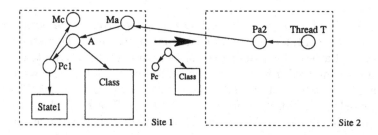

**Fig. 6.** The object is invoked remotely (1)

Figure 6 shows what happens when thread T invokes A from Site 2. At first, only the proxy Pa2 is present on Site 2, not the object itself. The proxy asks its manager for a copy of the object record. This causes an access structure to be created for the state pointer, with a manager Mc and one proxy Pc1. The class record is copied eagerly and does not have a global name. A message containing the class record and a state pointer proxy is sent to Site 2. The object's state remains on Site 1.

Figure 7 shows what happens when the message arrives. A second proxy Pc2 is created for the state pointer. The class record is copied to Site 2 and proxy Pa2 becomes the object record A. The mobile state protocol (see Section 4) then atomically transfers the state pointer to Site 2. The object record has a global name. This implies that any further messages to Site 2 containing object references will immediately refer to the local copy of the object record. No additional network operations are needed.

Figure 8 shows what happens after the state pointer is transferred to Site 2. The new state, State2, is created on Site 2 and will contain the updated object

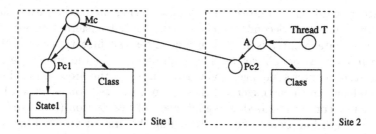

**Fig. 7.** The object is invoked remotely (2)

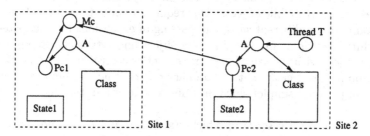

**Fig. 8.** The object is invoked remotely (3)

state after the method finishes. The old state, State1, may continue to exist on Site 1 but the state pointer no longer points to it.

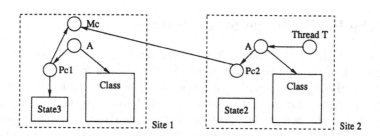

**Fig. 9.** The object moves back to Site 1

Figure 9 shows what happens if Site 1 invokes the object again. The state pointer is transferred back to Site 1. The new state, State3, is created on Site 1 and will contain the updated object state after the method finishes. The old state, State2, may continue to exist on Site 2 but the state pointer no longer points to it.

## 3.1 Discussion

There are several interesting things going on here. First, the object is always executed locally. The state pointer is always localized before the method starts executing, and it is guaranteed to stay local during the method execution while the object is locked. Second, the class code is only transferred once to any site. Only the state pointer is moved around after the first transfer. This makes object mobility very lightweight. Third, all requests for the object are serialized by the state pointer's manager node. This simplifies the protocol but introduces a dependency on the manager site (i.e., the protocol is "home-based" [12]). This dependency can be removed at higher levels of abstraction (e.g., see [3], which is also a migration protocol) or by extending the present protocol (see [16] for a simple solution).

A stationary object can be defined in a system in which the only mobile entities are freely mobile objects. This requires remote thread creation, synchronization between different sites, and passing of exceptions between sites. An Oz procedure that takes any freely mobile object and returns a reference to a stationary object with the same language semantics is given in [19]. The procedure's definition makes it clear that a stationary object is not a simple concept. Freely mobile objects are simpler since they always execute in the thread that invokes them.

There is a precise sense in which stationary and freely mobile objects are duals of each other. With a stationary object, the object state remains on one site, and the thread conceptually moves to that site, to execute there. With a freely mobile object, it is the reverse: the thread remains on one site, and the object state moves to that site. Since moving object state is simpler than moving a thread (see, e.g., [10, 14]), this confirms that freely mobile objects are simpler than stationary objects.

## 4   The Basic Mobile State Protocol

The mobile objects of Section 3 are compound entities that use several distributed algorithms. The object record is copied once lazily (when the object is first invoked), the methods are copied along with it, and the object's state pointer is moved between sites that request it. The protocol that moves the state pointer, the *mobile state* protocol, is particularly interesting because of the way it is integrated into the object system. In this section we give the basic protocol that assumes there is no failure. Section 5 explains how the protocol is extended with failure detection.

The protocol must guarantee consistency between consecutive states. If the consecutive states are on different sites, then this requires an atomic transfer of the state pointer between the sites. A site that wants the state pointer requests it from the state pointer's manager, and the latter sends a forwarding command to the site that has (or will eventually have[1]) the state pointer. Therefore, in the basic protocol, the manager only needs to store one piece of information, namely the site that will eventually contain the state pointer [19].

We show how the protocol works by means of an example. Figure 10 shows a state pointer C referenced from two sites. The state pointer is initially on Site

---

[1] In the temporal logic sense [1].

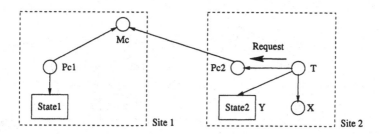

**Fig. 10.** The state pointer is referenced by Pc1; thread T requests a state update

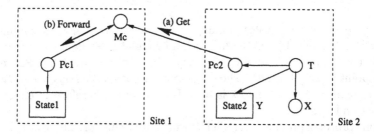

**Fig. 11.** (a) Pc2 requests the state pointer; (b) Pc1 is asked to forward it

1; proxy Pc1 has the state pointer and proxy Pc2 does not. Thread T executes on Site 2 an object method that will update the object state. At some point, T requests a state update by sending a **Request** message to Pc2. The thread references the new state through variable Y. When the update completes then the thread will also reference the old state through variable X.

Since proxy Pc2 does not have the state pointer, it must ask its manager. Figure 11 shows (a) Pc2 requesting the state pointer by sending a **Get** message to manager Mc, and (b) the manager sending a **Forward** message to the proxy that will eventually have the state pointer, namely Pc1. Therefore the manager can accept another request immediately; it does not need to wait until the state pointer's transfer is complete.

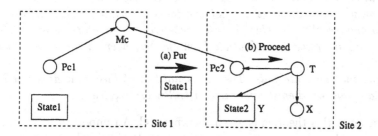

**Fig. 12.** (a) Pc1 forwards the state pointer; (b) Pc2 informs thread T

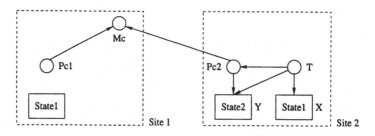

**Fig. 13.** Pc2 has the state pointer; T references the old and new states

Figure 12 shows (a) Pc1 sending to Pc2 a Put message containing the old state, State1, and (b) Pc2 sending to T a Proceed message informing it that the transfer is complete. The old state may still exist on Site 1 but Pc1 no longer has a pointer to it. Figure 13 shows the final situation. Pc2 has the state pointer, which points to State2, and X is bound to State1. Therefore T references both State1 and State2.

This protocol provides a predictable network behavior. There are a maximum of three network hops for the state pointer to change sites; only two if the manager is on the source or destination site; zero if the state pointer is on the requesting site. The protocol maintains sequential consistency, that is, updates to the state pointer are done in a globally consistent order.

## 5 The Reliable Mobile State Protocol

We extend the basic protocol to obtain a new protocol that provides reliable failure detection and that is a sufficient foundation for building fault tolerance abstractions. The resulting protocol satisfies the following theorem:

**Theorem 1 (Failure detection theorem).** *If the state pointer is requested at proxy P, then exactly one of the following three statements is eventually true:*

1. *The manager site does not fail and the state pointer is never lost. Then P will eventually receive the state pointer exactly once.*
2. *The manager site does not fail and the state pointer is lost before the state pointer reaches P. Then P will never receive the state pointer, but it will eventually receive notification from the manager that the state pointer is lost.*
3. *The manager site fails. Then P is notified of this. If it does not have the state pointer, then it infers that it will never receive it.*

The proof of this theorem is given elsewhere [4]. An important corollary of this theorem is that the protocol has no time outs. Deciding whether or not to time out is left to the application.

Figure 14 gives the essential parts of the thread, proxy, and manager state diagrams for the basic protocol and its reliable extension. Each circle represents

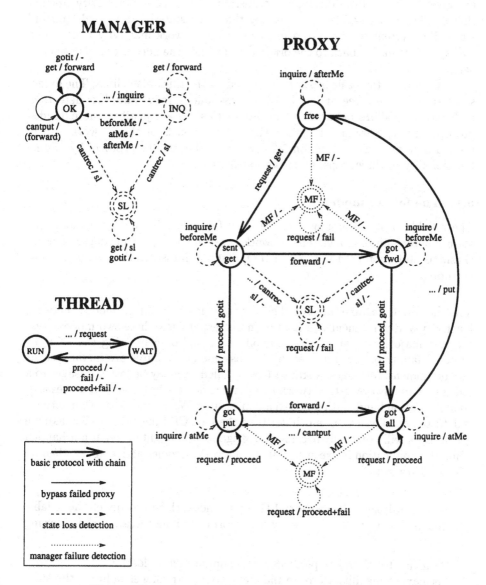

**Fig. 14.** State diagrams of the basic and reliable protocols

a proxy state or manager state. A transition arrow represents an atomic state change; each arrow is optionally labeled *Condition / Action*. Here *Condition* is the firing condition (often a received message, but possibly a network condition), and *Action* is an action to be performed on firing (often a sent message). MF means "manager failure," SL means "state lost," and "-" means no action. To avoid overloading the figure, message arguments are left out and some conditions are given as "...". In addition, the transitions for network inactivity are not shown. They can be added by assuming that each state has a second "mirror" state. The system transfers to a mirror state if network inactivity is detected. The system transfers back to the original state when the network becomes active again.

In Figure 14, the basic protocol is defined by the thick black lines. The extensions are given in three further steps: bypass failed proxy, state loss detection, and manager failure detection. The rest of this section justifies the extended protocol. First, Section 5.1 defines the failure models of the network and of the state pointer. Then, Section 5.2 constructs the reliable protocol by adding functionality in three steps, as shown in the figure.

## 5.1 The failure models

The reliable protocol assumes the network failure model and implements the state pointer failure model. The network is assumed to send messages in asynchronous and unordered (i.e., non-FIFO) fashion. Messages that arrive are not corrupted.

**The network failure model** The network has two failure modes: network inactivity and permanent site failure. In our experience, these two modes cover the vast majority of failures in an application environment using the TCP/IP protocol family on the Internet [6]. We assume site failures are instantaneous and permanent. Messages in transit from a failed site may be lost. Messages to a failed site are always lost. Network inactivity is detected as a sudden decrease in communication bandwidth between a pair of sites. We assume network inactivity is detected quickly, e.g., in much less time than a TCP time out. We also assume the network will eventually become active again. This might or might not happen while the application is executing. If the network becomes active again, then no messages are lost.

**The state pointer failure model** Given the network failure model, the reliable protocol is designed so that a proxy can inform a calling thread of the following problems:

- Permanent inability to perform a state update (state lost).
- Permanent inability to move the state pointer (manager failure); the state pointer may or may not be local.
- Current inability to perform a state update (network inactivity). This may go away, if the network inactivity goes away.

– Current inability to move the state pointer (network inactivity); the state
pointer may or may not be local. This may go away, if the network inactivity
goes away.

The Mozart system can be configured at run-time to detect these failures syn-
chronously or asynchronously, and to raise an exception or call a user-defined
procedure when a particular failure is encountered on a given state pointer [18].

## 5.2   Stepwise construction of the reliable protocol

We construct the reliable protocol in stepwise fashion from its nonreliable an-
cestor, following the steps of Figure 14. We first introduce the concept of *proxy
chain*, which at any instant is the sequence of proxy nodes that the state pointer
will eventually traverse. If several proxies send Get messages in quick succession,
then it may take some time before the state pointer has visited them all. The
proxy chain represents at any instant the sequence of proxies that are still waiting for the state pointer [19]. In the basic protocol, the proxy chain is stored as
a distributed data structure.

**Basic protocol with chain**   The first improvement is to let the manager maintain a conservative approximation to the proxy chain (see Figure 15). This is
very simple: when the manager receives a Get message, it appends the requesting proxy to the proxy chain. It then sends a Forward message to the preceding
proxy, so that the latter forwards the state pointer to the requesting proxy. When
a proxy receives a Put message containing the state pointer, it sends a new message, Gotit, to the manager. The Gotit message does not exist in the basic
protocol. When the manager receives the Gotit, then it removes from the proxy
chain all proxies before the one that sent the Gotit. Moving the state pointer
costs four messages instead of three for the basic protocol, but the message
latency does not change, i.e., it is still three messages.

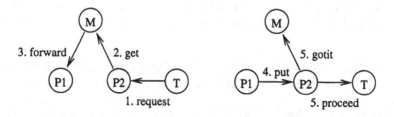

**Fig. 15.** Basic protocol with chain

**Bypass failed proxy** The second improvement consists in checking whether a proxy is working before forwarding the state pointer to that proxy (see Figure 16). Suppose proxy $P_1$ has to forward the content to proxy $P_2$. If $P_1$ detects that $P_2$ has failed, then it sends a new message, Cantput, to the manager. The manager then sends another Forward message to $P_1$ to bypass the failed proxy. Therefore the state pointer can survive crashes of sites that do not possess it.

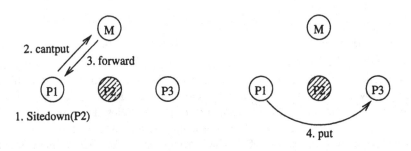

**Fig. 16.** Bypass failed proxy

**State loss detection** The third improvement is to add an inquiry protocol that determines when the state pointer is definitely lost. This loss can happen in two ways:

- The state pointer is at proxy P and P's site crashes.
- The state pointer has been sent over the network in a Put message and the message is lost because of a site failure (of the sender or the receiver).

The inquiry protocol is implemented at the manager node. The inquiry protocol traverses the chain and asks each proxy where the state pointer is. The proxy answers with beforeMe, atMe, or afterMe. The basic idea is to bracket the state pointer's location. If the protocol finds two proxies that answer afterMe and beforeMe, and all proxies between them have crashed, and there is nothing in the network, then the state pointer is lost.

**Manager failure detection** The fourth and last improvement is to allow proxies to detect a manager failure. This is useful in the following situations:

- Proxy P does not have the state pointer and wishes to obtain it. The proxy infers that it will never receive the state pointer and it can directly signal that fact to the thread.
- Proxy P has the state pointer and cannot forward it. The proxy infers that it will keep the state pointer forever.

# 6 Conclusions and Reflections

This paper presents the main ideas of an efficient, reliable object migration protocol that preserves centralized object semantics and allows for precise prediction of network behavior. The main limitation of the protocol is its dependency on the manager site. This limitation will be removed in the future [16]. The migration protocol is completely implemented as part of Mozart, a platform for distributed application development based on the Oz language [11]. We are using Mozart to write efficient and robust distributed applications (e.g., [7]).

We introduce the concept of "freely mobile object," whose distributed semantics are implemented by the migration protocol. Freely mobile objects are interesting because they are always executed locally, i.e., each method is executed in the thread that invokes it. The same property holds for centralized objects. Stationary objects, which are always executed on the same site, are more complex beasts on any system. For example, Java RMI semantics must define which threads are used for remote calls and when new threads are created [14]. In Oz, one can define stationary objects *in* the language. They require remote thread creation, synchronization between threads on different sites, and passing exceptions between threads on different sites.

We provide evidence that a freely mobile object is a useful basis for a system with migratory objects. Freely mobile objects behave as state caches, and as such provide a mechanism for latency tolerance. Furthermore, arbitrary mobility behavior can be programmed at the language level by restricting the mobility of freely mobile objects. At all times, the language semantics of objects are respected.

## Acknowledgements

This research is partially financed by the Walloon Region of Belgium. The reliable migration protocol was designed by Per Brand and the first version of the Mozart network layer was implemented by him. We thank Erik Klintskog for his implementation of fault-tolerant objects in Oz using the protocol presented here. We thank Iliès Alouini for his implementation of a fault-tolerant transactional store in Oz. Finally, we thank all the other contributors and developers of the Mozart Programming System.

## References

1. Mack W. Alford, Leslie Lamport, and Geoff P. Mullery. chapter 2. Lecture Notes in Computer Science, vol. 190. Springer Verlag, 1985. Basic Concepts, in Distributed Systems–Methods and Tools for Specification, An Advanced Course.
2. Iliès Alouini and Peter Van Roy. Le protocole réparti de Distributed Oz (The distributed protocol of Distributed Oz) (in French). In *Colloque Francophone sur l'Ingénierie des Protocoles (CFIP 99)*, pages 283–298. Hermès Science Publications, April 1999.

3. Iliès Alouini and Peter Van Roy. An open distributed fault-tolerant transactional store in Mozart. In preparation, 2000.

4. Per Brand, Peter Van Roy, Raphaël Collet, and Erik Klintskog. A fault-tolerant mobile-state protocol and its language interface. In preparation, 1999.

5. Luca Cardelli. A language with distributed scope. In *Principles of Programming Languages (POPL)*, pages 286–297, January 1995.

6. Douglas E. Comer. *Internetworking with TCP/IP. Vol. 1: Principles, Protocols, and Architecture*. Prentice-Hall, Englewood Cliffs, N.J., 1995.

7. Donatien Grolaux. Editeur graphique réparti basé sur un modèle transactionnel (A distributed graphic editor based on a transactional model) (in French). Technical report, Université catholique de Louvain, June 1998. Mémoire de fin d'études (Master's project).

8. Seif Haridi and Nils Franzén. Tutorial of Oz. Technical report, 1999. Draft. In Mozart documentation, available at http://www.mozart-oz.org.

9. Seif Haridi, Peter Van Roy, Per Brand, and Christian Schulte. Programming languages for distributed applications. *New Generation Computing*, 16(3), May 1998.

10. Eric Jul, Henry Levy, Norman Hutchinson, and Andrew Black. Fine-grained mobility in the Emerald system. *ACM Transactions on Computer Systems*, 6(1):109–133, February 1988.

11. Mozart Consortium (DFKI, SICS, UCL, UdS). The Mozart programming system (Oz 3), January 1999. Available at http://www.mozart-oz.org.

12. James D. Solomon. *Mobile IP–The Internet Unplugged*. PTR Prentice Hall, Upper Saddle River, New Jersey, 1998.

13. Sun Microsystems. *The Java Series*. Mountain View, Calif., 1996. Available at http://www.aw.com/cp/javaseries.html.

14. Sun Microsystems. *The Remote Method Invocation Specification*. Sun Microsystems, Mountain View, Calif., 1997. Available at http://www.javasoft.com.

15. Tommy Thorn. Programming languages for mobile code. *ACM Computing Surveys*, 29(3):213–239, September 1997.

16. Peter Van Roy. Eliminating manager dependency in mobile cell protocol, August 1999. Message on internal Mozart mailing list.

17. Peter Van Roy. On the separation of aspects in distributed programming: Application to distribution structure and fault tolerance in Mozart. In *International Workshop on Parallel and Distributed Computing for Symbolic and Irregular Applications (PDSIA 99)*, Tohoku University, Sendai, Japan, July 1999.

18. Peter Van Roy, Seif Haridi, and Per Brand. Distributed programming in Mozart – A tutorial introduction. Technical report, Mozart Consortium, 1999. Draft. In Mozart documentation, available at http://www.mozart-oz.org.

19. Peter Van Roy, Seif Haridi, Per Brand, Gert Smolka, Michael Mehl, and Ralf Scheidhauer. Mobile objects in Distributed Oz. *ACM Transactions on Programming Languages and Systems*, 19(5):804–851, September 1997.

# Seal: A Framework for Secure Mobile Computations

Jan Vitek[1] and Giuseppe Castagna[2]

[1] Object Systems Group, CUI, Université de Genève, Suisse
[2] C.N.R.S, Laboratoire d'Informatique de l'Ecole Normale Supérieure, Paris, France

**Abstract.** The Seal calculus is a distributed process calculus with localities and mobility of computational entities called seals. Seal is also a framework for writing secure distributed applications over large scale open networks such as the Internet. This paper motivates our design choices, presents the syntax and reduction semantics of the calculus, and demonstrates its expressiveness by examples focused on security and management distributed systems.

## 1 Introduction

Advances in computer communications and computer hardware are changing the landscape of computing. Networking is now cheap and pervasive. The Internet has become a platform for large scale distributed programming. What is needed now is programming languages that support the development of Internet applications.

In the last couple of years a number of process calculi have been designed to model programming large scale distributed systems over open networks. Several of these calculi [12, 19, 34, 21] advocate programming models based on the notion of mobile computations. These mobile calculi give a semantics to programs structured as systems of communicating mobile computations also referred to as mobile agents.

We present a low level language called Seal which has been designed for distributed computing over large scale open networks such as the Internet. The language is based on a model of computing in which program mobility and resource access control are essential mechanisms. We introduce Seal as a fairly simple language, an extension of Milner's $\pi$-calculus, with the goal of being able to express the essential properties of Internet programs. We view Seal as a framework for exploring the design space of security and mobility features. For this reason rather than striving for minimality, Seal tries to express key features of Internet programming directly.

### 1.1 Internet design principles

The Seal language adheres to five design principles that are particularly suited to Internet programming. These principle are the following.

### 1.1.1 No reliance on global state

The physical size and number of hosts require solutions that scale to wide area networks of millions of nodes. At this size, the language in which programs are expressed can not afford to assume any shared state. Thus, algorithms that require synchronization over sets of machines or up-to-date information about the state of groups of processors are prohibited. For example, automatic memory management on the Internet would require synchronization of the whole system to collect all unreferenced objects, this means stopping the Internet for "a couple of instants" [29].

### 1.1.2 Explicit localities

Fluctuations in bandwidth, latency and reliability are so common that they can not be papered over in the language semantics [38]. The location where computation occurs and the location of its resources are essential to the efficiency and the fault tolerance of a distributed program. Locations should thus appear at the programming level and be under the program's control.

### 1.1.3 Restricted connectivity

Failures of machines and communication links can occur without warning or detection [31]. Some of these failures may be temporary as machines may be restarted and connection reestablished, but others may be permanent. Furthermore, firewalls impose purposeful restriction on communication abilities of programs. This means that, at a given time, a computation may be able to communicate with only a subsets of the other entities on the network. At the extreme, a computation may have to operate disconnected.

### 1.1.4 Dynamic configuration

In an open network new hosts and communication links are added with no advance notice, hosts may disappear and even reappear under a new name and address. The topology both in the physical sense and in the logical sense of services and resources available is thus changing over time. Programming the Internet thus requires working in dynamically evolving environment. Ideally, the location of all elements of a distributed computation should be controlled by the computation itself, allowing it to adapt to changes in its environment.

### 1.1.5 Access control

Finally, security is the *conditio sine qua non* of every discussion of the Internet. Security requirements vary from application to application, policies must be tailored to the specific requirements of applications or application domains. At best, a language can provide mechanisms for protecting resources to facilitate the enforcement of policies.

## 1.2 Models of Internet Programming

These principles are a basis for designing a distributed programming language. Unfortunately, full-fledged computer languages are usually cluttered with semantic noise coming from the many features not directly pertinent to distribution. We focus on a model of distributed programming as a miniature programming language composed of only the core features needed for mobile computations.

Distributed programming is an inherently concurrent activity, quite naturally concurrent language and distributed ones have common roots. The advantage of extending an existing concurrent model for distribution are that some of the theory can be reused as well. We consider three models of concurrency: *Linda, Actors*, and the *π-calculus*.

Linda is a coordination model; it specifies only how a community of concurrent, and possibly distributed, processes can communicate and synchronize their activities using a shared data structure called a tuple space [20]. Linda has been used successfully in small-scale configurations, but its scalability is limited by the synchronous nature of tuple space operations. In essence, the presence of single shared data structure contradicts our first design principle as it is a form of global state.

The Actor model described by Agha [3] presents a distributed computation as a group of named entities, actors, which communicate by asynchronous message passing. Communication is tied to knowledge of names; knowing the name of another actor suffices to be allowed to communicate with it. As names are values, name-passing models evolving patterns of cooperation amongst groups of actors. From our point of view, Actors are a step in the right direction as they forego the single shared data structure of Linda in favor of a message passing model which abides by our first design principle. Nevertheless, the calculus lacks a notion of locality: there are no distances between actors, nor are there means to restrict communication abilities.

The π-calculus [24], our last candidate, models concurrent computation by processes that exchange messages over named channels. Channel names play almost exactly the same role as actor names. Thus the π-calculus is also adequate to model evolving systems, but just as Actors, it lacks a suitable notion of location and has no direct means to model restricted connectivity. Two further features complicate a distributed interpretation of the π-calculus: synchronous message passing and choice, both imply synchronization consensus. Nevertheless, the π-calculus is attractive because of the solid theoretical basis developed over the years.

Further these three calculi lack resource access control mechanisms. They do not allow to model features like firewalls or sandbox commonly found in networks and programming languages.

**Structure** This paper is structured as follows. Section 2 presents our design choices and gives an informal introduction to the main features of the calculus. Section 3 details both syntax and operational semantics of the calculus. Section 4 presents some programming examples. Section 5 discusses related work. Finally, section 6 states some conclusions and outlines future directions of investigation.

# 2 The Seal Framework

This section outlines the main features of the Seal calculus, a distributed model of computing for large scale open networks. We briefly present our design choices, discuss the objectives of the work and present the abstractions of the framework.

Seal can be roughly described as the $\pi$-calculus with hierarchical locations, mobility, and resource access control. Unlike many distributed programming languages, our goal is not to provide a high-level programming model that eases distributed programming by hiding localities, but rather its goal is to expose the network and hand over control of localities and low-level protection to the system programmer. The means to this end are powerful mobility and protection primitives. Another view of Seal is as a substrate for implementing higher level languages and advanced distributed services. In this light the Seal takes on the role of lowest common denominator between various Internet applications. Sophisticated services that require higher degrees of coherence and synchronization can be built on top of it. Examples of such services are distributed memory management, location independent secure messaging, and channels with quality of service guarantees.

What Seal does provide is a model of mobility which subsumes message passing, remote evaluation as well as process migration and which models user mobility and hardware mobility. Furthermore, the framework provides a hierarchical protection model, in which each level of the hierarchy can implement security policies by mediation — actions performed at a lower level in the hierarchy are scrutinized and controlled by higher levels. The hierarchical model guarantees that a policy defined at some level will not be bypassed or amended at lower levels. When coupled with mediation this gives rise to programming styles that emphasize interposition techniques [26, 17, 33].

## 2.1 Abstractions

Seal unifies several concepts from distributed programming into three abstractions: **locations**, **processes** and **resources**. Locations are meant to stand for physical places such as those delimited by the boundaries of address spaces, host machines, routers, firewalls, local area networks or wide area networks. Locations also embody logical boundaries such as protection domains, sandboxes and applications. The process abstraction stands for any flow of control such as a thread or operating system process. Finally, resources unify physical resources such as memory locations and peripheral device interfaces with services such as those offered by other applications, the operating system or a runtime system.

We now review the main features of the model and at the same time introduce the concrete syntax of the Seal language by examples.

### 2.1.1 Names

Names denote two kinds of computational entities, seals and channels; they are also values and as such can be exchanged in communication. New names are created by the restriction operator ($\nu$ _), they are considered distinct from any other name. Thus the expression ($\nu\, x)P$ creates a fresh name $x$ which can be used within the process $P$ without fear of name clash with any other name.

### 2.1.2 Processes

In a process calculus every expression denotes a process — a computation — running in parallel with other processes. The simplest Seal expression is the inert process **0**, a process with no behavior. A process $\alpha\,.\,P$ is composed of an action $\alpha$ and a continuation process $P$; this expression denotes a process waiting to perform $\alpha$ and then to behave like $P$. Actions consist of communication and moves and are explained later on. $P \mid Q$ denotes a process composed of two subprocesses, $P$ and $Q$ running in parallel. The replicated process $!\,P$ behaves like $P \mid \,!\,P$; it can be equivalently considered as a process that creates an infinite number of copies of $P$ running in parallel. Finally a process can also be a location with a process body, that is a *seal*, as we will see next.

### 2.1.3 Locations

*Seals* are named, hierarchically-structured, locations. The expression $n[P]$ denotes a seal named $n$ running process $P$. Since a seal encapsulate a process and a seal is also a process, then a seal can contain (the parallel composition of) several seals yielding a hierarchy of *subseals* of arbitrary depth. If $P$ contains one or more seals, say $\vec{m} = m_1 \ldots m_n$, then $n$ is the parent of $\vec{m}$ and $\vec{m}$ are the children of $n$. The transitive closure of the set of children is the set of *subseals* of $n$. A configuration is depicted graphically in Figure 1 which shows an outermost seal that represents the network its children are hosts, and their subseals are instances of application programs. Of course in an implementation we would not program the network — we do not plan to actually control the flow of bits along

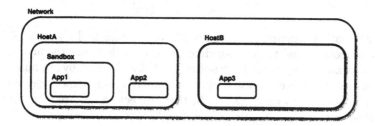

**Fig. 1.** Seal configuration.

wires — rather it would program the routers and such. Nevertheless it is elegant to be able to model the behavior of the network and of the programs that inhabit it within a single formalism. The configuration of Figure 1 corresponds to the expression appearing in Figure 2, where the processes $P, P'$ and $P''$ denote behaviors of the sandbox and two hosts, and $Q, Q'$ and $Q''$ denote the behaviors of the applications. An alternate graphical representation is the configuration tree in the same figure. In a configuration tree process-labeled vertices represent seals while edges represent seal inclusion. The position of seal names (on edges) emphasizes the weak association between names and seals, they are merely tags used by parents to tell their children apart.

NETWORK[
      HOSTA[$P'$ |
            SANDBOX[ $P$ | APP1[$Q$]] |
            APP2[$Q'$]] |
      HOSTB[$P''$ | APP3[$Q''$]]
      ]

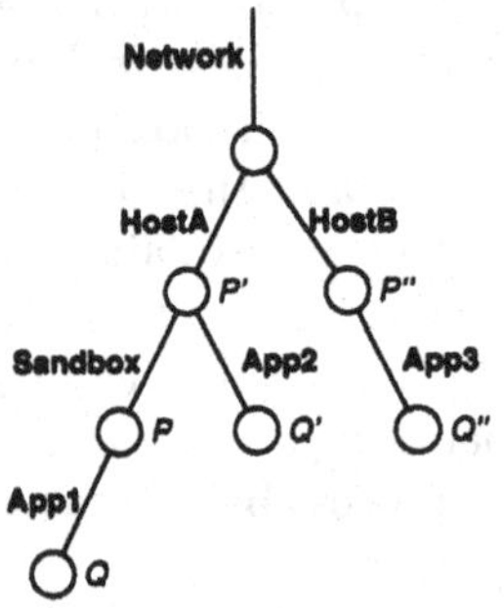

**Fig. 2.** Seal term and configuration tree.

### 2.1.4 Resources

The only resources in Seal are *channels*. Channels are named computational structures used to synchronize concurrent processes. As it happens for processes, channels are located. Channel denotations specify where channels are located. Thus, a channel $x$ is denoted by $x^\eta$, where $\eta$ is $\star$ when the channel is local, is $\uparrow$ when the channel is in the parent, and is the name of the seal when the channel is in a child. For example, consider the following process

$$n_1[\, P_1 \mid n_2[\, P_2 \mid n_3[P_3]\,] \,]$$

where the seal $n_1$ running the process $P_1$ has a child seal $n_2$; this child seal runs the process $P_2$ and has its own child the seal $n_3$ that runs the process $P_3$. A channel $x$ located in $n_2$ would be denoted as $x^{n_2}$ by $P_1$, as $x^\star$ by $P_2$, and as $x^\uparrow$ by $P_3$. Processes are allowed to use only the channels whose names they are aware of: it is not possible to guess names. In that respect names are communication capabilities, without propagation control and revocation, and provide a degree of protection and secrecy [1].

### 2.1.5 Communication

Seal allows only three distinct patterns of interaction shown in the figure below. We extend our graphical convention and use lozenges to denote channels and circles to denote processes.

There are two forms of *remote* interaction: a process located in the parent synchronizes with a process located in a child on a channel of the child (*down-sync*); a process in the parent synchronizes with a process in a child on a channel of

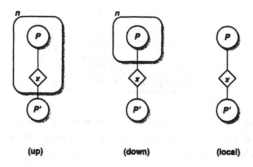

**(up)**         **(down)**         **(local)**

the parent (*up-sync*). And there is one form of *local* interaction: two co-located processes synchronize over a local channel. Channel synchronization is used both for communication (the channel is used to pass a name) and for mobility (the channel is used to move a seal). Each kind of interaction is specified by different actions.

There are two matching communication actions: $\overline{x}^\eta(y).P$ is a process that outputs the name $y$ on channel $x$ (located in $\eta$), and then behaves like $P$; $x^\eta(\lambda y).P$ is a process that waits for input on channel $x$ (located in $\eta$) and binds this input to all occurrences of $y$ in $P$.

When two processes running in parallel wait for matching actions on the same channel, the processes synchronizes and their actions are consumed. Thus a local communication is performed by processes of the form $x^\star(\lambda y).P \mid \overline{x}^\star(z).Q$. After the synchronization we obtain $P' \mid Q$ where $P'$ is obtained from $P$ by replacing all unbound occurrences of $y$ by $z$ (a standard notation for $P'$ is $P\{z/y\}$).

When a communication action acts on a non-local (respectively, local) channel we call it a *remote* (respectively, *local*) action. Remote actions produce *remote interactions*. So for remote communications we have, say, $x^n(\lambda y).P$ which tries to read a value emitted along channel $x$ located in child seal $n$, or $\overline{x}^\uparrow(y).P$ which tries to output a value along channel $x$ located in the parent. The matching action of a remote action is always a local action. Consider the following expression (note that this expression does not synchronize, the missing ingredient will be explained soon):

$$n[\, x^\star(\lambda y).P \,] \quad \mid \quad \overline{x}^n(z).P'$$

$x^\star(\lambda y).P$ is a process waiting to read a value from local channel $x$. $\overline{x}^n(z).P'$ is a process that wants to emit a value along the channel $x$ located in $n$. The remote action is matched by a local action.

Another way to view this form of interaction is that a local action is an "open" offer, that is, it does not prescribe which seal should provide a matching offer (it can also be matched by another local action). On the other hand, a remote action is a "closed" offer in the sense that the target seal is named explicitly. All combination of remote interaction in $P' \mid n[P]$ are summarized by the following table

|  |  | $P$ | $P'$ |
|---|---|---|---|
| (down-sync) | read | $x^\star(\lambda y).Q$ | $\overline{x}^n(z).Q'$ |
|  | write | $\overline{x}^\star(y).Q$ | $x^n(\lambda z).Q'$ |
| (up-sync) | read | $x^\uparrow(\lambda y).Q$ | $\overline{x}^\star(z).Q'$ |
|  | write | $\overline{x}^\uparrow(y).Q$ | $x^\star(\lambda z).Q'$ |

These interaction patterns are restrictive. For example, they do not allow processes located in sibling seals (and even less those located in arbitrary seals) to communicate directly. Communication across a seal configuration must be encoded; in other words every distributed interaction up to packet routing must be programmed.

## 2.2 Mobility

Seals may be moved over channels. The expression $\overline{x}^\star\{y\}.P$ denotes a process that is waiting to send a child seal $y$ along channel $x$ and then behave like $P$. The expression $x^\star\{z\}.P$ denotes a process waiting to receive a seal along channel $x$ and name it $z$.

Seal mobility is said *objective*, since a seal is moved by (a process in) the parent. The antithesis is *subjective* mobility in which a computational entity may move itself [12]. The computation encapsulated within a seal's boundary is not affected by the seal's mobility. Notification may be part of a mutually agreed upon mobility protocol, but in certain cases transparent mobility is desirable. For example, if the move occurred for load balancing reasons, the new parent will provide exactly the same services as the previous parent, and it is thus legitimate to hide mobility from seals.

A seal move action requires that a seal bearing the requested name is present otherwise the operations blocks. If several seals bear the same name, the send will select one of them randomly. Move actions can only send a single seal along a channel and the name of the seal may not be preserved by mobility. The full form of a receive action is shown by the expression $x^n\{\vec{y}\}.P$ (where $\vec{y} = y_1 \ldots y_n$) that denotes a process waiting to receive *one* seal and create $n$ identical copies of that seal under the names $\vec{y}$. The complementary action is the send action $\overline{x}^n\{n\}$ which sends a seal denoted by name $n$ over channel $x$. A first example of the use of mobility is a copy operation — typically used for fault tolerance to dynamically replicate running applications as new servers come online, or to improve availability by replicating computations. Let $y$ be a fresh name, we encode a copy operator as follows (we use small capitals to denote defined operators, which, for simplicity, may be infix and composed of several keywords):

$$\text{COPY}\,x\,\text{AS}\,z.P \quad \equiv \quad (\nu y)(\overline{y}^\star\{x\}.\mathbf{0} \mid y^\star\{x\,z\}.P)$$

Intuitively, $\text{COPY}\,n\,\text{AS}\,m.\mathbf{0} \mid n[P]$ reduces to $m[P] \mid n[P]$, that is, it creates a seal $m$ that is a copy of $n$. This is obtained by sending the seal denoted by $n$ on a local channel $y$ and reactivating two copies of it, one named $n$ the other named

$m$. More precisely, the operation first creates a brand new channel name $y$ (the purpose of this new name is to prevent any other process running in parallel from interfering with the protocol). Then, the subprocess on the right tries to move $n$ on the local channel, while the one on the left waits to receive the seal and instantiate two copies of it, one named $n$ and the other named $m$.

On the configuration tree, mobility corresponds to a tree rewriting operation. A move disconnects a subtree rooted at some seal $y$ and grafts it either onto the parent of $y$, or onto one of $y$ children, or back onto $y$ itself. The rewriting operation relabels the edge associated to the moved seal, and can create a finite number of copies of the subtree rooted at the moved seal. The diagrams below show an initial configuration $(a)$ and all three possible configurations obtained after a move. $(b)$ is obtained by moving $n$ into the parent and renaming it to $m$. $(c)$ is obtained by moving $n$ in $x$ and renaming it to $m$. $(d)$ is obtained by renaming $n$ to $m$ (local move). Each of these moves can also introduce copies.

(a)  (b)  (c)  (d)

For example, the initial configuration (a) depicted above corresponds to the expression $R \mid y[\, Q \mid x[P] \mid n[S] \,]$, while the final configuration (b) is described by the expression $R' \mid m[S] \mid y[\, Q' \mid x[P] \,]$. The processes involved in the move of $n$ are $Q$ (the sender) and $R$ (the receiver) and use a channel located either in $y$ or in its environment. If the channel, say $w$, is located in $y$ then $Q$ must perform the action $\overline{w}^{\star}\{n\}$ and $R$ the action $w^{n}\{m\}$, otherwise $Q$ must perform the action $\overline{w}^{\uparrow}\{n\}$ and $R$ the action $w^{\star}\{m\}$.

## 2.3 Protection

Use of non-local channels implies a threat to security, as an unknown process that may have migrated from an untrusted location has a way to access resources of its host. We propose several mechanisms to assist in the task of writing secure systems.

As a first line of defense, seals are not allowed to move about arbitrarily. Migration is always under the control of a seal's environment which decides when it occurs. Furthermore a seal must actually perform a receive action in order to allow a new seal to migrate from the outside and since it chooses the name for the new seal it can choose this name fresh and thus arbitrarily isolate the newcomer from the other processes. Nevertheless, accepting a seal is a risk and further protection mechanisms are required.

The second line of defense is keeping tight control of names of channels. That is, by not giving out a name of a service, we can guarantee that the service can not be called by migrant seals, of course this also somewhat reduces the usefulness of the service. Once a name has been given out, it may be difficult to control its propagation in the system, it is safe to assume that it quickly becomes public. One could envision a notion of trust playing a role here. For instance a trusted seal, would not willfully reveal a secret name. Of course, we would still have to prove that it does not do it by mistake.

The third security ingredient is tight control over local resources. We have already said that a local action is an "open" offer since it may synchronize either with another local action or with a remote action. The latter case constitutes an external accesses to a local resource. Therefore we want to strictly monitor these access by allowing the synchronization with a remote action only in presence of an explicit permission.

The protection mechanism we propose to control inter-seal communication is called *portal*. The idea is that if a seal $A$ wants to use seal $B$'s channel $x$, then $B$ must *open* a portal for $A$ at $x$. A portal is best viewed as an linear channel access permission. As soon as synchronization takes place, the portal is closed again. In the calculus the action to open a portal is $\mathbf{open}_n$ $\mathbf{x}$ where $\mathbf{x}$ is either $x$ (the action allows the seal $n$ to read once the local channel $x$) or $\overline{x}$ (the action allows the seal $n$ to write once on the local channel $x$). In Figure 3 we have a seal $n$ containing the process $P'$ and running in parallel with two processes $P$ and $S$. The latter processes interact on local channels $x'$ and $y'$, thus no portal is needed. $S$ interacts with $P'$ via a local channel $x$ monitored by a portal controlled by $S$, and via a channel $y$ in $n$ and monitored by a portal controlled by $P'$. Imagine that $P'$ wants to communicate to $S$ the name of its channel $y$ (possibly unknown

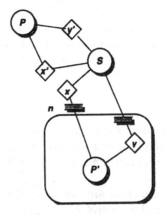

**Fig. 3.** Total mediation.

to $S$ and then wait an acknowledgment on $y$). Then $P'$ must send $y$ to $S$ via $x$ and open the portal to allow $S$ to write the acknowledgment on $y$ (the channel $y$ is used only for synchronization; to stress it we omit parameters and arguments of actions on it, and write $y^\eta()$ or $\bar{y}^\eta()$).

$$P' = (\bar{x}^\uparrow(y) \,.\, \mathbf{open}_\uparrow \, \bar{y} \,.\, P_1) \mid (y^\star() \,.\, P_2)$$

The process $S$ opens the portal to allow $n$ to write on local channel $x$, then it reads a name from a channel located in $n$ and, finally sends the acknowledgment along the name it just read:

$$S = (\mathbf{open}_n \, \bar{x} \,.\, S_1) \mid (x^\star(\lambda z) \,.\, \bar{z}^n() \,.\, S_2)$$

Thus we start by

$$\mathbf{open}_n \, \bar{x} \,.\, S_1 \mid x^\star(\lambda z) \,.\, \bar{z}^n() \,.\, S_2 \mid n[\bar{x}^\uparrow(y) \,.\, \mathbf{open}_\uparrow \, \bar{y} \,.\, P_1 \mid y^\star() \,.\, P_2] \qquad (1)$$

the processes synchronize on $x$ and the first opening action is consumed:

$$S_1 \mid \bar{y}^n() \,.\, S_2 \mid n[\mathbf{open}_\uparrow \, \bar{y} \,.\, P_1 \mid y^\star() \,.\, P_2] \qquad (2)$$

then the processes synchronize on $y$ and also the second opening is consumed:

$$S_1 \mid S_2 \mid n[P_1 \mid P_2]$$

If the local actions in (1) and (2) had not been in parallel with the corresponding opening actions, remote interaction would have been forbidden.

Now we can outline how a parent may implement total mediation. Total mediation implies that all observable actions (up-syncs and down-syncs) that involve one of its children are controlled by a security policy and that all the values exchanged are inspected. The mediation policy redirects all communications to the target seal passing them by a filter process, so that all values can be checked. Portals are opened only for channels that are allowed by the security policy. Note that if we allowed siblings to synchronize on a parent's channel, some interactions would not be subject to mediation. In Figure 3 process $S$ is implementing an interposition policy, that provides channels $x'$ and $y'$ to $P$. The policy is in charge of opening the portal for $x$ (the portal for $y$ is opened within $n$) and of checking the values sent along both channels.

## 2.4  Discussion

Let us return to our five designing principles and discuss how the calculus addresses them. First, the seal model clearly does not rely on any global state. A seal knows only the names of its direct children and can communicate with them and its parent. This means synchronization involves at most two nested locations. Second, localities are explicit and the model clearly differentiates between local resources, and remote resources. Third, communication is restricted to local and neighbor (parent or children) interaction. Any further form of communication must be explicitly programmed. This mean that we can easily model disconnected operations or the effects of a firewall. Fourth, dynamic reconfiguration is obtained by three ingredients: mobility, name passing, and dynamic binding. Mobility supports seal migration and duplication and can model topological reconfiguration of locations. Name passing can be used to explicitly reconfigure a migrated seal for the new environment while implicit configuration is obtained by dynamic binding of the ↑ identifier. This tag denotes the parent environment and it is dynamically bound to the current parent. This allows a dynamic reconfiguration of the seal after migration, and the possibility to transparently update the services provided by the environment to its seals. Finally, portals allow to control access to local resources at a fine granularity.

## 3   The Seal Language

In this section the syntax and operational semantics of Seal are given. The language is an extension of Milner's synchronous polyadic $\pi$-calculus without matching and choice operators.

### 3.1   Syntax

We assume infinite sets $\mathcal{N}$ of *names* and $\overline{\mathcal{N}}$ of *co-names* disjoint and in bijection via $(\overline{\phantom{x}})$; we declare $\overline{\overline{x}} = x$. The set of location denotations extends names with two symbols $(\star, \uparrow)$. Bold font variables denote either a name or the corresponding co-name, thus $\mathbf{x}$ may be either $x$ or $\overline{x}$.

$$
\begin{array}{lll}
\mathcal{N} & m, n, \ldots, x, y, z & \text{names} \\
\overline{\mathcal{N}} & \overline{m}, \overline{n}, \ldots, \overline{x}, \overline{y}, \overline{z} & \text{co-names} \\
& \mathbf{x} ::= x \mid \overline{x} &
\end{array}
\qquad
\begin{array}{lll}
\mathscr{L} & \eta ::= x \mid \uparrow \mid \star \text{ locations} \\
\mathscr{X} & X & \text{process variables}
\end{array}
$$

The set of *processes*, ranged over by $P, Q, R, S$ and *actions*, ranged over by $\alpha$, are defined by the following grammars:

**Table 1:** Processes and Actions

| Processes | | Actions | |
|---|---|---|---|
| $P ::= \mathbf{0}$ | inactivity | | |
| $\mid \quad P \mid Q$ | composition | $\alpha ::= \overline{x}^{\eta}(\vec{y})$ | name output |
| $\mid \quad (\nu x)P$ | restriction | $\mid \quad x^{\eta}(\lambda \vec{y})$ | name input |
| $\mid \quad \alpha \,.\, P$ | action | $\mid \quad \overline{x}^{\eta}\{y\}$ | seal send |
| $\mid \quad !\,P$ | replication | $\mid \quad x^{\eta}\{\vec{y}\}$ | seal receive |
| $\mid \quad x[P]$ | seal | $\mid \quad \mathbf{open}_{\eta}\, \mathbf{x}$ | portal open |
| $\mid \quad x[X]$ | abstract seal | | |

**0** denotes the inert process. $P \mid Q$ denotes parallel composition. $(\nu\, x)P$ denotes restriction. $\alpha\,.\,P$ denotes an action $\alpha$ and a continuation $P$. $!\,P$ denotes replication. Finally, $x[P]$ and $x[X]$ denote, respectively, a seal named $x$ with body process $P$ and a seal $x$ with body a process variable $X$.

**Definition 1.** *A process $P$ is well-formed if and only if it contains no abstract seal $x[X]$ and no action of the form* $\mathbf{open}_\star\, \mathbf{x}$ *(portal local open).*

Subsequently, we shall deal only with well-formed processes.

Following accepted terminology, the polarity of actions on names is positive and the polarity of actions on co-names is negative. $\overline{x}^\eta(\vec{y})\,.\,P$ denotes a process offering $\vec{y}$ at channel $x$ located in seal $\eta$ with a continuation $P$. The process $x^\eta(\lambda \vec{y})\,.\,P$ denotes a process ready to input distinct names $\vec{y}$ at $x$ in $\eta$. The $\lambda$ is a visual cue to remind the reader the $\vec{y}$ are bound in $P$. $\overline{x}^\eta\{y\}\,.\,P$ denotes the sender process offering at $x$ in $\eta$ a seal named $y$. The process $x^\eta\{\vec{y}\}\,.\,P$ denotes the receiver process waiting to read a seal at $x$ in $\eta$ and start $n$ copies of it under names $y_1 \ldots y_n$. Note that this action is not binding. Finally, $\mathbf{open}_\eta\, x\,.\,P$ (respectively $\mathbf{open}_\eta\, \overline{x}\,.\,P$) denotes a process offering to open a portal for seal $\eta$ to perform a positive (respectively negative) action on local channel $x$ and then behave as $P$.

$\{^y/_x\}$ and $\{^Q/_X\}$ are meta-notations for substitutions. Thus $P\{^{\vec{y}}/_{\vec{x}}\}$ denotes the term obtained from $P$ by simultaneous substitution of $y_1 \ldots y_n$ for the free occurrences of distinct names $x_1 \ldots x_n$, and $P\{^Q/_X\}$ denotes the term obtained from $P$ by substituting process $Q$ for all free occurrences of process variable $X$. Substitutions are ranged over by $\sigma$.

Location denotations $\star, \uparrow$ and $n$ denote respectively the current seal, the parent seal and a sub-seal bearing name $n$. The location denotations refer to the seal in which synchronization occurs. The simple case, which reduces to the $\pi$-calculus, is local synchronization, thus $P = \overline{x}^\star(y)\,.\,\mathbf{0}$ is willing to emit name $y$ along $x$ and then become inert. $Q = x^\star(\lambda z)\,.\,\overline{x}^\star(z)\,.\,\mathbf{0}$ is a repeater which reads a name form $x$ and emits it on the same channel. Local communication is always allowed, so the composition of the above mentioned processes reduces in one step:

$$P \mid Q \quad \to \quad \mathbf{0} \mid \overline{x}^\star(y)\,.\,\mathbf{0}$$

Consider now the processes $P = \overline{x}^\uparrow(y)\,.\,P'$, $Q = x^\star(\lambda z)\,.\,Q'$ and $S = \mathbf{open}_n\, \overline{x}\,.\,S'$. The following configuration also reduces in one step:

$$n[P] \mid Q \mid S \quad \to \quad n[P'] \mid Q'\{^y/_z\} \mid S'$$

The case above involves a sub-seal trying to use a resource located in its environment; the symmetric case occurs when a process tries to access resources located in a sub-seal. Here for example, let $P = x^n(\lambda y)\,.\,P'$, $Q = \overline{x}^\star(z)\,.\,Q'$ and $S = \mathbf{open}_\uparrow\, x\,.\,S'$. The following configuration reduces in one step:

$$P \mid n[Q \mid S] \quad \to \quad P'\{^z/_y\} \mid n[Q' \mid S']$$

**Notation** We often omit the $\star$ at the index of local communication and trailing **0** processes are elided, thus $x^\star(\lambda y).\mathbf{0}$ becomes $x(\lambda y)$. When communication is used purely to synchronize processes, we abbreviate $\overline{x}^\eta(y)$ to $\overline{x}^\eta()$ and input $x^\eta(\lambda y)$ to $x^\eta()$. Actions bind tighter than composition and composition bind tighter than restrictions, so that for instance $(\nu x)x().\overline{y}() \mid \overline{x}()$ means $(\nu x)((x().\overline{y}()) \mid \overline{x}())$.

## 3.2 Reduction semantics

The *reduction relation* $\to$ is defined over processes and represents one step of computation. Reduction is defined by means of two auxiliary notions: *structural congruence* and *heating*.

### 3.2.1 Structural congruence

Structural congruence, $\equiv$, is the least congruence on processes satisfying the following axioms and rules:

---

**Table 2:** Structural congruence.

| | | |
|---|---|---|
| $P \mid \mathbf{0} \equiv P$ | | (Struct Dead Par) |
| $P \mid Q \equiv Q \mid P$ | | (Struct Par Comm) |
| $(P \mid Q) \mid R \equiv P \mid (Q \mid R)$ | | (Struct Par Assoc) |
| $!P \equiv P \mid !P$ | | (Struct Repl Par) |
| $(\nu x)\mathbf{0} \equiv \mathbf{0}$ | | (Struct Dead Res) |
| $(\nu x)(\nu y)P \equiv (\nu y)(\nu x)P$ | | (Struct Res Res) |
| $b(\nu x)(P \mid Q) \equiv P \mid (\nu x)Q$ | if $x \notin fn(P)$ | (Struct Res Par) |

---

The set $fn(P)$ of *free names* of a process $P$ is defined in a standard way (e.g., see [24]).

Intuitively, this relation does not correspond to any step of computation, instead it allows processes to be rearranged so that reduction can take place.

For example, we already saw that local synchronization is enabled when two complementary actions on a channel appear at the same level:

$$x(\lambda y).\overline{y}() \mid \overline{x}(z) \quad \to \quad \overline{y}() \mid \mathbf{0} \tag{3}$$

But, if the emitting process were $(\nu z)\overline{x}(z)$, then the $\nu$-abstraction would hide the output action and thus prevent synchronization. Structural congruence rearranges the term so that can reduce:

$$x(\lambda y).\overline{y}() \mid (\nu z)\overline{x}(z) \equiv (\nu z)(x(\lambda y).\overline{y}() \mid \overline{x}(z)) \to (\nu z)(\overline{z}() \mid \mathbf{0}) \tag{4}$$

This result is obtained by alternating $\to$ and $\equiv$ rewritings, that is, by allowing replacement of terms by structurally equivalent terms. Structural congruence also handles the semantics of replicated actions and performs some house-keeping by sweeping out dead processes.

Structural congruence does not handle renaming of bound variables. Instead, we consider that alpha-conversions are silently performed whenever needed.

### 3.2.2 Heating

Although structural congruence provides a convenient way of rearranging terms to enable local synchronization, it does not suffice for non-local synchronization. Communication across seal boundaries requires special treatment. To illustrate this point let's modify example (3) so that the emitting process is located in a sub-seal:

$$\mathbf{open}_n \overline{x} \mid x^\star(\lambda y) . \overline{y}() \mid n[\, \overline{x}^\uparrow(z) \,] \quad \to \quad \mathbf{0} \mid \overline{z}() \mid n[\mathbf{0}]$$

Now, if like in (4) we $\nu$-abstract the argument of the output, we expect the $\nu$-abstraction to extrude the seal boundary and wrap around the input process, that is, informally the following should hold:

$$\mathbf{open}_n \overline{x} \mid x^\star(\lambda y) . \overline{y}() \mid n[\, (\nu\, z)\overline{x}^\uparrow(z) \,] \quad \to \quad (\nu\, z)(\, \mathbf{0} \mid \overline{z}() \mid n[\mathbf{0}] \,)$$

This would require an equivalence such as $n[(\nu\, x)P] \equiv (\nu\, x)n[P]$. However, it would be an error to define these terms as equivalent, because we allow seal duplication [1]. Indeed, if we compose both terms with the copier process defined earlier $Q = \text{COPY } n \text{ AS } m$ we obtain:

$$n[(\nu\, x)P] \mid Q \to n[(\nu\, x)P] \mid m[(\nu\, x)P] \text{ and } (\nu\, x)n[P] \mid Q \to (\nu\, x)n[P] \mid m[P]$$

The first term yields a configuration where seals $n$ and $m$ have each a private channel $x$, while in the other case, they share a common channel $x$. Our solution is to forego structural congruence at this point and perform the extrusion together with synchronization. To this end we define a *heating* relation on terms (we borrow the terminology of Berry and Boudol's Chemical Abstract Machine [7]). A term is "heated" to allow synchronization. Heating singles out all the $\nu-$abstractions that must be extruded, that is, those that bind arguments of the negative action about to be performed. Heating will extrude as few $\nu$-abstractions as possible. So for example the term

$$\mathbf{open}_n \overline{x} \mid x^\star(\lambda y) . \overline{y}() \mid n[(\nu\, w)(\nu\, z)\overline{x}^\uparrow(z)]$$

reduces to $\mathbf{0} \mid (\nu\, z)(\overline{z}() \mid n[(\nu\, w)\mathbf{0}])$ rather than to $\mathbf{0} \mid (\nu\, w)(\nu\, z)(\overline{z}() \mid n[\mathbf{0}])$.

More precisely, consider the term $(\nu\, w)(\nu\, z)\overline{x}^\uparrow(z)$. Heating will tell us that to synchronize on $\overline{x}^\uparrow$ it is necessary to extrude $(\nu\, z)$. This is expressed by the following heating relation pair:

$$(\nu\, w)(\nu\, z)\overline{x}^\uparrow(z) \quad \prec \quad \overline{x}^\uparrow . (\nu\, z)\langle z\rangle((\nu\, w)\mathbf{0})$$

channel ——⌐      ⌐—— residual

names to extrude ——————⌐   ⌐—————— arguments

The heated form resembles Milner's *agents* [23]. The channel name comes first, it is followed by a list of extruded names, $(\nu\, x)$ in this case, the arguments, $z$,

---

[1] The Ambient Calculus [12] does not allow duplication and thus the equivalence holds.

and the residual process, $(\nu\,w)0$. The argument values include both names and processes.

A term in heated form is called an *agent*. Agents are written $\omega P$ where $\omega$ is an agent prefix and $P$ is a process. The set of *agent prefixes* ranged over by $\omega$ is defined by the following grammar:

---

**Table 3:** Agent prefixes

$$
\begin{aligned}
\omega ::= \ &\epsilon & &\text{empty prefix}\\
|\ &(\nu\,\vec{x})\langle\vec{y}\rangle & &\text{name concretion}\\
|\ &(\nu\,\vec{x})\langle P\rangle & &\text{process concretion}\\
|\ &\langle\lambda\vec{y}\rangle & &\text{name abstraction}\\
|\ &\langle\lambda X\rangle & &\text{process abstraction}
\end{aligned}
$$

---

The sets $fn(\omega)$ of *free names* of an agent prefix and $bn(\omega)$ *bound names* of an agent prefix have standard definitions.

In order to simplify the presentation of the reduction rules we introduce the set $\overline{\mathscr{L}}$ of *co-locations* (that is in bijection with $\mathscr{L}$ via $(^-)$) and the set of sync-locations. Their use is explained later on.

---

$\overline{\mathscr{L}}\ \bar{\eta} ::= \bar{x} \mid \bar{\uparrow} \mid \bar{\ast}$ co-locations $\qquad\qquad\qquad$ $\eta ::= \eta \mid \bar{\eta} \mid \mathbf{x}[]$ sync-locations

---

The heating relation $\prec$ relates a well-formed process to a term of the form $\mathbf{x}^{\eta}.\omega P$ and is defined as the least relation respecting the following axioms and rules (where $\boldsymbol{\eta}$ denotes either $\eta$ or $\bar{x}$):

---

**Table 4:** Heating.

$$
\begin{array}{lr}
\bar{x}^{\eta}(\vec{y}).P \prec \bar{x}^{\eta}.\langle\vec{y}\rangle P & \text{(Heat Out)}\\[4pt]
x^{\eta}(\lambda\vec{y}).P \prec x^{\eta}.\langle\lambda\vec{y}\rangle P & \text{(Heat In)}\\[4pt]
\bar{x}^{\eta}\{y\}.P \mid y[Q] \prec \bar{x}^{\eta}.\langle Q\rangle P & \text{(Heat Send)}\\[4pt]
x^{\eta}\{y_1,\ldots,y_n\}.P \prec x^{\eta}.\langle\lambda X\rangle(P\mid y_1[X]\mid\ldots\mid y_n[X]) & \text{(Heat Recv)}\\[4pt]
y\notin fn(\omega), y\notin\{x,\eta\}, P\prec \mathbf{x}^{\eta}.\omega P' \ \Rightarrow\ (\nu\,y)P \prec \mathbf{x}^{\eta}.\omega(\nu\,y)P' & \text{(Heat Res-1)}\\[4pt]
y\in fn(\omega), y\notin\{x,\eta\}, P\prec \mathbf{x}^{\eta}.\omega P' \ \Rightarrow\ (\nu\,y)P \prec \mathbf{x}^{\eta}.(\nu\,y)\omega P' & \text{(Heat Res-2)}\\[4pt]
bn(\omega)\cap fn(Q)=\emptyset, P\prec \mathbf{x}^{\eta}.\omega P' \ \Rightarrow\ P\mid Q \prec \mathbf{x}^{\eta}.\omega(P'\mid Q) & \text{(Heat Par)}\\[4pt]
bn(\omega)\cap fn(Q)=\emptyset, P\prec \mathbf{x}^{\ast}.\omega P' \ \Rightarrow\ P\mid \mathbf{open}_{\eta}\,\bar{x}.Q \prec \mathbf{x}^{\bar{\eta}}.\omega(P'\mid Q) & \text{(Heat Open)}\\[4pt]
y\notin bn(\omega), P\prec \mathbf{x}^{\uparrow}.\omega P' \ \Rightarrow\ y[P] \prec \mathbf{x}^{y[]}.\omega y[P'] & \text{(Heat Seal-1)}\\[4pt]
y\notin bn(\omega), P\prec \mathbf{x}^{\bar{\uparrow}}.\omega P' \ \Rightarrow\ y[P] \prec \mathbf{x}^{\bar{y}[]}.\omega y[P'] & \text{(Heat Seal-2)}
\end{array}
$$

---

The first two axioms handle synchronization for communication. In particular the first axiom states that an output process does not need to extrude any name. The (Heat Send) and (Heat Recv) axioms deal with synchronization for mobility. (Heat Send) states that a negative action offers as argument the body of a seal. The fourth axiom says that a positive action heats into an abstraction where the process variable $X$ stands for the body of the seals specified by $\vec{y}$, after synchronization the residual consists of the continuation $P$ in parallel with the seals where $X$ has been substituted by some process $Q$.

The following two rules select the names that will be extruded. If a $\nu$-abstracted name does not occur free in the agent prefix $\omega$ then (Heat Res-1) applies and the name is not extruded. Instead, if a $\nu$-abstracted name does occur free in $\omega$ then (Heat Res-2) applies and the name is extruded. The rule (Heat Par) simply propagates restrictions taking care of name conflicts. Note that it is always possible to alpha-convert *bound* variables so that name clashes are avoided.

The rule (Heat Open) combines a local action on some channel $x$ and a permission to interact with a matching action from a process located in seal $\eta$. This is represented by changing the action label from $x^\star$ to $x^{\overline{\eta}}$.

Finally the last two rules allow actions originating from a seal $y$ to synchronize with matching actions in the parent. When they flow through the boundaries of seal $y$ the action labels are changed from $x^\dagger$ to $x^{y\Box}$ and from $x^{\overline{\dagger}}$ to $x^{\overline{y}\Box}$ in the process to prevent accidental matches and further propagation. In summary, $x^{\overline{y}\Box}$ means that the seal $y$ is ready to synchronize on its own channel $x$ with the environment (it opened the channel to the environment and *committed* — see [13]— to perform an action on it), while $x^{\overline{y}}$ means that the environment is ready to synchronize $y$ on the local channel $x$ with the seal $y$ (it opened the channel to $y$ and committed to perform an action on it).

### 3.2.3 Reduction

We define the reduction relation $\rightarrow$ as the least relation on well-formed processes that satisfies:

**Table 5:** Reduction.

<br>

(Red Res)
$$\frac{P \rightarrow Q}{(\nu\,x)P \rightarrow (\nu\,x)Q}$$

(Red Par)
$$\frac{P \rightarrow Q}{P \mid R \rightarrow Q \mid R}$$

(Red Seal)
$$\frac{P \rightarrow Q}{x[P] \rightarrow x[Q]}$$

(Red $\equiv$)
$$\frac{P \equiv P' \quad P' \rightarrow Q' \quad Q' \equiv Q}{P \rightarrow Q}$$

(Red Local)
$$\frac{P \prec x^\star.\omega_1 P' \quad Q \prec \overline{x}^\star.\omega_2 Q'}{P \mid Q \rightarrow (\omega_1 P') \bullet (\omega_2 Q')}$$

(Red Remote)
$$\frac{P \prec x^{\overline{y}}.\omega_1 P' \quad Q \prec \overline{x}^{y\Box}.\omega_2 Q'}{P \mid Q \rightarrow (\omega_1 P') \bullet (\omega_2 Q')}$$

The *pseudoapplication* relation $(\_) \bullet (\_)$ used in the definition of synchronization is a partial *commutative* binary function from agents to processes. Let $\vec{y}, \vec{x}$ be vectors of the same arity and $\vec{x} \notin fn(P)$, then we define pseudoapplication as:

---

1. $(\langle \lambda \vec{y} \rangle P) \bullet ((\nu \, \vec{x})\langle \vec{z} \rangle Q) = (\nu \, \vec{x})(P\{^{\vec{z}}/_{\vec{y}}\} \mid Q)$

2. $(\langle \lambda X \rangle P) \bullet ((\nu \, \vec{x})\langle R \rangle Q) = (\nu \, \vec{x})(P\{^{R}/_{X}\} \mid Q)$

3. Undefined otherwise.

---

Of course, (Red Local) and (Red Remote) apply only provided that the inferred pseudoapplication is defined.

The first three rules perform reduction within restrictions, seals and parallel composition. The rule (Red $\equiv$) allows structural rearrangements to take place around a step of reduction.

The core of the semantics is given by the last two rules. They describe synchronization on a channel that is respectively local or remote. The combined use of heating and pseudoapplication allows us to compact severals rules into a single one. For example, every single rule describes the synchronization in case of both communication and mobility. Let us show how the rules work by a couple of examples, starting with (Red Local).

*Example 1.* Consider the process $x(\lambda y) . P \mid \overline{x}(z) . Q$. By definition of heating we have $x(\lambda y) . P \prec x . \langle \lambda y \rangle P$ and $\overline{x}(z) . Q \prec \overline{x} . \langle z \rangle Q$, thus by (Red Local) the process reduces to $(\langle \lambda y \rangle P) \bullet (\langle z \rangle Q)$, that is $P\{^{z}/_{y}\} \mid Q$. In summary, $x(\lambda y) . P \mid \overline{x}(z) . Q \rightarrow P\{^{z}/_{y}\} \mid Q$. $\square$

In case of local synchronization the notational additions collapse two rules, communication and mobility, into the single (Red Local) rule. In the case of (Red Remote) the advantage is greater since in the absence of such notation we would be obliged to specify different rules for mobility and communication and also rule for positive and negative actions.

In order to understand the (Red Remote) rule let us show a second example of communication.

*Example 2.* Consider the process $x^\star(\lambda y) . P \mid \mathbf{open}_n \overline{x} . R \mid n[(\nu \, w)(\nu \, z)\overline{x}^\uparrow(z) . Q]$. By silent alpha conversion, we can consider, without loss of generality, that $y \notin fn(R)$, and $z \notin fn(P \mid R)$. By (Heat In), we have $x^\star(\lambda y) . P \prec x^\star . \langle \lambda y \rangle P$. By (Heat Open) and the fact that $y \notin fn(R)$, we obtain $x^\star(\lambda y) . P \mid \mathbf{open}_n \overline{x} . R \prec x^{\overline{n}} . \langle \lambda y \rangle (P \mid R)$. Turning now to the seal, (Heat Out), (Heat Res-2) and (Heat Res-1) give us $(\nu \, w)(\nu \, z)\overline{x}^\uparrow(z) . Q \prec \overline{x}^\uparrow . (\nu \, z)\langle z \rangle(\nu \, w)Q$. Therefore, by (Heat Seal), we get

$$n[(\nu \, w)(\nu \, z)\overline{x}^\uparrow(z) . Q] \prec \overline{x}^{n[]} . (\nu \, z)\langle z \rangle n[(\nu \, w)Q]$$

The side conditions of pseudoapplication in (Red Remote) being satisfied we obtain

$$(\langle \lambda y \rangle(P \mid R)) \bullet ((\nu \, z)\langle z \rangle n[(\nu \, w)Q]) = (\nu \, z)((P \mid R)\{^{z}/_{y}\} \mid n[(\nu \, w)Q])$$

Finally, since $y \notin fn(R)$ we have $(P \mid R)\{z/y\} = P\{z/y\} \mid R$. In summary we have

$$x^\star(\lambda y) . P \mid \textbf{open}_n \, \overline{x} . R \mid n[(\nu w)(\nu z)\overline{x}^\uparrow(z) . Q] \;\to\; (\nu z)(P\{z/y\} \mid R \mid n[(\nu w)Q])$$

$\square$

We conclude this section on reduction semantics by two remarks. First, as the second example shows, it is always possible to make terms satisfy the side conditions of pseudoapplication and heating rules. In fact, these conditions are on bound variables, that can be always alpha-converted to match the constraints. Secondly, we can show that reduction preserves well-formedness:

**Lemma 1.** *If $P$ is well-formed and $P \prec x^\eta . \omega Q$ then either $Q$ is well formed or $\omega = \langle \lambda X \rangle$ and $Q\{R/X\}$ is well-formed for any well-formed $R$.*

*Proof.* By induction on structure of the derivation of $P \prec x^\eta . \omega Q$.

**Lemma 2.** *Given a well-formed term $P$, if $P \to Q$ then $Q$ is well formed.*

*Proof.* By induction on the structure of the derivation of $P \to Q$. For the rules of communication simply note that by (HeatSend) and (Heat Res-2) if $P'$ is well-formed and $P' \prec \overline{x}^\eta . (\nu \vec{x})\langle Q' \rangle P''$, then also $Q'$ is well-formed; use then Lemma 1.

## 4  Programming examples

We consider a distributed application management example in which the license of an application is to be extended automatically. The license string is a function of the host serial number and an expiration date. To extend the duration of the license it is necessary to regenerate a new license string for each instance of the application. If a customer decides to renew the license for a set of machines (designated by their IP numbers), the software manufacturer can generate a small mobile computation that will go around this set of machines, stopping at each machine long enough to obtain its serial number and run the password generation function on it. The overall configuration is shown in Figure 4. We will now present a Seal solution to this problem, outlining some of the necessary security properties. We start with the definition of two operators that will be used in the example.

### 4.1  Implementing the upgrade protocol

**Renaming**   Seal renaming, $x \, \text{BE} \, y$, atomically renames a seal bearing name $x$ to $y$. This operator is defined as follows:

$$x \, \text{BE} \, y.P = (\nu n)\,\overline{n}\{x\} \mid n\{y\}.P$$

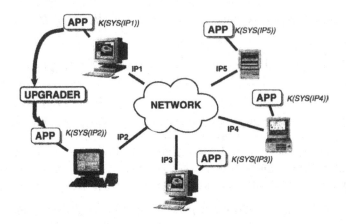

**Fig. 4.** Mobile upgrade agent.

Renaming is implemented by a local move. The action $\overline{n}\{x\}$ moves seal $x$ along channel $n$. $n\{y\}$ receives a seal and names it $y$. In order to avoid interferences, the temporary fresh name $n$ is used for the local channel.[2]

**Linking**  A communication link allows two siblings to interact:

$$\text{LINK } n\, m \text{ VIA } c\,.P = c^n(\lambda x).\overline{c}^m(x).P$$

The process reads $x$ on channel $c$ located in seal $n$ and transmits it on a channel with the same name located in $m$. An example of linking is $n[\overline{x}(y) \mid \mathbf{open}_\uparrow x] \mid$ LINK $n\, m$ VIA $x \mid m[x(\lambda z).P \mid \mathbf{open}_\uparrow x]$ which first reduces in one step $x^n(\lambda z)$. $\overline{x}^m(z) \mid n[\overline{x}(y) \mid \mathbf{open}_\uparrow x] \mid m[x(\lambda z).P \mid \mathbf{open}_\uparrow x] \rightarrow \overline{x}^m(y) \mid n[] \mid m[ x(\lambda z).P \mid \mathbf{open}_\uparrow x] \equiv \overline{x}^m(y) \mid m[x(\lambda z).P \mid \mathbf{open}_\uparrow x] \mid n[]$ to finally reduce to $m[P\{y/z\}] \mid n[]$.

**Network**  A very simplified network can be modeled by a single seal, with as many sub-seals as there are machines. Machines are designated by their IP number and for each machine a process takes care of routing packets sent to other machines on the net. The overall configuration is therefore:

$$\text{MACH } ip_1\, P_1 \mid \ldots \mid \text{MACH } ip_n\, P_n$$

More precisely, MACH is the description of three things: the actual machine (a seal whose name is the machine's IP number); the protocol that allows the machine to send out packets; the portion of the network transport layer that takes care of routing a packet to a given machine and port.

---

[2] Contrast this to renaming in the Ambient Calculus [12]: in our formalism renaming is performed by a process in the parent seal while in the Ambient Calculus ambients (that is, seals) rename themselves.

MACH $ip\,P\;=$
$$!(\nu\,pk)\;out^{ip}\{pk\}$$
$$.hdr^{pk}(\lambda ipdest\,port)$$
$$\overline{.port}^{ipdest}\{pk\}$$

$$|\;ip[\,!out\{leave\}\;|\,!\mathbf{open}_\uparrow\,out\;|\;P\,]$$

The network waits for the machine $ip$ to send a new packet on channel $out$, it generates a new name $pk$ for it, asks it on the header port $hdr$ its destination machine and port, and routes it there. Besides running some generic process $P$, the machine $ip$ moves out every packet whose name is $leave$.

**Packets**   A packet is characterized by a seal $n$ that represents the encapsulated information, and the IP number and port of destination that it publishes on its header port $hdr$. The seal $n$ is encapsulated in and extracted from the packet through channels $in$ and $out$ respectively. We do not give a general description of how incoming packets are handled by machines, since this would be too specific. In general every process $P$ on a machine will run a suite of protocols that listen to given ports and accordingly perform some operations. However, it possible to define two general operators that machines will use to handle packets. These operators named PACK and UNPACK are defined as follows:

PACK $n\,ip\,port$ AS $p\,.P =$
$$(\nu\,x)\;x[\,in\{k\}$$
$$.\overline{hdr}(ip\,port)$$
$$\overline{.out}\{k\}$$
$$|\;\mathbf{open}_\uparrow\,\overline{in}.\mathbf{open}_\uparrow\,hdr.\mathbf{open}_\uparrow\,out\,]$$

$$|\;\overline{in}^x\{n\}.\,x\;\text{BE}\;p\,.P$$

The action PACK $n\,ip\,port$ AS $p$ creates a packet named $p$, encapsulating the seal $n$, and with destination $ip$ and $port$. Creation uses a temporary seal $x$ to avoid external interferences during construction. Thus PACK $n\,ip1\,pt2$ AS $p\;|\;n[P]$ reduces to $p[\overline{hdr}(ip1\,pt2).\overline{out}\{k\}\;|\;k[P]\;|\;\mathbf{open}_\uparrow\,hdr.\mathbf{open}_\uparrow\,out]$.

UNPACK $p$ AS $q\,.P =$
$$(\nu\,x)$$
$$p\;\text{BE}\;x$$
$$.out^x\{q\}.P$$

The action UNPACK $p$ AS $q$ extracts the seal encapsulated in packet $p$ and names it $q$; the renaming is performed so that after the extraction $p$ has become $(\nu\,x)x[]$, which is equivalent to the inactive process. Thus UNPACK $p$ AS $n$ $|$ $p[\overline{out}\{k\}\;|\;k[P]\;|\;\mathbf{open}_\uparrow\,out]$ reduces to $n[P]\;|\;(\nu\,x)x[]$.

**Upgrade protocol**   The only application specific protocol we describe in detail is the UPGRADE_PROTOCOL that listens on the *upgrade* port for mobile programs that upgrade the licence password of an application. This protocol must be run (possibly inside a replication) by every machine that wants to allow licence upgrades. For the sake of simplicity we do not handle the cases in which the upgrade fails. The definition of the protocol is:

UPGRADE_PROTOCOL.$P =$
    **open**$_\uparrow$ $upgrade$ |
    $(\nu\, upg\, pkt)$   $upgrade\{pkt\}$
        .UNPACK $pkt$ AS $upg$
        .$request^{upg}(\lambda app\, chn)$
        .$\overline{sys}^{upg}(vv)$
        .LINK $upg$ $app$ VIA $chn$
        .$next^{upg}(\lambda ip)$
        .PACK $upg$ $ip$ $upgrade$ AS $leave.P$

Let us describe it in detail. The protocol waits on the port *upgrade* for a packet that contains an upgrade application. The protocol extracts the upgrader application from the packet and names it with the fresh name *upg*. It then waits for *upg* to request a communication with a seal *app* (the application to upgrade) on channel *chn*. The protocol sends the machine serial number *vv* (used to generate the new license) to *upg* and allows a single communication from *upg* to *app* to take place. Finally the protocol asks *upg* its next destination and sends it out within a new packet.

**Mobile upgrader application** The upgrader application sequentially upgrades the application *app* in the various machines:

$$upgrader[\text{UPGRADE } ip_1.\text{UPGRADE } ip_2....]$$

For simplicity we do not consider the cases in which one or more machines are down, or unreachable or fail during the upgrading.

The steps performed to upgrade a single machine *ip* are:

UPGRADE $ip.P =$
    $\overline{next}(ip)$
    .$\overline{request}(app\, chn)$
    .$sysinfo(\lambda vv)$
    .$\overline{chn}(\text{NEW\_LICENSE } vv)$ |
    **open**$_\uparrow$ $request.$**open**$_\uparrow$ $\overline{sysinfo}.$**open**$_\uparrow$ $chn.P$

First the upgrader broadcasts the *ip* it wants to visit. Then it requests a communication channel *chn* to the application *app*. This action is performed only after that the upgrader has arrived at its destination. It also expects to receive some system information, before communicating the new license password (its computation not described here) to *app* via *chn*.

Upgrading the machines in a random order is obtained by running several upgrade processes in parallel within the same upgrader, $upgrader[\text{UPGRADE } ip_1 \mid \text{UPGRADE } ip_2 \mid ...]$.

## 4.2 Security issues

The development of the Seal calculus emphasizes security issues. Indeed, we look for a calculus that allows context independent proofs of security, that is, our goal is to be able to localize security code in small, well-delineated portions of a system and to be able to reason about security properties without having to resort to whole program analysis.

The first property that we want to obtain is what [12] calls the *perfect firewall equation*: this says that an arbitrary process can be completely prevented from any communication, and is formally written[3]

$$(\nu\, x)\, x[P] \simeq 0$$

Here $\simeq$ denotes some action-based observational equivalence on process. A formal example of definition of $\simeq$ can be found in [13], but for the purposes of this section it suffices to consider as equivalent two processes that perform at the top level the same sequences of channel writings.

Intuitively, the perfect firewall equation holds in the Seal calculus because if a seal is given a fresh name that is not known by any other process, then there can be no portal open for that name (such as $\mathbf{open}_x\ \mathbf{y}$), nor can there be a located communication (such as $\mathbf{y}^x\{...\}$). This property is preserved by reduction. (Note that the formal proof that this equation holds is far more complicated than the simple reasoning in the lines above: see [13]). It is a useful property as it guarantees that once a seal is in a firewall it cannot divulge any information, nor perform any externally visible action for that matter.

One difference between our approach and ambients is that here it is possible to force a seal into a firewall: the following operation will eventually trap a seal $x$

$$\textsc{trap}\ x = (\nu\ ct)\,\bar{c}\{x\}\mid c\{t\}$$

If portals are viewed as capabilities, the TRAP operator is a non reversible form of revocation while renaming is a reversible revocation.

More generally, we would like to guarantee that some code or protocol has given security properties. For example, in the case of the upgrade application one wants to guarantee, by simple examination of the upgrade protocol, that every mobile upgrader, however it is defined, can only interact with the application *app* that it requested explicitly upon arrival, and that every interaction with the rest of the machine is mediated by the protocol.

More precisely, let **P** denote the part of the update protocol that does not handle packet reception and dispatching:

$\mathbf{P} = request^{upg}(\lambda app, chn)$
$\quad.\overline{sys}^{upg}(vv)$
$\quad.\text{LINK}\ upg,\ app\ \text{VIA}\ chn$
$\quad.next^{upg}(\lambda ip)$

---

[3] In [12] there is the extra requirement that $x$ does not appear free in $P$.

If $U$ is the body of the upgrader then the situation after migration is:

$$ip[((\nu\,upg)\mathbf{P} \mid upg[U]) \mid Q]$$

Note that by the move (more precisely by the definition of substitution) *upg* cannot appear free in $U$. Then, for every process $U$ in which *upg* is not free we can reason as follows:

1. Since *upg* never appears free in the argument of a negative action in $\mathbf{P}$, then: (a) *upg* cannot move, and (b) *upg* cannot appear free in any reductum of $Q$.
2. The two points above imply that there cannot be any interaction between $upg[U]$ and $Q$ (if *upg* could move then it could be renamed and escape the restriction on *upg*). Therefore every remote interaction of $upg[U]$ is with $\mathbf{P}$.
3. From the previous point we have that the only process that may access resources located in *upg* is $\mathbf{P}$, and that *upg* can only access the external resources granted by $\mathbf{P}$ (actually, none). Furthermore, since $\mathbf{P}$ is a sequential process (there is no fork) we can also determine the exact order in which remote interactions (may) happen.
4. In conclusion whatever the upgrade program is, it can only send a single name (via the total mediation of the protocol) to the seal *app* specified on the *request* channel, and read the serial number *vv* provided by the $\mathbf{P}$ protocol.

These security results can be declined in some more general properties:

1. *Bound communication:* The entering seal cannot communicate with anyone but with the seal requested on the channel *request*. In particular, this is true even in the case that two seals agreed on some communication protocol and entered independently the machine: only the hosting machine can allow them to communicate.
2. *No hitchhiking:* Unwanted seals cannot use a seal entering by the *upgrade* port as a Trojan horse to sneak into the machine, nor once the upgrading seal entered the machine can it be used to surreptitiously carry away some (partner) seal.[4]

The above mentioned security properties relate to protection of the host from the actions of mobile computations. To present a comprehensive solution we should also devise a protocol that provides some guarantees to mobile computations. Although the host may not modify the internal behavior of the upgrader, a malicious host may (1) lie about its serial number, (2) learn the itinerary of an upgrader, (3) trap an upgrader, (4) impersonate an upgrader, (5) listen in on the conversation between an upgrader and the upgraded application.

---

[4] Hitchhiking is allowed in the Ambient calculus [12]. In the train example (see [11]) ambients representing passengers enter train stations, and then board trains. In the untyped calculus, there is no way of limiting the number of passengers that board a train and nothing prevents a passenger from hiding a potentially infinite number of hitchhikers that will come out as soon as the passenger is on the train.

In this section we reasoned about some security properties. The deductions we hinted cannot be considered as "proofs" of security. They are intentionally informal and *ad hoc*. For Seal to be used to state and prove security properties it is necessary to define a theory of proof, to develop some techniques of proof, and to define suitable notions of "observation", "test", and "specification" (see *e.g.* [1]). We are working in this direction [13, 33].

# 5 Related Work

**Ambients** The Ambient calculus of Cardelli and Gordon [12] has been one of the inspirations of this work. Ambients resemble seals in the sense that they are named places with a hierarchical structure. The main difference between the models is that in the Ambient setting, mobility is triggered and controlled by the ambient itself and mobility control is based on capabilities. An ambient that has been given a capability to enter another ambient may do so at any time. Our model gives full control of mobility to the environment, thus it is always the environment that decides when a move may occur. In an ambient system trapping a migrating ambient is not entirely straightforward, while in Seal, the environment can enforce confinement on any seal running within it. Another important difference is that the boundary around an ambient can be dissolved, thus releasing the ambient's content in the current environment. Such an operation is quite dangerous as the ambient being opened may contain any kind of code. Seal does not allow boundaries to be dissolved. Finally, the Ambient calculus is more minimal than Seal, with ambients computation is mobility. In Seal computation can be carried out in the $\pi$-calculus core.

**Distributed calculi** The difficulties of modeling some key aspects of distributed computing, in particular failures, within the $\pi$-calculus have driven a number of researchers to specifying distributed extensions [5, 28].[5] The Linda model was extended with explicit localities and the ability to evaluate (dynamically scoped) processes at a given locality [15]. The distributed join-calculus of Fournet and Gonthier is a calculus specially designed for a distributed implementation [18] in which every channel is rooted at a given location. All of these calculi adopt a higher level view than Seal, allowing direct communication with remote processes. In particular, the perfect firewall equation typically does not hold. In programming terms this means that a mobile entity may always communicate with its creator and thus leak any information that it gleaned along the way. So policies such as the strong sandbox of Java can not be straightforwardly implemented. More subtly, the lack of syntactic difference between local and remote resources promotes a programming style in which computations are spread over a number of different nodes, thus increasing the degree of interdependency and making computation much more sensitive to failures. Our goal with mobility is to emphasize local interaction.

---

[5] In the Seal, failures are modeled by trap operator which eventually entraps its target and prevents it from interacting with the environment.

**Local vs. global** The $\alpha$-conversion involved in extrusion has unpleasant computational implications if the scope of a name is extended over a number of hosts. It is therefore desirable to control tightly the scope of names and be prepared to promote a locally unique name to global uniqueness. One approach for avoiding $\alpha$-conversion is to use a location-aware naming scheme, such as the one described in the work of Bodei, Degano and Priami [9] who proposed that names be tied to their creation point in the syntax tree and that relative paths in the syntax tree be used to differentiate between equal names. In our setting this approach would fail as processes may move requiring tracking or forwarding services. A less elegant implementation techniques that avoids $\alpha$-conversion is to generate name randomly and rely on the small likelyhood of collisions. Nevertheless, generating and computing with such names may degrade efficiency of an application. Ideally, one would prefer to generate globally unique names only when they are needed. Peter Sewell proposed to use a type system to capture locality of names [32]. This approach would permit optimizations such as the use of simpler representations for local names.

**Types for security** Several researchers have proposed to rely on types for resource access control [21, 14, 32]. The work of Hennessy and Riely is innovative as it deals with open networks where a subset of hosts may be malicious. This raises very interesting problems: for instance, handing out an ill-typed value to a mobile application can not be detected right away if the value is a non-local channel name but may break the application later on. Their type system detects these kinds of error before the value is used, but this remains a genuine attack (if the goal is to prevent the mobile agent from carrying out its task). In Seal we did not choose types for controlling access to resources as we feel that resource allocation in real systems is very dynamic, typically the set of resources (memory, communication channels, cpu time, etc.) available to an entity will evolve over time. Types appear too rigid to model this aspect well. For our part, we plan to study the use of type systems for constraining other characteristics of the behavior of seals.

**Cryptography** The spi-calculus is an elegant extension of the $\pi$-calculus with cryptographic primitives developed by Abadi and Gordon [1]. In essence, they add public-key encryption to the $\pi$-calculus, interestingly it is possible to express this extension in the Seal calculus. But, the main contributions of this work are proof techniques for security protocols which we plan to adapt to our setting.

**From Seal to $\pi$** Sangiorgi devised a technique for translating a higher order $\pi$-calculus in the plain $\pi$ [30] (see also [4]). In his technique, process sending is encoded by triggers. Instead of sending a whole process $P$, just a fresh name $x$ is sent. The process $P$ is guarded by an input on $x$ and placed within a replication: $!x.P$. Thus, any output on $x$ will release a copy of $P$. The same technique cannot be used here because seal mobility is defined on "running" processes. Consider the term $\overline{x}\{y\} \mid y[P]$. The rules of our calculus allow $P$ to reduce to some $P'$ before the seal is captured by the move action. In general, the set of $\{P'|P \to^* P'\}$ is not finite, and we would need as many triggers as there are different $P'$s. Another translation from a mobile agent setting into the join-calculus was given in [19]. There, the translation relied on message routing. It can not be used for Seal because mobility also involves process copying.

**Static and dynamic scoping**  We have already discussed that we do not allow the scope of a $\nu$-abstraction to extrude outside a seal: $s[(\nu x)P] \not\equiv (\nu x)s[P]$. This complicated the definition of intra-seal interaction since the reduction must also handle extrusion of the restrictions over an outgoing argument. A different way to handle this problem would be to follow Bent Thomsen's CHOCS and adopt dynamic scoping of $\nu$-abstracted names [35]. In that case it would be possible to send a name outside of its static scope. However, this would clash with security, since dynamic binding would permit names to be "guessed", *i.e.* our proof of security in the example of section 4 relied on the fact that restricted names were not known outside of their scope and that names would be alpha-converted to avoid conflicts. Without this, all security code becomes more complex and in general programs become more fragile. It is interesting to note that Thomsen himself later amended the definition of CHOCS to static scoping [36].

Inspection of our syntax for concretions and abstraction reveals that our calculus, like CHOCS, sends processes as values. But, for safety (and implementation) reasons, we restrict the occurrences of process variables to be encapsulated within seals. In fact our syntax ensure that a seal abstraction will always have the form: $x^\eta.[\lambda X] \ldots (P \mid y_1[X] \mid \ldots \mid y_n[X]) \ldots$ where the only occurrences of a process variable are the bodies of seals $y_1$ through $y_n$. The guarantees that migrating processes will always be protected by boundaries and that their parent will not be able to compose them with arbitrary processes ($y[X \mid P]$ is forbidden as $P$ may be a virus). One of the side effects of this restriction is that our calculus does not allow the open operation of Ambients.[6]

**Asynchrony and synchrony**  Many recent works in concurrency theory and distribution have argued for asynchronous calculi. Boudol [10] gives a well motivated argument in favor of asynchrony in the framework of the $\pi$-calculus, while the Ambient Calculus adopts it in a distributed setting (see [11] for an extensive justification of this choice). The usual motivation for this is by a two-pronged argument: (1) synchronous communication does not sit well with a large scale distributed system as it requires global distributed consensus. (2) Synchronous communication can be implemented in an asynchronous setting, by means of a mutual inclusion protocol in which a sender waits for an acknowledgment. Boudol proved the adequacy of such an implementation w.r.t. a testing preorder [10].

---

[6] An ambient can be opened, releasing its body in the environment. Without our syntactic restrictions, open could be coded in the seal calculus as: OPEN $n.P = \overline{x}\{n\} \mid x.[\lambda X](X|P)$, the concretion releases the seal's body process in environment.

While the first part of the argument is certainly true, the second part of the argument fails in a mobile environment. Mobility exposes the difference between asynchronous primitives and synchronous ones, differences become observable by processes. If a seal moves after a request has been issued and before the acknowledgment is sent, it will not receive the acknowledgment. This may mean, in programming terms, that the seal may try to request the same service a second time. One option would be to forward messages, but tracking mobile entities on a system such as the Internet would require an unrealistic amount of support and cooperation.

We consider that synchronous interactions are frequent and quite natural. Thus, the Seal calculus takes the opposite approach and all communications, including seal mobility, are synchronous. Note however that communication in our model is localized. Synchronization is either local to a seal or restricted to synchronization between parent and child (*e.g.* a machine and an application, a local area network and a machine). All other patterns of interaction must be implemented as sequences of synchronous exchanges and are thus asynchronous. Communications across machine boundaries in an implementation of seal will only require synchronization of adjacent seals. Mobility will likewise not require more than synchronization between adjacent seals.

So we are in presence of two different disciplines of communication. Our model supports only local and parent-child communication. This is synchronous, it requires synchronization consensus but this is limited in scope. Any other pattern of communication must be implemented in terms of our primitives and, in general, will be asynchronous. More powerful distributed communication mechanisms, *e.g.* incorporating distributed failure detection, are likely to be application specific and must be provided as derived operations.

**Objects**   Many distributed programming languages have adopted the object-oriented model as a basis for structuring distributed services. At the outset this was also our view, as witnessed by the original title of this work: "a calculus of sealed objects". The name was shortened to seals when we realized that the abstractions involved were more basic than those of the object paradigm. It also became clear early on that hierarchical protection would be very difficult to obtain in an object system, this mostly due to pervasive aliasing (the object spaghetti) [25]. Furthermore, we also came to understand that seals are coarser abstractions than objects. This point is echoed in our current implementation effort, JavaSeal, which represents seals by systems of objects [37].

# 6   Conclusion and Future Work

The Seal calculus is a programming language suited for modeling Internet applications. Seal captures their inherent parallelism, the repartition of computational elements amongst multiple locations, the mobility of resources and locations, as well as the protection domains that arise from different security policies.

We already mentioned several points that are under investigation: the definition of suitable notions of observation, specification, and equivalence, in order to develop some general techniques and patterns of proofs of security properties.

The next step of this research will be the definition of leaner calculus. The most important criterion for its definition will be minimality. Therefore we will try to reduce the forms of synchronization, and simplify the semantics of portals. For example, if we separe channels for local and remote communications portals for up-sync would become useless. Further issues to consider include:

- Specification. Should/could the leaner calculus be used for specification? Is the formal system of this article a better candidate?
- Testing. Do standard definitions of testing for the process algebras suffice to test mobile software?
- Which properties could/must be captured by the calculus and which ones should instead be delegated to static analysis or dynamic checking?
- Since the synchronism of remote communications is cumbersome to implement, could/should it be weakened?

Moreover, the notion of resources must be extended to encompass memory and cpu-time, if denial of service attacks are to be considered. Furthermore, we are looking at types as means to provide security guarantees, in other words, types should not be just the means to check that channels transport well typed data, they should constrain the behavior of mobile computations so as to facilitate proofs of their security properties.

The long-term and much more ambitious goal is to provide a complete set of tools for software engineering. One essential component should be a specification language for conceptual design (analogous to UML for object-oriented languages) that can be automatically translated into the Seal calculus. The Seal calculus would then constitute a language in which to provide an intermediate representation of mobile software. This representation could be then be transformed either into a representation in a calculus in which test and formal proofs could be performed, or into a executable representations in Seal-based languages such as JavaSeal [37].

*Acknowledgments*

Our work benefited greatly from multiple discussion with Martín Abadi and Luca Cardelli, we are grateful for their insightful advice which prevented us for straying too far off the track. We also wish to thank Karen Bernstein, Walter Binder, Ciarán Bryce and Laurent Dami for comments and inspiration. The first author is funded by the Swiss PP project *ASAP: Agent System Architectures and Platforms* No 5003-45335.

# References

1. M. Abadi and A. D. Gordon. A calculus for cryptographic protocols: The Spi calculus. In *Proceedings of the Fourth ACM Conference on Computer and Communications Security, Zürich, April 1997*. ACM Press, 1997. Long version as Technical Report 414, University of Cambridge.

2. ACM. *Proceedings of the 23rd Annual Symposium on Principles of Programming Languages (POPL) (St. Petersburg Beach, Florida)*, Jan. 1996.

3. G. Agha. *Actors – A model of concurrent computation in distributed systems*. The MIT Press, 1986.

4. R. M. Amadio. On the reduction of CHOCS bisimulation to $\pi$-calculus bisimulation. In Best [8], pages 112–126. Extended version as Rapport de Recherche, INRIA-Lorraine, 1993.

5. R. M. Amadio. An asynchronous model of locality, failure, and process mobility. In *Proceedings of COORDINATION '97*. Springer-Verlag, 1997. Full version as Rapport Interne, LIM Marseille, and Rapport de Recherche RR-3109, INRIA Sophia-Antipolis, 1997.

6. F. M. auf der Heide and B. Monien, editors. *23rd Colloquium on Automata, Languages and Programming (ICALP) (Paderborn, Germany)*, volume 1099 of *Lecture Notes in Computer Science*. Springer-Verlag, 1996.

7. G. Berry and G. Boudol. The chemical abstract machine. *Theoretical Computer Science*, 96:217–248, 1992.

8. E. Best, editor. *CONCUR'93, $4^{th}$ International Conference on Concurrency Theory*, volume 715 of *Lecture Notes in Computer Science*. Springer-Verlag, 1993.

9. C. Bodei, P. Degano, and C. Priami. Mobile processes with a distributed environment. In auf der Heide and Monien [6], pages 490–501. Full version as Università di Pisa Technical Report *Handling Locally Names of Mobile Agents*, 1996.

10. G. Boudol. Asynchrony and the $\pi$-calculus (Note). Rapport de Recherche 1702, INRIA Sofia-Antipolis, May 1992.

11. L. Cardelli. Abstractions for mobile computation. In J. Vitek and C. Jensen, editors, *Secure Internet Programming: Security Issues for Distributed and Mobile Objects*. Springer Verlag, 1999.

12. L. Cardelli and A. D. Gordon. Mobile Ambients. In M. Nivat, editor, *Foundations of Software Science and Computational Structures*, number 1378 in LNCE, pages 140—155. Springer-Verlag, 1998.

13. G. Castagna and J. Vitek. Commitment and confinement for the seal calculus. Technical report, Laboratoire d'Informatique de l'École Normale Supérieure, 1999.

14. R. De Nicola, G. Ferrari, and R. Pugliese. Coordinating mobile agents via blackboards and access rights. In *Proceedings of COORDINATION'97*. Springer-Verlag, 1997.

15. R. De Nicola, G. Ferrari, and R. Pugliese. Locality based Linda: programming with explicit localities. In *Proceedings of FASE-TAPSOFT'97*. Springer-Verlag, 1997.

16. P. Degano, R. Gorrieri, and A. Marchetti-Spaccamela, editors. *24rd Colloquium on Automata, Languages and Programming (ICALP) (Bologna, Italy)*, volume 1256 of *Lecture Notes in Computer Science*. Springer-Verlag, 1997.

17. B. Ford, B. Hibler, J. Lepreau, P. Tullmann, G. Back, and S. Clawson. Microkernels Meet Recursive Virtual Machines. In *Proceedings Symposium on Operating Systems Design and Implementation(OSDI'96)*. ACM Press, Oct. 1996.

18. C. Fournet and G. Gonthier. The reflexive chemical abstract machine and the join-calculus. In POPL'96 [2], pages 372–385.

19. C. Fournet, G. Gonthier, J.-J. Lévy, L. Maranget, and D. Rémy. A calculus of mobile agents. In *CONCUR96*, pages 406–421, 1996.

20. D. Gelernter. Generative communication in Linda. *ACM Trans. Prog. Lang. Syst.*, 7(1):80–112, Jan. 1985.

21. M. Hennessy and J. Riely. Type-safe execution of mobile agents in anonymous networks. In *Proceedings of the Workshop on Internet Programming Languages, (WIPL)*. Chicago, Ill., 1998.

22. K. G. Larsen, S. Skyum, and G. Winskel, editors. *25rd Colloquium on Automata, Languages and Programming (ICALP) (Aalborg, Denmark)*, volume 1443 of *Lecture Notes in Computer Science*. Springer-Verlag, 1998.

23. R. Milner. The polyadic $\pi$-calculus: a tutorial. Technical Report ECS-LFCS-91-180, Laboratory for Foundations of Computer Science, Department of Computer Science, University of Edinburgh, UK, Oct. 1991. Also in *Logic and Algebra of Specification*, ed. F. L. Bauer, W. Brauer and H. Schwichtenberg, Springer-Verlag, 1993.

24. R. Milner, J. Parrow, and D. Walker. A calculus of mobile processes, Parts I and II. *Journal of Information and Computation*, 100:1-77, Sept. 1992.

25. J. Noble, J. Vitek, and J. Potter. Flexible alias protection. In *ECOOP'98 – Object-Oriented Programming, 12th European Conference Proceedings*. Brussels, Belgium, Springer-Verlag, July 1998.

26. P. Pardyak, S. Savage, and B. N. Bershad. Language and runtime support for dynamic interposition of system code. Nov. 1995.

27. *Proceedings of the Sixteenth Annual Symposium on Principles of Programming Languages (POPL) (Austin, TX)*. ACM Press, Austin Texas, January 1989.

28. J. Riely and M. Hennessy. Distributed processes and location failures. In Degano et al. [16], pages 471-481. Full version as Report 2/97, University of Sussex, Brighton.

29. H. Rodrigues and R. Jones. Cyclic distributed garbage collection with group merger. In *ECOOP'98 – Object-Oriented Programming, 12th European Conference Proceedings*. Brussels, Belgium, Springer-Verlag, July 1998.

30. D. Sangiorgi. *Expressing Mobility in Process Algebras: First-Order and Higher-Order Paradigms*. PhD thesis, Department of Computer Science, University of Edinburgh, UK, 1993.

31. F. Schneider. What Good are Models and What Models are Good? In S. Mullender, editor, *Distributed Systems (2nd Ed.)*. ACM Frontier Press, 1993.

32. P. Sewell. Global/local subtyping and capability inference for a distributed $\pi$-calculus. In Larsen et al. [22].

33. P. Sewell and J. Vitek. Secure composition of insecure components. In *Computer Security Foundations Workshop (CSFW-12)*. Mordano, Italy, June 1999.

34. P. Sewell, P. Wojciechowski, and B. Pierce. Location independence for mobile agents. In *Proceedings of the 1998 Workshop on Internet Programming Languages*, Chicago, Ill., May 1998.

35. B. Thomsen. A calculus of Higher Order Communicating Systems. In POPL'89 [27], pages 143-154.

36. B. Thomsen. Plain CHOCS. A second generation calculus for higher order processes. *Acta Informatica*, 30(1):1-59, 1993.

37. J. Vitek, C. Bryce, and W. Binder. Designing JavaSeal: or How to make Java safe for agents. In D. Tsichritzis, editor, *Electronic Commerce Objects*. University of Geneva, 1998.

38. J. Waldo, G. Wyant, A. Wollrath, and S. Kendall. A note on distributed computing. In J. Vitek and C. Tschudin, editors, *Mobile Object Systems: Towards the programmable Internet*. Springer-Verlag, 1997.

# A Run-Time System for WCL

Antony Rowstron[1] and Stuart Wray[2]

[1] Engineering Department, Cambridge University,
Trumpington Street, Cambridge, CB2 1PZ, UK.
`aitr2@eng.cam.ac.uk`
[2] Cambridge University Computer Laboratory,
Pembroke Street, Cambridge, CB2 3QG, UK.

**Abstract.** WCL is an inter-agent co-ordination language designed for Internet and Web based agent systems. WCL is based on shared associative memories called tuple spaces, as introduced in Linda.

In this paper we describe a novel run-time system for WCL. This distributed run-time system is radically different from traditional run-time systems supporting tuple spaces because it performs on-the-fly analysis of the usage of tuple spaces and moves tuple-space data between machines dynamically. Experimental results show that this approach provides significant speed improvements.

## 1 Introduction

Linda has been used with considerable success since the mid eighties [1–3] for inter-process co-ordination in the field of parallel processing. The early implementations were all "closed" in the sense that all the processes wishing to communicate had to be known at compile time. In the last few years there has been a drive to produce "open" implementations for workstations on a LAN, which do not require all the communicating processes to be known at compile time [4]. Still more recently, there have been attempts to create tuple space systems which support geographically distributed computing over the Internet. Announcements by Sun Microsystems about JavaSpaces show the level of commercial interest in the use of tuple spaces for inter-agent co-ordination over the Internet.

This recent work on tuple space systems for the Internet falls into two categories: new access primitives and new run-time systems. New tuple-space access primitives include WCL [5], BONITA [6], Sun JavaSpaces [7] and IBM TSpaces [8]. Examples of run-time systems supporting tuple spaces over the Internet are PageSpace [9] and $C^2AS$ [10].

This paper outlines the run-time system currently being developed for WCL. All other tuple space run-time systems for Internet based co-ordination have been developed by making incremental adjustments to LAN based implementations, such as in PageSpace [9], $C^2AS$ [10], and WWW-Paradise.

WCL is designed to provide general purpose support for geographically distributed applications – not for high performance parallel computing. For example, the run-time described in this paper will not provide high performance for parallel image processing. The sort of applications we have been working on to date are small example applications; such as talk tools, shared white boards, asynchronous conferencing tools, event based applications, and agent based information gathering applications.

In this paper we describe a new distributed run-time system (or "kernel") used to support WCL. This run-time system builds on experience of creating LAN implementations, in particular the York Kernel II [11], but utilizes more much advanced on-the-fly analysis of tuple space usage to enable the migration of tuple spaces around a group of machines which are collectively running the kernel. This allows the system to tune itself automatically and dynamically to provide better performance, and this happens with no extra load being placed on the programmer using WCL. The kernel exploits the location transparency inherent in tuple space based co-ordination languages.

Although the system described in this paper is currently a prototype system, it demonstrates the advantages and speed of such a system. It should also be noted, that although designed to support WCL, this kernel could support any set of access primitives. It is a general purpose tuple space management system.

Section 2 briefly describes WCL, Section 3 describes the architecture of the run-time system, Section 4 shows some initial results for the kernel, and Section 6 describes the problems of transactions and how we plan to overcome them in this WCL implementation.

## 2 WCL

BONITA [6] was a first attempt at creating a new set of access primitives for tuple spaces that did not use *synchronous* tuple space access. The traditional Linda primitives are synchronous: the primitives block the thread of execution which performs the operation. Latency is high over the Internet, and synchronous primitives often block for significant periods. WCL was created after gaining the practical experience of using BONITA for real applications. Currently, *all* other tuple space languages use synchronous tuple space access[1]. The fundamental objects of WCL are the same as in all tuple space systems inspired by Linda: tuples, templates and tuple spaces:

**Tuple** A tuple is an ordered collection of typed fields. For example the tuple $\langle 10_{int}$, "Hello World"$_{str}$ $\rangle$, contains two fields.

**Template** A template is similar to a tuple, but the fields do not need to have values. The templates: $\langle |10_{int}$, "Hello World"$_{str}$ $|\rangle$ and $\langle |10_{int}$, $\square_{str}$ $|\rangle$ will

---

[1] From an agents point of view primitives like inp and rdp provide *synchronous* tuple space access. The thread of execution in the agent performing the operation blocks until the tuple space has been searched for the tuple – if the tuple space is stored on the other side of the world then the time this takes can be considerable because of network latency. Hence, from an agents perspective the operation is synchronous *with respect to the tuple space*. A more detailed description is presented in Rowstron [6]

both match the tuple above. Matching is performed associatively. The number of fields in the template and tuple must be equal, the type of every field must match, and either the value of the fields must be the same, or the template field must have the "unspecified" value, represented here by □.

**Tuple space** A tuple space is a *logical shared associative memory* that is used to store tuples. A tuple space implements a *bag* or *multi-set*, so it can contain multiple identical tuples. There is no ordering of the tuples within a tuple space.

Agents communicate by inserting tuples into, and removing tuples from, shared tuple spaces. Note that while Linda originally had only one tuple space, used by all agents, WCL provides for many separate tuple spaces, as is usual for modern implementations. WCL does provide a global tuple space. Tuple space handles can be passed between agents in tuples inserted in tuple spaces. Co-ordination through tuple spaces provides two basic properties: temporal and spatial separation of agents. Temporal separation means that two agents can communicate even though they do not exist concurrently, because the tuple spaces through which the agents communicate can persist longer than the lifetimes of individual agents. Spatial separation means that agents can be anonymous, and other agents do not need to know their location or indeed their identity in order to communicate with them. These properties make the use of tuple spaces over the Internet ideal, and they allow the designer of run-time systems much freedom.

WCL is only a co-ordination language, and has to be embedded into a host computation language. Currently, bindings for Java and C++ have been developed. It should be noted that agents written in one language can communicate with agents written in another.

The access primitives provided in WCL are described in detail in Rowstron [5] and a detailed justification of why there are so many primitives is also given. Amongst the primitives provided by WCL there are asynchronous versions of the traditional **in**, **out** and **rd** Linda primitives and asynchronous versions of the bulk primitives **collect** [12] and **copy-collect** [13], as well as primitives supporting the streaming of tuples which also provide a simple event model. A brief overview of the WCL primitives is now presented:

First the operation used to create new tuple spaces.

**tscreate()** Create a tuple space and return the handle to that tuple space.

Next are the classic synchronous Linda operations, and their asynchronous equivalents.

**out_sync(ts, tuple)** Insert *tuple* into the tuple space *ts*. When the primitive terminates the tuple is guaranteed to be present (visible) in the tuple space.

**in_sync(ts, template)** This destructively retrieves a tuple which matches the *template* from the tuple space *ts*. The matched tuple is returned. The primitive is synchronous so the executing agent will block until a matching tuple becomes available.

**rd_sync(ts, template)** This is the same as in_sync except the tuple is not removed.

**out_async(ts, tuple)** Insert *tuple* into the tuple space *ts*. When the primitive terminates the tuple is *not* guaranteed to be present in the tuple space, but will appear in the tuple space as soon as possible.

**reply_id = in_async(ts, template)** This is an asynchronous destructive request for a tuple that matches the template *template* from tuple space *ts*. The primitive returns a reply identifier (*reply_id*) immediately and *does* not wait until a tuple matching the template is available (hence it is an asynchronous primitive).

**reply_id = rd_async(ts, template)** This is the same as in_async except the tuple is not removed.

The next operations provide a combined out and in.

**touch_sync(ts, tuple)** This primitive inserts the *tuple* into the tuple space *ts* and then attempts to destructively read it from the tuple space. This primitive is synchronous and when the primitive returns the tuple *tuple* is no longer present in the tuple space. When the tuple is inserted in the tuple space if there are other primitives blocked that could match the tuple being inserted then they compete for the inserted tuple and the winner is non-deterministic.

**touch_async(ts, tuple)** This primitive is the same as touch_sync except the primitive does not block.

Next we have operations to check on and if necessary to abandon pending asynchronous operations.

**check_async(reply_id)** This primitive is used to check if the tuple associated with the reply identifier *reply_id* is available. This primitive is asynchronous, so if the associated tuple is available then it is returned, but if it is not available then an empty tuple is returned. The primitive does not block.

**check_sync(reply_id)** This primitive is the same as check_async except it blocks until the result associated with *reply_id* is available.

**cancel(reply_id)** This primitive cancels the request associated with the reply identifier *reply_id*.

The move and copy operations provide for bulk transfer of tuples between tuple spaces. These operations are all considered to be atomic.

**move_sync(ts$_{src}$, ts$_{dest}$, template)** This moves all the tuples that match the template *template* from the tuple space *ts$_{src}$* to the tuple space *ts$_{dest}$*. The primitive returns a count of the number of tuples moved. If the source and destination tuple space are the same, then the 'moved' tuples are always visible.

**copy_sync(ts$_{src}$, ts$_{dest}$, template)** This primitive is the same as move_sync except the matched tuples are copied from the source to the destination tuple space. A count of the number of tuples copied is returned.

**reply_id = move_async(ts$_{src}$, ts$_{dest}$, template)** This moves all the tuples that match the template *template* from the tuple space *ts$_{src}$* to the tuple space *ts$_{dest}$*. The movement operation does return a count of the number of tuples moved, but unlike the synchronous version, the primitive does not block and returns a request identifier, which is used with either **check_sync** or **check_async** to actually retrieve the number of tuples moved.

**reply_id = copy_async(ts$_{src}$, ts$_{dest}$, template)** This primitive is the same as **move_async** except the matched tuples are copied from the source to the destination tuple space.

These last operations speed up bulk transfer of tuples to an agent and provide a basic event mechanism.

**reply_id = bulk_in_async(ts, template)** This primitive is used to retrieve all tuples that match the template *template* from the tuple space *ts*. The matched tuples are removed from the tuple space *ts*. The primitive returns a reply identifier *reply_id* which is then used in conjunction with the **check_async** and **check_sync** primitives to retrieve the matched tuples, one tuple at a time. The tuples can be considered as being streamed to the user agent. It should be noted that *there is no way* to determine the number of tuples returned, but this primitive can be used in conjunction with the **copy** and **move** family of primitives.

**reply_id = bulk_rd_async(ts, template)** This primitive is the same as the **bulk_in_async** primitive except the returned tuples are not removed from the tuple space it ts.

**reply_id = monitor(ts, template)** This places a monitor on a tuple space for tuples that match the template *template*. All the tuples within the tuple space *ts* that match the template *template* are streamed back to the user agent, and any tuples subsequently inserted are also sent to the user agent. The primitives returns a reply identifier *reply_id* which is used in conjunction with the **check_async** and **check_sync** primitives to retrieve the returned tuples, one tuple at a time. A **monitor** is guaranteed to match and return any tuple inserted that matches the template, regardless of whether the tuple is also matched by another primitive.

It should be noted that *reply_id* values returned by some of asynchronous primitives has no meaning other than for use with the **check_sync** and **check_async** primitives and the *reply_id* only has any context within the agent that performed the asynchronous primitive. It can not be passed to another agent and then that agent use it to retrieve the result.

## 3 Run-Time System Architecture

The run-time System architecture has been designed from the beginning to use data location transparency and to support geographically distributed computing. The entire run-time system, usually running across several machines, is called the kernel. The kernel is composed of three distinct sections; the control system, the tuple management system and the agent libraries. The current implementation is very much an experiment to discover techniques that are useful for creating tuple space support on a large scale. The initial aim has been to demonstrate that the bulk movement of tuples is a useful tool for developing such kernels. Only the agent libraries are specific to WCL, the other parts of the kernel provide a generic tuple space management system. The architecture of the kernel is designed to be independent of the host language and to support multiple host languages.

The tuple management system uses multiple tuple servers. A tuple server is designed to provide agents with an efficient data access service. It processes instructions to insert tuples, instructions to return tuples, and instructions to move tuple spaces. A separate layer, the control system, determines when a tuple space should be moved, and dispatches the instructions to the individual tuple servers. Agents connect to the control layer, and to the tuple servers as required.

The separation between the control layer and the tuple storage layer has been made so that the tuple servers can be as efficient as possible. The tuple servers are the potential bottleneck of the system, therefore the quicker they can service requests the sooner blocked agents can continue. The control role is separated from the tuple management role, and performed on different machines, and even at different geographical locations.

## 3.1 Tuple management system

The tuple servers are distributed geographically around the area being supported. Each tuple server manages many entire tuple spaces. To use the analogy of Douglas [4] the tuple spaces can be considered as layers of a layered cake. Most LAN based run-time systems have tuple servers managing a slice of the cake, so each tuple server manages a small part of many tuple spaces. Alternatively, some LAN based systems have all the tuple spaces managed by a single centralized server (the entire cake). In our system each tuple server manages one *or more* layers of the cake, in other words each server manages multiple entire tuple spaces. This has an advantage from the point of view of fault tolerance, as it makes it cheap to take a snapshot of a tuple space, since there is no need for global synchronization between different tuple servers.

The approach of storing an entire tuple space on one of many single servers is different from other kernels. This approach makes the system bad for 'high performance parallel processing'[2] because multiple processes can not concurrently access the data, where as when the tuples of a single tuple space are distributed over multiple servers then multiple access to different tuples which are from the same tuple space is possible. Indeed, we have been involved in the development of several such run-time systems [4, 14, 11]. However, in such run-times providing fault tolerance of tuple spaces is difficult, supporting many of the more complex access primitives is difficult (requiring global synchronization between all servers storing the tuple spaces). Across a LAN this can be achieved but if this is then

---

[2] Or at least no worse than for traditional single process centralized kernels!

further distributed the latency between tuple servers impairs the performance greatly - this has been demonstrated when we attempted to run the $C^2AS$ [10] kernel across multiple sites in Europe.

However, there is nothing theoretically to stop a single tuple server in this context in fact being distributed across several machines connected by a fast LAN. In many ways the work on this kernel was an experiment to see if storing entire tuple spaces on a single server really could work and if the migration of these tuple spaces between single servers was possible and still provide reasonable performance.

Finally, it should be noted that the tuple servers are written in C++ and use sockets directly so as to have complete control over their communication.

## 3.2 Control system

The control system acts as a manager, with which the tuple servers register, and the control system also presents agents with their entry point to the system. Currently, the control system uses a "well known" Internet address and port. When an agent is started this is either provided on the command line or read from an initialization file. When an agent connects to the control system it tells the control system its geographical location, and is passed a handle for the universally accessible tuple space, called the *Global Tuple Space*. The geographical location of an agent is also specified either on the command line or in the initialization file.

When the tuple servers register with the control layer they specify their geographical location, and this defines the areas over which they provide the best coverage. The geographical model used is one in which named regions are completely contained within other named regions, forming a tree structure like a file system directory structure (see figure 1 for a graphical representation). Currently, the locations are fairly large and the name space is fairly shallow, so for example a location might be *Cambridge-UK-Europe*. However, the granularity of locations can be as fine as required. For example, a tuple server running on our machine might for example use the location *428-Austin-CL-CU-Cambridge-Anglia-England-UK-Europe-World*. Where 428 is the office number, Austin is the building, CL is the department, CU is Cambridge University, Cambridge is the town, Anglia the region, UK the country etc. An agent on the same machine would share the same location description. It should be noted that a tuple server can serve tuples to and accept tuples from an agent running anywhere.

The aim of the geographical descriptions is to provide a gross indication to the run-time system of where tuple spaces should be stored when being accessed by agents. Therefore, the tuple server running on a machine in Cambridge would not be a good choice to store a tuple space being used only by agents currently running in California. However, if they were all running in England it may well be a good choice. When a tuple server registers, as well as telling the control layer its geographical location, it also provides information about its processing power. This enables the control system to ensure that the load placed upon the tuple server is acceptable for its power. This information could be obtained automatically by making the tuple servers perform tests when they initialize, and then the servers could monitor the load on the machine and reduce or increase their processing power co-efficient with the control layer as appropriate.

In the prototype control system, agents can come and go freely. Tuple servers can join at any time, but currently can not leave. In a full implementation of the system this would of course be necessary and there are no fundamental reasons why this is hard. The control system would need to be told that a tuple server wanted to leave and it could then arrange to move all tuple spaces from that tuple space server to other servers. It should be noted that an agent can re-register to provide different geographical location information. This is important if migrating agents are to be supported.

The control system generates tuple space handles (global names for tuple spaces), monitors tuple space usage and decides when tuple spaces should be moved. Every time an agent becomes capable of using a tuple space the control system is informed, and every time an agent loses the ability to use a tuple space the control system is informed. Therefore, the control system maintains an overview of all the tuple spaces, and which agents are currently using them. Although, the control system is currently centralized, the kernel has been designed to allow the control system to lag behind, thus overcoming the problem of it becoming a bottleneck. We are currently investigating the possibility of a decentralized control system. However, a centralized control system does have the advantage that it can perform garbage collection using the method of Menezes and Wood [15].

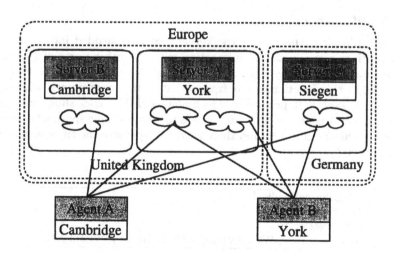

**Fig. 1.** Information stored in control system.

Figure 1 shows the information stored and managed in the control system. It shows three tuple servers, one in Siegen, one in Cambridge and one in York. All the servers are grouped geographically and hierarchically (eg. Europe contains both the United Kingdom and Germany). There are also two agents, whose locations are York and Cambridge. The clouds represent tuple spaces, and their position shows which tuple server is physically looking after them.

The control system attempts to optimize the performance of the system by moving tuple spaces to the best position within the entire system. Therefore, in Figure 1 the control system analyses its usage and location information and observes that the two agents using the tuple space stored at Siegen are in fact in the United Kingdom. Therefore, it decides to move the tuple space. If both the agents were at the same physical location then the tuple space would be moved to the tuple server at that location. However, either of the tuple servers in the United Kingdom could be just as good, therefore the control system looks at the number of tuple spaces on each and then makes a decision to migrate it to either Cambridge or York. As more agents use it, the position of the tuple space may change again.

The current prototype system uses a very simple heuristic to decide when tuple spaces should be moved. It is based solely on the geographical information provided when the agents and tuple servers are started. Section 5 describes our current work on how this can be extended.

The replication of tuple spaces is not currently supported, mainly because access controls to tuple spaces have not yet been implemented. Access controls will provide information needed to sensibly decide when to replicate tuple spaces. It should also be noted that like the tuple servers, the control system is also written in C++ and uses sockets directly.

## 3.3 Agent library

The agent library is the part of the kernel that is embedded into each agent. These routines manage all the interaction with the other parts of the kernel, provide local tuple storage data structures, and determine where to find tuple spaces. All of this functionality is transparent to the programmer, who simply uses the high level WCL primitives. The fragment of C++ code shown in Figure 2 demonstrates the code a programmer writes to create a tuple space whose handle is stored in the variable TS1 and then inserts a tuple into the tuple space of the form $[x_{int}, \text{``D''}_{str}]$.

```
TupleSpaceHandle TS1;
int x = 10;
TS1.createts();
out_async(TS1, WCL_INT(x), WCL_STR("D"), WCL_END);
```

**Fig. 2.** Example using WCL primitives embedded in C++.

So far, agent libraries have been written for C++ and Java. Agents written in one language can communicate with agents written in other languages. It should be noted that the Java embedding supports only the basic primitive types in Java, rather than objects. However, the control system and the tuple management system are unaware of the types embedded within a tuple. Therefore, a language embedding could add types, provided the new 'type codes' do not interfere with existing embeddings. Currently, we control the type codes strictly, but we are considering schemes that would support the dynamic allocation of type codes managed by the control system.

The Java embedding is written in Java and can be used in either applets or stand-alone applications. If it is being used in an applet it detects this and connects to a proxy which is running on the web server which provided the applet. The proxy server is then able to forward the requests to the appropriate servers. Once the security model in Java is relaxed, the applets will be able to communicate directly with the servers.

## 3.4 Tuple space management and migration

In the last sections we have described the basic structure of the kernel, and now we consider briefly how the interaction between the agent library and the tuple server and control layer is managed.

Since tuple spaces migrate around the system, how does an agent know where to find a particular tuple space? Tuple spaces are identified by tuple space handles, which contain a globally unique tag and information (IP address and port number plus other information) about which tuple server is thought to be storing the tuple space. When an agent wishes to access a tuple space it looks at this information and if a connection is not already open to the appropriate tuple server, it opens a new connection and sends the requests to that tuple server. If that tuple server still holds the tuple space then the appropriate operations are performed there and the results returned to the agent. However, if the tuple space has migrated, then the tuple server will return to the agent a "forwarding address", in the form of a new tuple space handle with more up-to-date location information, but the same unique tag as before. The agent stores this and uses this new tuple space handle whenever it is presented with the superseded tuple space handle. It is not feasible to expect a tuple server to maintain a list of all tuple spaces it has ever seen for all of its life, so the tables are periodically flushed. If the tuple server receives operations on a tuple space it no longer knows about, then the agent which sent the operations is informed. That agent must then query the control system to find the current location of the tuple space. The same mechanism can be used to allow servers to be removed. If the agent can not connect to a tuple server, it can ask the control layer where a tuple space is. The control system, given any tuple space handle, can provide an up-to-date version of that tuple space handle because it controls the movement of tuple spaces, so it knows their current locations. Because of the globally unique tag within a tuple space handle it is not necessary for the control system to store all tuple space handles ever associated with a tuple space; outdated tuple space handles can always be matched by the control system to the up-to-date one.

The current kernel is scalable and could support thousands of tuple spaces and agents, but performs best when there are a small number of agents using each tuple space. Because a tuple space is stored on a single tuple server at a particular location all the access for that tuple space must be sent to that tuple server. However, if several 'popular' tuple spaces are stored on a single tuple server, one or more of them can be moved to other tuple servers, so as to balance the load between them. It is safe to say that this kernel supports more agents, and provides better access, over the whole system, than existing LAN based implementations extended for use over the Internet.

The migration of a tuple space is not as simple as it may at first seem; often there will be operations pending on a migrating tuple space and care must be taken that these complete correctly. Another concern is that there are primitives in WCL that must be applied to all the tuples in a tuple space rather than a subset. A problem is introduced because an agent can be informed that a tuple space has been moved to a new tuple server, and then contact that tuple server, *before* the messages containing the tuple space is received by the next tuple server. Therefore, some primitives have to be queued because otherwise it is possible to introduce race conditions. The tuple space handle has information encoded in it that allows a tuple server to know whether the tuple space handle represents a new tuple space, or whether a tuple space handle represents a tuple space being moved. Therefore we ensure that commands to a new tuple space are never queued awaiting the arrival of non-existent tuples.

## 4    Experimental Results

The aim of the prototype is to investigate the migration of tuple spaces, and we now present some experimental results which demonstrate the effectiveness of tuple space migration in kernels for Internet based co-ordination. The experimental results were obtained by running the kernel across three sites; Cambridge University (UK), the University of York (UK) and the University of Siegen (Germany). At Cambridge the tuple server was run on a Linux PC workstation, at Siegen on a DEC Alpha workstation and at York on a SGI Indy workstation.

The results shown in Figure 3 show the time taken to insert (out_sync) and retrieve (in_sync) 2500 tuples from a tuple space. The columns show the location of the agent performing the insertion or retrieval. The rows show where the tuple space was being stored at the start of the test. For the retrieval timings two times are given, marked ( *"disabled"* and *"enabled"*). The row marked *"disabled"* shows the time when the migration of tuple spaces was disabled, and the row marked *"enabled"* shows the time when it was enabled. It should be noted that the retrieval timings include the time taken to register with the system, so this ensures that the times represent the time to move the tuple space as well as retrieve the tuples. This is important because if the time taken to fetch and move the tuples was greater than just fetching them then there is no point in migrating the tuples. When the migration is enabled the final location of the tuple space will be the same location as the agent performing the retrieval operation. The speedup (number of times faster) obtained when using tuple space migration is shown on the row below the two retrieval results.

Obviously, the results are highly dependent on network load, and the results presented here were gathered early on a Sunday morning, when network traffic in Europe was low. It should also be noted that the insertion timings are for synchronous insertion.

| Tuplespace | Type of | Agent Location | | |
| Location | Operation | York | Cambridge | Siegen |
|---|---|---|---|---|
| York | 2500 out_sync | 6.79 | 60.44 | 114.55 |
| | (disabled) 2500 in_sync | 11.35 | 56.31 | 115.56 |
| | (enabled) 2500 in_sync | 11.35 | 2.94 | 9.73 |
| | Speedup | - | 19.2 | 11.9 |
| Cambridge | 2500 out_sync | 63.11 | 1.50 | 106.16 |
| | (disabled) 2500 in_sync | 62.64 | 2.32 | 112.91 |
| | (enabled) 2500 in_sync | 11.65 | 2.32 | 8.40 |
| | Speedup | 5.4 | - | 13.4 |
| Siegen | 2500 out_sync | 108.21 | 110.23 | 4.51 |
| | (disabled) 2500 in_sync | 120.22 | 112.23 | 7.57 |
| | (enabled) 2500 in_sync | 11.86 | 3.77 | 7.57 |
| | Speedup | 10.1 | 29.8 | - |

**Fig. 3.** Insertion (out_sync) and retrieval (in_sync) timings.

These results demonstrate that the use of bulk movement of tuple spaces within the kernel gives a large increase in performance. This performance increase is due to reduced communication across the Internet, the ability to tune packet sizes to an optimum size for routing through the Internet, and the much lower latency of performing local operations compared to operations at a remote site. It should be noted that the results presented here do not deal with concurrent access to tuple spaces by more than one agent – this is because of the difficulty of setting up experiments over multiple sites that test this repeatably enough to present results in this paper. The tests of concurrent access to a tuple space by multiple agents does show a speedup when using migration. Indeed, this demonstrated that some care might have to be taken to prevent continuous migration between tuple servers. However, the nature of most tuple space applications makes this unlikely anyway, and a "resistance" to migrating too often can be added in the control layer.

It should be noted that the migration of a tuple space may result in faster access for some agents accessing the tuple space, whilst providing slower access for other agents. However, the aim is that on *average* all the agents can access the tuple space quicker. If this is not the case then the migration of a tuple space can be regarded as a failure.

# 5 Migration Control Experiments

Some consideration has been made as to how the simplistic heuristic of when to move a tuple space can be extended, for example by adding dynamic checking of communication latency between agents and tuple servers and by using historical data. Our initial investigations have concentrated on using the "historical" load on the Internet as a way to predict when and where network load will again be high. This was motivated by an observation from using the Internet that at some times of the day access to many countries is far slower than at other times of the day. For example, from the UK access in the afternoon to USA is very slow.

We set up an experiment to use the UNIX ping tool every fifteen minutes to measure the time taken for a round-trip to a number of sites. Each time 10 packets were sent, and the results then analyzed. Figure 4 provides the average packet round trip time from a machine at the Computer Laboratory at Cambridge University to a number of other computers around the world. The results are shown for only three days, starting 00:00 on the 20th May 1998 GMT, and the last reading is at 00:00 on the 23rd May 1998 GMT. This represents three days during the working week. We monitored many sites during the time, and sites were chosen because of their geographical location and because of the routers that were 'normally' chosen to reach them (we detected this using the UNIX traceroute tool).

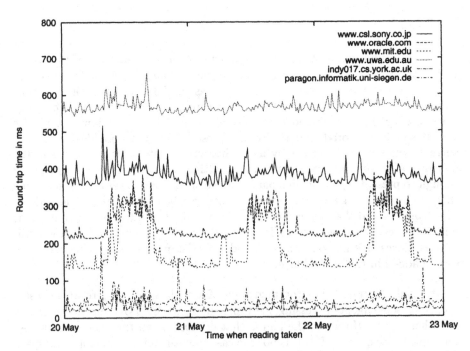

**Fig. 4.** Round trip time for a packet.

What is interesting is that the round trip time to the machines in the USA increases noticeably when America goes to work, and drops again when working day finishes. The traces for the weekends interestingly show no such increase. What is also interesting is that there is no such peak for machines located outside the USA. The latency remains constant.

This was interesting because we had expected to see latency increase whenever a country was at work! Ping uses ICMP packets, so there is no retransmission of lost packets, as there would be for the TCP connections used by the WCL system. Therefore, we next examined the number of lost packets. Figures 5 and 7 show respectively the results for the sites outside Europe and the results for the two sites in Europe (used in the previous experiment).

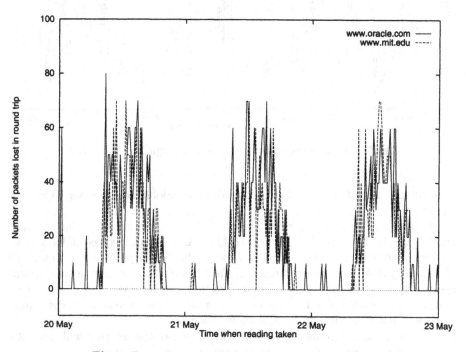

**Fig. 5.** Percentage of packets lost to North America.

It is interesting that the number of packets to all countries outside Europe rises when the USA is working. By contrast, the number of packets lost in Europe is very small.

By using traceroute to these addresses and to other randomly chosen class C addresses we were able to investigate where the packet loss was occurring. Traffic from Cambridge to sites in the USA travel from external-gw.ja.net across the Atlantic to teleglobe.net and thence via other Teleglobe routers to other service providers. Unsurprisingly, most of the delay is introduced on the link across the Atlantic. However, hardly any packets were dropped on our side of the Atlantic

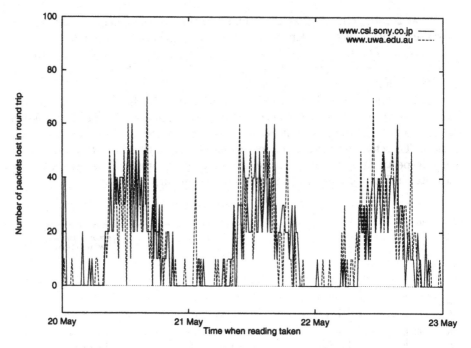

**Fig. 6.** Percentage of packets lost going through North America.

— most of the lost packets were dropped by telegloble.net or other Teleglobe routers.

Although geographical position provides a strong indication of latency and traffic capacity between sites (if for no other reason than the speed of light!), we have come to the conclusion that in many ways the *service providers (who provide the routers) define the true geography of the Internet.* Rather than using physical geography we need to build an "image" of how the Internet is interconnected, and the times when certain key routers are liable to be busy in order to determine when a it is a good time to move a tuple space.

Future work on taming the current wild nature of the Internet will dramatically affect how one should both measure network capacity and how to use these measurements to decide when to migrate data. For example, end-to-end bandwidth negotiation and traffic-smoothing gateways would both have a big impact in this area.

## 6 Further Work

The existing prototype needs improvement in a number of areas before it is sophisticated and robust enough for wider use:

**Surviving agent failure** The kernel can survive agent failure, but agent failure is still a problem for applications. Agents must remove tuples from a

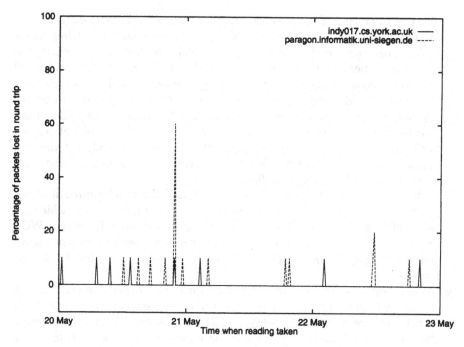

**Fig. 7.** Percentage of packets lost to Siegen and York.

tuple space, for example to increment a counter or claim a lock. If an agent terminates unexpectedly while holding such a tuple, then the whole application may deadlock.

Some implementations [16, 17, 7] offer solutions to this problem based on transactions, but none of them are completely satisfactory.

All the implementations take a similar approach. Two new commands are added, START and COMMIT. The START command causes all tuples inserted to be held, and all tuples removed by the co-ordination commands in between the START and the COMMIT to be held. When the COMMIT occurs any inserted tuple appear in the tuple space. This way, if the COMMIT is never reached the inserted tuples do not appear in the tuple spaces and any removed tuples can be replaced in the tuple spaces.

The problem with extra locking operations like START and COMMIT is that they alter the underlying semantics of the co-ordination fragments they are placed around. This is demonstrated by the code fragments given in Figure 8.

| Fragment One | Fragment Two |
|---|---|
| $out(10_{integer})$; | $in(10_{integer})$; |
| $in(11_{integer})$; | $out(11_{integer})$; |

**Fig. 8.** Example of transaction problems.

The two fragments of pseudo code shown in Figure 8 are assumed to be performed on the same tuple space, and represent a trivial but yet important co-ordination construct using tuple spaces. This construct is an explicit synchronization between the two fragments. If the START and COMMIT are placed around the co-ordination construct in Fragment two then this does not alter the semantics. However, if the START and COMMIT are placed around the co-ordination construct in Fragment one then Fragment two will deadlock. The tuple inserted in Fragment one into the tuple space will not appear until after the tuple inserted in Fragment two has been read, but this can not occur until after the tuple inserted in Fragment two appears in the tuple space, thus the Fragments deadlock.

In order to overcome this problem we have used the novel approach of migrating "co-ordination fragments" from agents to tuple servers, which we have called mobile co-ordination [18]. These fragments will contain WCL operations with Java. This technique has also improved latency since fewer round-trips are necessary, and it reduces the bandwidth needed for similar reasons.

**Surviving tuple server failure** The development of a fault tolerant kernel will be facilitated by our approach of storing a tuple space on a single tuple server, because this makes it easy to take a snapshot of a tuple space, as in the LAN-based PLinda [16]. It will be necessary to replicate the tuple space over perhaps multiple sites.

**Control system** The control system is centralized, and for reliability and load sharing this needs to be changed to a distributed version. Also we need to work on the algorithms and techniques used to control when tuple spaces are moved. This will include taking account of network topology, capacity and recent and historic load.

**Tuple and tuple space management** We need to add access control mechanisms to tuple spaces and potentially tuples. This will also allow us to consider garbage collection of tuple spaces and tuples.

## 7  Conclusions

In this paper we have described a novel implementation of a distributed kernel supporting tuple spaces, which can be used for the co-ordination of geographically distributed agents over the Internet. The kernel uses tuple space usage analysis to transparently move tuple spaces to the tuple servers which can best support the dynamically changing access patterns of the agents.

Recent interest in tuple space based systems for the Internet and recent product announcements shows the importance that tuple spaces may play in the future. If the true potential of the tuple space paradigm is to be fulfilled the development of run-time systems which support them in a scalable and efficient manner must be developed. We are currently addressing this, and the current prototype implementation represents an initial step in the right direction.

The work on implementations has revealed a weakness both in the current prototype and the WCL languages, in their inability to support fault tolerance.

This is to be addressed with the concept of mobile co-ordination. This should be seen as complementary to the mobile tuple space concept presented in this paper.

Some implementors of tuple space systems for wide area use have suggested that centralized implementations are preferable to distributed ones. However, the experimental results from our prototype distributed kernel show the potential performance gains from bulk data migration. In some cases we have observed a 30-fold speed increase. These figures argue compellingly for distributed tuple space run-time systems.

## Acknowledgements

We would like to thank Prof. Andy Hopper and the Olivetti and Oracle Research Laboratory for funding this work. We would also like to thank Alan Wood (York University) and Thilo Kielmann (Siegen University) for allowing us to use their computing resources. We would also like to thank Sheng Li for his advice.

## References

1. N. Carriero. *Implementation of Tuple Space Machines*. PhD thesis, Yale University, 1987. YALEU/DCS/RR-567.
2. N. Carriero and D. Gelernter. Linda in context. *Communications of the ACM*, 32(4):444–458, 1989.
3. D. Gelernter. Generative communication in linda. *ACM Transactions on Programming Languages and Systems*, 7(1):80–112, 1985.
4. A. Douglas, A. Wood, and A. Rowstron. Linda implementation revisited. In *Transputer and occam developments*, pages 125–138. IOS Press, 1995.
5. A. Rowstron. WCL: A web co-ordination language. *World Wide Web Journal*, 1998.
6. A. Rowstron and A. Wood. BONITA: A set of tuple space primitives for distributed coordination. In *HICSS-30*, volume 1, pages 379–388. IEEE CS Press, 1997.
7. Sun Microsystems. Javaspace specification, revision 0.4. Unpublished beta draft specification., 1997.
8. Peter Wyckoff, Stephen McLaughry, Tobin Lehman, and Daniel Ford. TSpaces. To appear in *IBM Systems Journal*, August, 1998.
9. P. Ciancarini, A. Knocke, R. Tolksdorf, and F. Vitali. PageSpace: An architecture to coordinate distributed applications on the web. In *5th International World Wide Web Conference*, 1995.
10. A. Rowstron, S. Li, and S. Radina. $C^2$AS: A system supporting distributed web applications composed of collaborating agents. In *WETICE*, pages 87–92, 1997.
11. A. Rowstron. *Bulk primitives in Linda run-time systems*. PhD thesis, Department of Computer Science, University of York, 1997.
12. P. Butcher, A. Wood, and M. Atkins. Global synchronisation in Linda. *Concurrency: Practice and Experience*, 6(6):505–516, 1994.
13. A. Rowstron and A. Wood. Solving the linda multiple rd problem using copy-collect. *Science of Computer Programming*, 31(2-3), July 1998.

14. A. Rowstron and A. Wood. An efficient distributed tuple space implementation for networks of workstations. In L. Bougé, P. Fraigniaud, A. Mignotte, and Y. Robert, editors, *Euro-Par'96*, volume 1123 of *Lecture Notes in Computer Science*, pages 510–513. Springer-Verlang, 1996.

15. R. Menezes and A. Wood. Garbage Collection in Open Distributed Tuple Space Sys tems. In *Proceedings of 15th Brazilian Computer Networks Symposi um - SBRC'97*, 1997.

16. B. Anderson and D. Shasha. Persistent Linda: Linda + Transactions + Query Processing. In *Research Directions in High-Level Parallel Programming Languages*, LNCS 574, 1991.

17. Scientific Computing Associates. *Paradise: User's guide and reference manual.* Scientific Computing Associates, 1996.

18. A. Rowstron. Mobile co-ordination: Providing fault tolerance in tuple space based co-ordination languages. In *To appear Coordination'99*. Springer Verlag, 1999.

# PML: A Language Interface to Distributed Voice-Response Units

J. Christopher Ramming

AT&T Labs, 75 Willow Road, Menlo Park, CA 94025

**Abstract.** Wide-area networks such as the Internet support distributed applications that occasionally incorporate services owned and operated by third parties. These third-party network services must be reliable and secure; they must support efficient and responsive applications; finally, they must be cost-effective. Can programming languages contribute to achieving these goals? This paper responds to that question by relating experience with the Phone Markup Language (PML), and its role in a project code-named "PhoneWeb". The PhoneWeb provides Voice Response Unit (VRU) capabilities to untrusted remote clients by accepting PML programs and executing them: PML acts as the PhoneWeb "service interface". By using a language as the service interface, we have obtained the performance benefits due to mobile code; and through restrictions on our language we have achieved security and reliability. The resulting service allows us to timeshare the underlying hardware, yielding a solution that is more cost-effective than its alternatives.

## 1 Introduction

Computer networks support the integration of widely distributed components. The motivation for such distributed systems varies: a corporate database (particularly one that is dynamically updated) might not easily be replicated and maintained on a given processor; or, an application such as speech recognition may require unusually powerful compute servers; or perhaps there is specialized hardware such as a fax modem bank that handles some aspect of the application. In each instance, there is a natural separation of concerns dictated by the characteristics of the remote resource and by the processing that is associated with that resource. In the these examples, the servers might locally perform query processing, recognition grammar compilation, and fax formatting; other aspects of the application would be performed elsewhere.

*Wide-area* networks support distributed applications as well, but additionally present the problem that there may be significant latency in the interprocessor communication. Minimizing the effects of such latency then becomes a crucial design issue.

*Public* wide-area networks such as the Internet introduce a new twist: namely, that the remote resource may not even be owned and operated by the same group that creates the application. In addition to suggesting commercial opportunities (since the use of the resource can be for-fee), this distinction has design ramifications, since it becomes important to protect such a resource from untrusted clients (alternately, from trusted but sometimes inept clients). When the resource is shared amongst multiple clients, then it becomes even more important to ensure that users cannot affect each other, either by damaging the resource or by exploiting security flaws to spy on and affect other users' activity.

We have developed a network service (the PhoneWeb) which performs the specialized activity required of Interactive Voice Response[1] (IVR) applications. This service uses a domain-specific language as its user interface and demonstrates that domain-specific languages, in addition to providing convenience to programmers, have allowed us to expose a shared resource on a public network in a way that overcomes some performance and security problems that might be considered typical of public wide-area networks such as the Internet.

## 2   Interactive Voice-Response Systems

Our service, the PhoneWeb, is intended for use as a component of Interactive Voice Response (IVR) applications. Examples of these applications include bank-by-phone systems, the package-tracking systems offered by several overnight delivery services, answering machines, and the kind of activity one performs when using telephone calling cards. Recently, a number of interesting IVR applications have also been created to access Internet-resident data (such as data from personal information managers and electronic mail).

At commercial scale, IVR applications are implemented with expensive, specialized computers called VRUs. VRUs include processors, network interface cards, DSP cards that perform speech synthesis (e.g., text-to-speech) and automatic speech recognition (ASR). VRUs, in addition to being single-purpose computers with high purchase price, are also expensive to maintain because one must lease capacity from the telephone network and any necessary data networks. These leases involve both fixed monthly fees in addition to usage-dependent charges, strongly suggesting that VRUs should never be idle.

In an IVR application the system interacts extensively with callers: answering the call, reacting to touchtone DTMF (dual-tone multi-frequency) signals, recording speech, playing sound files, and performing speech synthesis and recognition. The application typically performs information retrieval (stock quotes, weather, news, balance inquiries), transactions (ticket purchases, votes, message creation, paging), or call control activity (transfers, bridging) according to the logic of the application.

It is reasonable to draw the analogy between an IVR application and an ordinary computer application. The difference is largely one of user interface: one case there is as full qwerty keyboard, mouse, and screen; in the other, there is a 12-digit keyboard, a a microphone, and a speaker. The analogy breaks down and becomes interesting because the processing and the terminal are not necessarily co-located; in fact, for the majority of existing telephones, most processing must take place in the network, on the Voice Response Units.

VRUs are typically owned and operated by the same group that programs its IVR applications. However, VRU hardware is sufficiently specialized that it suggests a separation of concerns in the form of an architecture in which the application logic and the VRU are distributed. In the Internet environment, this separation might be realized in the form of a VRU service, in which the hardware is hired on a per-transaction basis and controlled by external programs. From a client's perspective, such a network service is attractive because it is a basis for cost reductions due to economies of scale, resource time sharing, maintenance offloading, and other benefits that derive from location independence such as redundancy, dynamic routing, and overload-capacity management. From a service operator's perspective, the challenges are to meet customers' cost, reliability, and performance requirements.

The VRU represents a component of IVR applications that is a "natural service": a VRU is comprised of specialized, expensive equipment, and in addition there are high usage-independent operating costs such as leased connections to the Public Switched Telephone Network (PSTN); these characteristics strongly favor timesharing to fully saturate the equipment and yield the lowest per-transaction cost. At the same time, aggregation can yield efficiencies where unshared installations would have to plan for capacity at peak usage (or forgo opportunities), yielding VRUs that would necessarily be underutilized a large percentage of the time.

The idea of a VRU as service interface suffers from three problems. First, VRU service provider is motivated to minimize the amount of customization performed on behalf of any given application (there is a preference for solutions which have sublinear cost growth). Second, the service provider wishes to timeshare equipment despite the existence of untrusted programmers, whose malicious or naive efforts ought nonetheless be incapable of harming other customers. Third, if the solution is distributed one, there are significant concerns involving network efficiency which must be addressed.

This paper describes a distributed architecture for IVR applications which includes a VRU service component. The VRU uses a domain-specific language, the Phone Markup Language (PML) as its interface. The use of a domain-specific language as the service interface confers certain advantages to both the service provider and client; these advantages are the topic of this paper.

## 3 The Web and PhoneWeb Architectures

The inspiration for our particular IVR architecture derives from the Web, but the idea of the Web is essentially inverted in the PhoneWeb. The Web supports distributed applications in a way that prevents untrusted code from harming the end-user clients (usually PCs); the PhoneWeb marshals the same approach in order to protected a shared network resource (the VRU).

Web applications are distributed applications. A Web browser controls a resource (the terminal device) to display graphics and support user interaction with the keyboard and mouse. The substance of the application resides transparently at a remote server, which executes all the service logic, e.g., the control flow and database queries or transactions which implement an application. The interface to the terminal device is HTML, and HTML code will be mobile in the sense that it originates at the remote server[1] HTML, in combination with an interpreting browser, insulates the terminal device against flawed or malicious service logic: the language is simply incapable of expressing harmful activity. The use of HTML also increases efficiency by defining an architecture in which the layout, scrolling, and certain input activities are encapsulated and abstracted away from the components of a service that execute at the HTTP daemon: the browser operates independently of the HTTP daemon, reducing the need for round-trips at every instance.

The PhoneWeb architecture (see Figure 1) is based on the ordinary Web architecture, since IVR applications can be viewed as analogous to Web applications. The goal of the PhoneWeb is to deliver services through a telephone, rather than via an ordinary visual browser. Both the Web and the PhoneWeb employ HTTP daemons, which serve up Web pages and perform any arbitrary computation not supported by the mobile code language; however, in the PhoneWeb that language is used as the interface to a network resource, the VRU. The PhoneWeb "browsers" are located (conceptually) within the telephone network (on arbitrarily located VRUs); the "browsers' control both a telephone set and aspects of the telephone network. In order to implement this scheme, certain telephone numbers are designated by the network as special: they are routed to the PhoneWeb VRUs. There is also a mapping from these telephone numbers and to customers' URLs. When one of these special telephone numbers is dialed, the call is routed to a PhoneWeb VRU, which launches a Web browser and interprets the document at that URL. That document must be written in PML, rather than in HyperText Markup Language (HTML) [2].

The PhoneWeb architecture is fundamentally the same as the Web architecture, permitting application programmers to drive both Web and IVR applications from the same HTTP servers and data. However, the mobile code language is slightly different depending on which terminal device is being controlled, and the resource being protected is an end-user device in one case and a shared network resource in the other.

We apply the Web architecture to IVR systems to support a separation between application *service logic*: the Web pages and scripts that are invoked through the Common Gateway Interface (CGI) convention and VRU-specific logic. We maintain a correspondence between PML and HTML to allow service providers to use the same programming techniques, and to encourage the creation of applications that link the PhoneWeb and the Web, for instance by using the Web to configure the telephone or vice-versa.

---

[1] Unlike some forms of mobile code, only the program text is transmitted, not a running process. Furthermore, unlike some languages supporting mobile code, mobility is an artifact of the environment, not a first-class concept within the language.

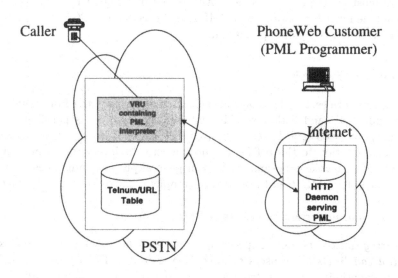

**Fig. 1.** The PhoneWeb Architecture. Application "service logic" is separated from the Voice Response Units; a restricted language serves as the VRU interface as a form of protection, and mobile code in this language is used to achieve location transparency.

## 4 PML and Its Implementation

PML is an imperative language containing primitives that allow a programmer to specify behavior of the VRU; it is geared toward form-oriented user interaction with an HTTP daemon, and is used in conjunction with HTTP daemon-side gateway scripts for implementation of complete IVR applications.

PML is a variant of HTML; although they share many tags and thus have an intuitive correspondence, their semantics are markedly different: HTML is declarative, whereas PML is a sequential imperative language. The difference is essential because the the functional goal of the PhoneWeb is *not* to help users browse Web pages on the phone, but rather to build telephone services using ordinary Web programming techniques. Telephone interactions inherently take place sequentially over time (for instance, telephone service will re-prompt for input if timeouts are triggered), whereas Web services typically involve instantaneous visual display.

Unlike many domain-specific languages, the role of PML as a convenient programming language is secondary to its role as a network-service interface. In other words, the primary function of PML is to allow programmers to control a shared VRU, not necessarily to be the single language in which IVR applications are most conveniently specified. We assume that higher-level interfaces can be developed which generate both PML and the associated CGI scripts that together represent a complete application.

## 4.1 Language Synopsis

PML has at its core certain language constructs that support the functionality offered by our VRU and little else. This minimalist approach is possible precisely because the Web (and PhoneWeb) architectures relegate transactions and arbitrary computation to the HTTP daemon, where the interfaces (commonly CGI) are used to invoke programs written in general-purpose languages. Thus there is no need for PML itself to be Turing-complete, nor to have a wide range of primitives.

There are four important categories of PML construct:

- *Rendering constructs* control speech synthesis and the playing of audio files.
- *Control constructs* allow users to affect the logic of a PML program with switch-like primitive for constructing menu trees and gotos corresponding to the hyperlinks of HTML.
- *Input constructs* collect voice recordings, DTMF input, and menu selections. Input is grouped using the same form construct as is present in HTML, and results in name-value pairs that are communicated to the application server.
- *Call-control constructs* perform telephone operations such as transferring or hanging up on a call.

As with HTML, the concrete syntax for PML is based on SGML.

Although PML and HTML are syntactically similar, they are semantically distinct. The PML interpreter linearizes its input programs, since they cannot be displayed statically to a caller using an ordinary old-fashioned telephone. As an analogy, consider the difference between displaying a song's lyrics visually and actually singing the lyrics. The two can be related if an animation, such as a bouncing ball in a karaoke system, follows the progress of the performance. The contrast between the interpretation of ordinary Web pages and telephone-oriented PML pages is similar. In the dynamic rendering of some audio content, there must be something analogous to a the bouncing ball: a program counter.

The idea of sequencing leads naturally to the need for control constructs. Extending the analogy: musical notations contains declarative control constructs (lyrics labeled as a refrain have implications for the progress of the karaoke animation) and imperative constructs (such as explicit directives to repeat a particular passage). Similarly, IVR applications motivate some declarative constructs (such as those which support hierarchichal telephone trees) and imperative constructs (such as hyperlinks, which have a natural interpretation as GOTO statements).

```
<body>
<dl>
<dt>To leave a message</dt>
<dd>
    <form action="/cgi-bin/message.pl" method="POST">
    Please leave a message at the sound of the tone.
    <input name=rec itype=recording maxlength=120s>
    <input type=submit>
    </form>
</dd>
<dt>To send a page message</dt>
<dd>
    <form action="/cgi-bin/pagerbot.pl" method="POST">
    <input type=hidden name="notify" value="650-555-1212">
    Please enter your numeric message followed
    by a pound sign.
    <input type=text name="pager-info" size=10>
    <input type=submit>
    </form>
</dd>
</body>
```

**Fig. 2.** A sample PML program that collects either a voice recording or a page message. PML's concrete syntax resembles that of HTML. This example is part of IVR application that serves as an answering system.

PML's datatypes include only strings, enumerations, and digitized sound files. There are no data abstraction facilities in the language. Variables are not declared directly, but rather arise as the byproduct of form input fields. Variables are set by the activity of the telephone user, who uses the telephone keypad to enter a sequence of digits, or the handset to offer a voice recording. The only operations on variables are assignment (which takes place implicitly as the result of caller activity) or to test their value as part of a conditional branch operation, or to reset them (useful if the user chooses to abandon an input activity). Given these rather drastic restrictions, the only significant use of PML data values is on the part of the HTTP daemon, which receives these input values in sets of name-value pairs according to HTTP's POST method in accordance with established HTML conventions (HTML, CGI, and the HTTP protocol are detailed extensively in IETF standards-track documents).

As a matter of programming convenience, the re-use of HTML's concrete syntax has worked well in practice (it has simplified learning and allowed programmers to re-use common Web infrastructure, such as ordinary browsers, which can serve as a debugging tool for PML applications). In addition, PML's form-

```
program: head body

head:   HEAD title pragma*

body:
    ( rendering-construct
    | control-construct
    | input-construct
    | call-control-construct
    )*

label:
    LABEL symbol   /* can serves as target of GOTO */

rendering-construct:
    ( PCDATA   /* text to be synthesized */
    | AUDIO url   /* audio file to be played */
    )

control-construct:
    ( SWITCH (OPTION body)* /* is a user-selectable switch */
    | GOTO target /* performs internal or external jump */
    | SUBMIT /* sends name-value pairs to HTTP daemon */
    | HANGUP /* hangs up the call */
    | LABEL symbol
    | FORM target body /* groups input (cannot be nested) */
    )

input-construct:
    (
    | GETRECORDING symbol   /* records voice */
    | GETDIGITS symbol /* gets a digit string */
    | SELECT symbol option*   /* multi-way choice */
    )

option:
    symbol PCDATA

call-control-construct:
    ( HANGUP /* terminates the current call */
    | TRANSFER telnum /* transfers current call */
    )

url:
    ( href /* unqualified URL */
    | href symbol /* label-qualified URL */
    | symbol /* label in the current document */
    )
```

**Fig. 3.** Abstract syntax for a core subset of PML.

based user-input paradigm is appropriate in a telephone context. However, the primary benefits derive from the properties of PML as a service interface.

## 4.2 Example

A simple example can serve to illustrate the use of PML. The following figures show a series of pages that would be retrieved by the PML interpreter in the implementation of a simple binary-search guessing game. The game rejects unregistered users, and the winner is transfered to a live operator.

The PML session begins when a phone call is placed to a number provisioned as a phone-web telephone number. That call is then diverted to a VRU running a PML interpreter, and the PML interpreter retrieves and interprets a page from the URL previously associated with that telephone number.

For this example, the body of the first page retrieved is shown in Figure 4.

```
<BODY>
<FORM ACTION="/cgi-bin/guess">
Please enter your user ID.
<INPUT NAME=userid INTERACTION=basic>
Please enter your password.
<INPUT TYPE=PASSWORD NAME=password>
I have picked a number between 1 and 100.
Try to guess the number!
<INPUT NAME=guess INTERACTION=basic>
<INPUT TYPE=SUBMIT>
</FORM>
</BODY>
```

**Fig. 4.** The first form in the call-in game.

The page shown in Figure 4 collects three values from a caller and submits them to the Web server. Text sentences appearing in this page are synthesized by a text-to-speech engine for the caller, and input is performed using a DTMF keypad.

Note that this first page requests the caller's ID and password; the analysis of the user's input must be done at the Web site associated with this example, not within the VRU. It is this separation of concerns that allows PML to be useful even though it is not Turing-complete.

A sequence of pages such as that shown in Figure 5 must be presented until the user guesses the hidden number.

Finally, the user that guesses correctly is transferred to the prize department according to the directions in Figure 6. After the live conversation terminates, the caller is thanked and the service concludes.

```
<BODY>
<FORM ACTION="/cgi-bin/guess">
Your guess was too high!  Try again.
<INPUT NAME=guess INTERACTION=basic>
<INPUT TYPE=SUBMIT>
</FORM>
</BODY>
```

**Fig. 5.** A form that is presented if the first guess was too high.

```
<BODY>
You guessed right!  We will now transfer
you to an operator.
<TRANSFER TELNO="2125551212" RETURN>
Thank you for calling the gaming hotline.
</BODY>
```

**Fig. 6.** A final page that transfers the user to a live operator.

## 4.3   PML Interface Properties

Network services must operate under the best possible performance, reliability, and security constraints. Services which perform arbitrarily complex tasks on behalf of clients pose special problems for all three goals.

First, a programmable resource presents a particular tension in a distributed setting because of latency and minimal user of bandwidth: a low-level protocol will suffer latency delays with each method invocation; the more complex the task, the more messages need to be passed, and the greater the overall latency and bandwidth utilization. Second, a programmable resource presents availability problems if its protocol is not stateless – there is potential for the allocation of embedded resources that might not be freed as quickly as possible, or at all. Third, a programmable service poses a security question, since it is crucial to ensure that clients cannot issue instructions that would compromise the integrity of the platform or another client's use of that platform. A restricted linguistic interface allows us to achieve all these goals, either at the language level or at the interpreter level.

**Network Efficiency** A language interface which allows users to aggregate more primitive requests will improve network performance because it will reduce the number of messaging round-trips between client and server: this is a fundamental and important characteristic of mobile code.

PML programs, like HTML pages, are transmitted from an HTTP daemon to an interpreter (which controls a VRU), which then executes them. In the case of PML, a large amount of activity — prompting the user, obtaining input, allowing the user to confirm or reenter data, handling timeouts — can take place entirely within the VRU, without any interaction between the HTTP daemon and the VRU. The alternative is less attractive: messaging interfaces (or a remote-procedure-call interface at a lower level) would necessarily involve a greater number of round-trip interactions, and that would be unacceptable in IVR applications where human perception of delay is acute.

Mobile-code solutions can also reduce the number of data transmitted over a network. There is a common savings in PhoneWeb applications due to reductions in the number of sound recordings communicated between the client and server. For instance, a given PML page can control a whole set of user interactions, including capturing, playback, cancelling, re-capturing, and confirming voice clips. A finite protocol language could solve this problem by offering primitives at the same level of abstraction, but this would reduce flexibility unless part of the protocol itself incorporated some sort of infinite language. Alternately, the voice clip could the stored on the server and messages could manipulate it as needed until retrieval time, but this again introduces the possibility that resources will be allocated and not freed depending on user error. The language solution is efficient, flexible, and foolproof.

**Static Analysis** Using a language (particularly a restricted language) as a service interface can also increase efficiency when static resource analysis and subsequent optimization is possible. In the PhoneWeb, since PML programs refer to audio files much as regular Web pages refer to graphic images, it is worthwhile to scan each program before running it to determine which audio files will be needed; the system then pre-fetches the audio resources. An improved scheme guesses the most likely path through a PML program, and orders the fetch requests appropriately. An even more sophisticated implementation would dynamically adjust the fetch order with respect to the current program counter value, to place highest emphasis on the voice file most likely to be needed next. Such analyses are not, in general, possible when a Turing-complete language is used. The result of analysis, in this example, is performance.

Because PML is based on a finite-state machine model, we can also imagine verifying user-specific safety properties. For instance, we might wish to verify that, regardless of context, PML users who press "*4" ("*H") will be transferred to a help facility. Work[3, 4] in the context of Esterel[5] suggests approaches that could be transferred to other languages based on finite-state machines, including to PML.

**Dynamic Guards** The language interface also supports dynamic guards that would be infeasible if none of an application's logic were available to the server. For instance, it is important to guard against error conditions that span multiple pages — in particular busy loops, which consume resources to no effect. A static analysis could not reveal such a problem, since pages are generated dynamically.

In order to detect infinite loops that cycle between two or more pages, we track hyperlink jumps, conservatively generating an error message if precisely the same URL is requested more than once without an intervening user event, such as a keypress. Thus, no application can loop indefinitely without direct user participation. A language interface offers the service more global knowledge about an application, enabling it to support such protections.

**Correctness by Construction** Any high-level programming language offers abstractions that represent a large quantity of lower-level computation. For instance, the procedural abstraction offered by C is implemented by compilers that generate code for passing parameters and for transferring control to and from the procedure, thereby eliminating the possibility of programmer error in that task (as well as enhancing programmer productivity). In many distributed applications, the lowest level of activity involves tremendously complex message-passing protocols. Our VRU, itself a distributed system, is no exception: its PML is a synchronous layer over a host of asynchronous events involving keypresses, call arrivals, hangups, timer events, network events, and concurrent Web activity.

The use of a linguistic interface, rather than the exposure of lower-level methods, inherently guarantees that the internal resources will be utilized properly in ways that even competent programmers have trouble ensuring: speech-synthesis resources are always deallocated as soon as they are no longer needed, the interpreter unfailingly reacts immediately when an audio event is interrupted, and so on. This kind of inherent guarantee is essential to a service offering, particularly in the treatment of shared resources, lest resource availability be reduced.

**Safety by Restriction** We can design a domain-specific language such that it cannot express a dangerous activity. For instance, neither does PML allow the `file://` protocol to be used in a URL, nor can PML programs invoke system calls directly, nor can they obtain information on activity performed by another caller. Such restrictions eliminate the need for some dynamic and static analyses.

**Sandboxing** If an interface language is implemented as an interpreter, then general constraints can be enforced on that interpreter for additional safety. For instance, we can restrict the entire interpreter to a subset of the file system, we can intercept all system calls issued by the interpreter and disallow certain calls (such as those creating external network connections). Sandboxing guards against both malicious users and faulty interpreter implementation.

**Usage Tracking** When we offer a network service — particularly one for which we charge — it is important to provide feedback to customers on how the resource is being used (both in terms of quantity, since that relates to cost, and activity, since that relates to how users are treating the system). The PML interface allows resource usage to be reported in terms of abstractions that are important to the customer. In the IVR environment, programmers of the VRU ask questions such as, "What choices do people make at this particular prompt?" "Which paths of a service are never used?" "Are users making errors or timing out at common points?" Because PML is a restricted language that offers these abstractions at the appropriate level, we can collect meaningful usage logs that support needed reports and visualizations.[6, 7, 8]

# 5  Related Work

There is an increasing trend toward the use of languages as service interfaces, and as a crucial element of distributed systems; in addition, there is an increasing quantity of research on techniques that support performance, availability, and security in the distributed application setting.

- *PostScript.* PostScript[9] provides a classic example of how we can obtain efficiency by using a linguistic interface to network resources: Programs to describe complex images are often smaller than bitmaps of the same image. However, like those related to the ordinary Web browser, the safety issues in protecting PostScript printers are perhaps less crucial than are those in protecting a VRU. Our VRU executes many PML programs simultaneously to maximize resource utilization, whereas printers execute one job at a time; our VRU is a hired resource rather than one owned by the application programmer; VRUs must respond in real time once a call has been initiated, whereas printers can reasonably operate in batch mode. Nonetheless each example employs language similarly.
- *Taint-PERL.* Implementations of languages such as PML can use knowledge of the program and its execution to enforce interesting constraints. Taint-PERL[10] offers a particularly interesting example of such enforcement, serving not only as an example of the power of domain-specific analysis, but also as an alternative to sandboxing, which offers a binary sort of protection — for instance, a sandbox must typically intercept and reject all system calls, given that it has no further information on which to discriminate between acceptable system calls and unacceptable system calls.

  The primary motivation of Taint-PERL appears to have been to employ the Unix "setuid" concept safely. The setuid facility allows a program to be run with permissions other than that of the user (for instance, to obtain access to a portion of the file system that would otherwise be forbidden to that user). Setuid programs are a frequent target of attack by hackers, who find ways of tricking the setuid program into performing an unanticipated action using another's permissions. In order to prevent such trickery, Taint-PERL refuses to permit any system call in which the arguments to that call were derived in any way from the environment or user input. In this way, unanticipated uses of the system calls are prevented but those used by the programmer are permitted. Interpreters of services such as PML would benefit from this kind of protection granularity, if it existed in any systems programming languages such as C or ML. The trusted programmer, who is implementing the service, has access to arbitrary system resources, yet is guaranteed that the service's potentially careless or malicious clients have no opportunities to subvert these system calls for their own purposes.

– *Proof-carrying-code.* One idea behind proof-carrying code is to specify a linguistic interface and to execute only that code that can be proven to meet predefined safety properties. Often, the proof is difficult or expensive to generate, but once the proof exists, it may be easy to verify that the proof applies to the imported code. This idea appears to be widely applicable to situations in which mobile code is used, and helps to avoid the need for run-time overhead in the same way that typechecking leads to generated code without any further dynamic-typechecking overhead. Restricted linguistic interfaces, such as those comprising PML, could conceivably support proofs that might be more difficult to construct in the setting of a general-purpose language. In any case, proof-carrying PML code could be used to enforce stylistic conventions and safety properties without incurring proof overhead entirely at runtime.

– *Active-networks research.* The premise behind active-networks research is that new protocols should be considerably easier to deploy than is currently the case in today's standards-based internet environment. One way to permit the rapid evolution of networks is a new network architecture in which the network routers are themselves programmable. Here too domain-specific languages are valuable interfaces to shared network resources: in the active networks example, restricted languages such as PLAN serve as the router interface. Variants of PLAN have been used to express application protocols that can be proven not to violate nontrivial safety and security properties, thus supporting the activity of untrusted application programmers on a shared resource.[11]

## 6    Future Challenges

In considering how to offer secure services in a public network, the question of flexibility and efficiency must be balanced against safety and reliability. Domain-specific languages as the interface to a service, together with a framework for transmitting that code from to the server from the client, form a nicely balanced solution.

The restrictions on PML are helpful, but they create a tension because programmers will invariably chafe against such restrictions; IVR application programmers always drive toward increasing control of the VRU. One challenge is to determine whether and under what circumstances restrictions on the interface languages can be loosened without sacrificing service integrity. In the PML case, offering flexibility might involve constructing arbitrary reactive programs to handle telephone events; more flexible (but still not Turing-complete) languages such as Esterel might be a way to obtain the benefits of PML without the loss of its particular advantages.

Regardless of what the base interface language is, the challenge is to balance flexibility against the necessary analyses: both dynamic and static, as well as universally applied and application specific. Network-service-interface languages offer new opportunities for us to apply formal methods in a setting other than software engineering.

## 7 Conclusion

The idea of a VRU as a shared public resource is justified because VRUs require expensive hardware and complex software that users have a strong incentive to share. A language interface confers the efficiency of mobile code along with flexibility; by restricting the language, we obtain enhanced security and availability. In conjunction with its interpreter, a domain-specific language offers both analysis and sandboxing opportunities. The domain-specific approach confers advantages whenever a shared centralized resource needs to be controlled by untrusted programmers.

## 8 Acknowledgments

The team that designed implemented the PhoneWeb as described in this experience report included Gerald Karam, Andrew Forrest, and Jim Pelletier. Nils Klarlund shaped an aspect of the language (not described here) which serves to customize input interactions.

The PhoneWeb derives indirectly from work with David Ladd on another Internet language, MAWL, for programming Web services. MAWL showed how to enforce a separation of concerns between the service logic and user interface component of Web applications; it therefore offered good support for browsers controlling different devices such as the telephone set — an idea that Ken Rehor helped articulate and prototype when we first conceived of the PhoneWeb service concept.

Lyn Dupre, Anne Rogers, and Kathleen Fisher offered much-appreciated comments on the draft of this report.

David Unger and Eric Sumner, Jr. have given funding and support to this project.

## References

1. D. Fischell, S. Kanwa., and D. Furman, "Interactive voice technology applications," *AT&T Technical Journal*, vol. 69, Sept./Oct. 1990. A good overview of IVR issues.
2. T. Berners-Lee and D. Connolly, "Hypertext markup language (html)," *Working Draft of the Internet Engineering Task Force*, 1993.
3. L. Jagadeesan, C. Puchol, and J. Von Olnhausen, "Safety property verification of ESTEREL programs and applications to telecommunications software," in *Proceedings of the 7th International Conference on Computer Aided Verification, Volume 939 of the Lecture Notes in Computer Science*, pp. 127–140, July 1995.

4. L. Jagadeesan, A. Porter, C. Puchol, J. C. Ramming, and L. G. Votta, "Specification-based testing of reactive software: Tools and experiments," in *The Nineteenth International Conference on Software Engineering*, pp. 525–535, May 1997.

5. G. Berry and G. Gonthier, "The ESTEREL synchronous programming language: design, se mantics, implementation," *Science of Computer Programming*, vol. 19, pp. 87–152, 1992.

6. Personal communication. Amy Ruth Ward, Stanford University and AT&T Labs.

7. D. Atkins, T. Ball, T. Baran, A. Benedikt, C. Cox, D. Ladd, P. Mataga, C. Puchol, J. Ramming, , K. Rehor, and C. Tuckey, "Integrated web and telephone service creation.," *The Bell Labs Technical Journal*, vol. 2, pp. 19–35, Winter 1997.

8. D. Atkins, T. Ball, A. Benedikt, G. Bruns, C. Cox, P. Mataga, , and K. Rehor, "Experience with a domain specific language for form-based services," in *Usenix Conference on Domain-Specific Languages*, 1997.

9. *PostScript Language Reference Manual.* Addison-Wesley, 1985.

10. L. Wall and R. L. Schwartz, *Programming PERL.* O'Reilly & Associates, 1990.

11. S. Thibault, C. Consel, and G. Muller, "Safe and efficient network programming," tech. rep., IRISA / INRIA - Universite de Rennes 1, February 1998. http://www.irisa.fr/compose.

# Derivatives: A Construct for Internet Programming

Dominic Duggan

Department of Computer Science,
Stevens Institute of Technology,
Castle Point on the Hudson,
Hoboken, New Jersey 07030.
dduggan@cs.stevens-tech.edu

**Abstract.** *Derivatives* are introduced to provide optimistic computation as a programming language construct. The motivation is in avoiding communication latency in wide-area distributed computing environments. A derivative represents a handle on a value that has not yet been received, where moreover the potential receiver may make assumptions about the value in order to proceed. Derivatives can therefore be seen as a generalization of futures and promises, which have also been introduced in order to deal with latency. A programming language, type system and operational semantics are provided supporting optimistic execution.

## 1 Introduction

Distributed programming over local area networks is now a mature and widely used technology. The situation for programming wide area networks is less successful. Despite the fact that the Internet has been in existence in one form or another for many years, electronic mail and electronic news are still the only major applications that have been developed in this environment. The advent of the World Wide Web, providing the promise of a vast global information system interconnecting individuals and organizations, has excited interest in exploiting the potential of the Internet. Nevertheless at the time of writing, the problems that have prevented the widespread development of Internet applications remain.

Programming over networks introduces problems of security, high latency, low bandwidth and partial failures. The latter includes network partitioning, where the desire may be for parts of an application to continue processing independently during the network failure. As a practical example, consider a network of automatic teller machines connected to a bank database. If a customer requests a withdrawal at a machine while the ATM is disconnected from the database, the withdrawal will be permitted provided the amount is within some reasonable limit. This limit is an overdraft withdrawal amount that the customer is permitted, to improve availability of the service. If upon reconnection it is found that the customer is overdrawn, then paper mechanisms are invoked to correct the situation.

*Derivatives* are introduced as a programming construct to provide this availability as a programming language construct for Internet programming. The essential idea of derivatives is "optimistic computation:" upon sending a request, the program makes an assumption about the result of that request, and proceeds accordingly. At some point the program needs to synchronize with the actual result of the request. If the request has completed successfully and with the expected result, then the program can "commit" to the computation performed since making the assumption about the result. If the request has not yet completed, then the program must wait for its completion. Finally if the request has completed, but not with the expected result, then the computation must be rolled back to the point at which the erroneous assumption was made about the result.

Derivatives can be viewed as a generalization of *futures* and *promises* [6, 11]. All are based on a lazy form of synchronization, motivated by high latency in message-passing communication, and lie somewhere between synchronous and asynchronous communication. With futures and promises, the requesting process blocks when it tries to use the result before the communication has completed. Derivatives generalize this by allowing the requesting process to optimistically make an assumption about the result. If the assumption is erroneous, then the process must be rolled back. This rolling back is where the most interesting problems arise, since the process may be in communication with other processes and these communications will need to be "undone" as part of the rolling back.

In the next section we give a language and type system for constructs supporting optimistic computation. In Sect. 3 we give a stock operational semantics, that does not incorporate optimistic computation. This is the yardstick for reasoning about the correctness of any semantics for optimistic computation. In Sect. 4 we give an alternative semantics that does incorporate optimistic computation. Finally in Sect. 5 we review related work and provide conclusions.

## 2 A Mini-Language With Derivatives

The following describes the syntax of our mini-language:

$$
\begin{aligned}
e ::=\ & x \mid (\lambda x : \tau.e) \mid (e_1\, e_2) \mid \{l_1 = e_1, \ldots, l_n = e_n\} \mid e.l \mid \\
& [l = e] \mid \text{case } e \text{ of } l \Rightarrow e' \mid \_ \Rightarrow e'' \mid \text{fork}(e) \mid \text{chan}_\tau() \mid \\
& \text{send}(e, e') \mid \text{receive}(e, e') \mid \text{sendout}(e, e') \\
\tau ::=\ & \tau_1 \rightarrow \tau_2 \mid \{l_1 : \tau_1, \ldots, l_n : \tau_n\} \mid [l_1 : \tau_1, \ldots, l_n : \tau_n] \mid \text{Chan}(\tau)
\end{aligned}
$$

The language has $\lambda$-abstractions (procedures), as well as records $\{l_1 = e_1, \ldots, l_n = e_n\}$ and variants (tagged unions) $[l = e]$. Records are accessed using field selection $e.l$, while variants are accessed using a case construct that provides a default if the value does not have the expected tag. The type rules are provided in Fig. 1.

The process constructs are provided in Fig. 2. They include a fork construct for creating new processes, and a chan construct for allocating new channels. The latter are typed communication channels. Values are communicated using a message send operation, whose first argument is a channel. Values are received on a channel using the receive operation. We make the simplifying assumption that any process with access to a channel can execute the receive operation on that channel; we do not provide an operation for binding a process to a channel.

The key constructs for derivatives are the receive operation and the case construct. The receive operation is non-blocking. It returns a *derivative*, a "handle" on

$$A \vdash x : A(x) \qquad\qquad\text{(HYP)}$$

$$\frac{A, x : \tau_1 \vdash e : \tau_2}{A \vdash (\lambda x : \tau_1.e) : \tau_1 \to \tau_2} \qquad\qquad\text{(ABS)}$$

$$\frac{A \vdash e_1 : \tau_2 \to \tau_1 \quad A \vdash e_2 : \tau_2}{A \vdash (e_1\, e_2) : \tau_1} \qquad\qquad\text{(APP)}$$

$$\frac{A \vdash e_i : \tau_i \text{ for } i = 1, \ldots, n}{A \vdash \{l_1 = e_1, \ldots, l_n = e_n\} : \{l_1 : \tau_1, \ldots, l_n : \tau_n\}} \qquad\qquad\text{(REC)}$$

$$\frac{A \vdash e : \{l_1 : \tau_1, \ldots, l_n : \tau_n\}}{A \vdash e.l_1 : \tau_1} \qquad\qquad\text{(SEL)}$$

$$\frac{A \vdash e_1 : \tau_1}{A \vdash [l_1 = e_1] : [l_1 : \tau_1, \ldots, l_n : \tau_n]} \qquad\qquad\text{(VAR)}$$

$$\frac{A \vdash e : [l_1 : \tau_1, \ldots, l_n : \tau_n]}{A \vdash e' : \tau_1 \to \tau \quad A \vdash e'' : \tau}{A \vdash (\text{case } e \text{ of } l_1 \Rightarrow e' \mid \_ \Rightarrow e'') : \tau} \qquad\qquad\text{(CASE)}$$

**Fig. 1.** Data Structure Language

$$\frac{A \vdash e : \text{unit} \to \text{unit}}{A \vdash \text{fork}(e) : \text{unit}} \qquad\qquad\text{(FORK)}$$

$$A \vdash \text{chan}_\tau() : \text{Chan}(\tau) \qquad\qquad\text{(CHAN)}$$

$$\frac{A \vdash e : \text{Chan}(\tau) \quad A \vdash e' : \tau}{A \vdash \text{send}(e, e') : \text{unit}} \qquad\qquad\text{(SEND)}$$

$$\frac{A \vdash e : \text{Chan}(\tau) \quad A \vdash e' : \tau \to \tau'}{A \vdash \text{receive}(e, e') : \tau'} \qquad\qquad\text{(RECV)}$$

$$\frac{A \vdash e : \text{Chan}(\tau) \quad A \vdash e' : \tau}{A \vdash \text{sendout}(e, e') : \text{unit}} \qquad\qquad\text{(SENDOUT)}$$

**Fig. 2.** Process Language

the actual value that will eventually be transmitted. The receiver is allowed to use this value in a way that makes assumptions about its eventual form. The key point where this is done is with the case construct for variants, where the receiver program may make an assumption about the tag associated with the variant.

If the communicated value contradicts this assumption, then the program rolls back its state to some point and resumes execution using the actual transmitted value. Our situation here is complicated by our commitment to supporting rollback with a stock runtime (in particular, not requiring any magic with the run-time stack, as would be required by continuations). The `case` construct introduces a breakpoint in program execution; should any assumption about the variant value be detected to be inconsistent with its actual value or other assumptions, then program execution may be rolled back to this breakpoint. The `receive` operation takes a continuation function as its second argument; the stack space allocated for this continuation is not discarded until the received value is committed by the sending process (so `receive` also introduces a breakpoint).

Both message sending and receiving are non-blocking in our semantics. The points of synchronization are in the continuation of a `receive` operation, and the branch of a `case` construct. When execution of such a continuation or `case` is finished, changes made by the execution must be committed. "Commitment" must wait until all receive events (which trap to that breakpoint) have rendezvoused with corresponding send events. Furthermore commitment must wait until the pending commits that the sending processes depend upon for finalization, dominate the pending commits (to the left) in the process trace for the process that executed the `receive` or `case`. "Dominates" means that if any of the pending commits in the sending processes are rolled back, then this will (eventually) cause some pending commit in the process executing the `receive` or `case` to be rolled back. Therefore there is nothing to be lost in discarding the program context saved during the initial execution of the `receive` or `case`. A simple example is the case where a receiver of a derivative waits for a non-speculative sender to communicate the actual value. Matters are complicated by the fact that both receivers and senders may depend on some optimistic computation.

In some situations it may be necessary to send a message that cannot be rolled back (for example, dispensing cash from an automatic teller machine). For this purpose we provide the `sendout` construct, that sends a message from a speculative execution. This construct checks that all speculative assumptions made to this point can be committed; however it cannot prevent the program from subsequently refuting one of these speculative assumptions. It is intended that the construct be used as the last instruction in a speculative execution. Caveat emptor.

## 3   Stock Semantics

$$(\lambda x : \tau.e_1)e_2 \longrightarrow \{e_2/x\}e_1$$
$$\{l_1 = e_1, \dots, l_n = e_n\}.l_i \longrightarrow e_i$$
$$\textbf{case}\,[l = e]\,\text{of}\,l \Rightarrow e' \mid \_ \Rightarrow e'' \longrightarrow e'(e)$$
$$\textbf{case}\,[l = e]\,\text{of}\,l' \Rightarrow e' \mid \_ \Rightarrow e'' \longrightarrow e''\,\text{if}\,l \neq l'$$
$$\frac{e \longrightarrow e'}{(\mathcal{V},\,\mathcal{E}[p \mapsto E[e]],\,S,\,T) \longrightarrow (\mathcal{V},\,\mathcal{E}[p \mapsto E[e']],\,S,\,T)}$$

**Fig. 3.** Expression Reduction Semantics

$$
\begin{array}{l}
(\mathcal{V}, (\mathcal{E}[p \mapsto E[\texttt{fork}(v)]]), \mathcal{S}, \mathcal{T}) \longrightarrow \\
\qquad (\mathcal{V} \cup \{p'\}, (\mathcal{E}[p \mapsto E[\{\}]][p' \mapsto v()]), \mathcal{S}, \mathcal{T} \oplus (p, \texttt{fork}(p'))) \text{ for some } p' \notin \mathcal{V} \\
(\mathcal{V}, (\mathcal{E}[p \mapsto E[\texttt{chan}_\tau()]]), \mathcal{S}, \mathcal{T}) \longrightarrow \\
\qquad (\mathcal{V} \cup \{c\}, (\mathcal{E}[p \mapsto E[c]]), \mathcal{S}, \mathcal{T} \oplus (p, \texttt{chan}_\tau(c))) \text{ for some } c \notin \mathcal{V} \\
(\mathcal{V}, (\mathcal{E}[p \mapsto E[\texttt{send}(c,v)]]), \mathcal{S}, \mathcal{T}) \longrightarrow \\
\qquad (\mathcal{V}, (\mathcal{E}[p \mapsto E[\{\}]]), (\mathcal{S}, \texttt{send}(c,v)), \mathcal{T} \oplus (p, \texttt{send}(c,v))) \\
(\mathcal{V}, (\mathcal{E}[p \mapsto E[\texttt{sendout}(c,v)]]), \mathcal{S}, \mathcal{T}) \longrightarrow \\
\qquad (\mathcal{V}, (\mathcal{E}[p \mapsto E[\{\}]]), (\mathcal{S}, \texttt{send}(c,v)), \mathcal{T} \oplus (p, \texttt{sendout}(c,v))) \\
(\mathcal{V}, (\mathcal{E}[p \mapsto E[\texttt{receive}(c,v)]]), (\mathcal{S}, \texttt{send}(c,v')), \mathcal{T}) \longrightarrow \\
\qquad (\mathcal{V}, (\mathcal{E}[p \mapsto E[v(v')]]), \mathcal{S}, \mathcal{T} \oplus (p, v' = \texttt{receive}(c))) \\
(\mathcal{V}, (\mathcal{E}[p \mapsto E[\texttt{commit}(X,e,v)]]), \mathcal{S}, \mathcal{T}) \longrightarrow \\
\qquad (\mathcal{V}, (\mathcal{E}[p \mapsto E[v]]), \mathcal{S}, \mathcal{T} \oplus (p, \texttt{commit}(X)))
\end{array}
$$

**Fig. 4.** Stock Process Semantics

In this section we give the stock semantics for derivatives. This semantics does not assume optimistic computation, and is a yardstick for reasoning about the correctness of any semantics for optimistic computation.

We give a two-level reduction semantics, for expressions and for processes [4, 14]. Configurations of this semantics require some extensions to the syntax of expressions:

$$e ::= \ldots \mid c \mid \texttt{commit}(X, e, e')$$

We have the following sets of variables:

$$
\begin{aligned}
x, y, z, X, Y, Z \in \mathit{TermVar} &= \text{Program variables} \\
c \in \mathit{ChanVar} &= \text{Channel identifiers} \\
p \in \mathit{ProcVar} &= \text{Process identifiers}
\end{aligned}
$$

A type environment maps program variables $x$ to types $\tau$, and maps channel identifiers $c$ to channel types $\texttt{Chan}(\tau)$. We have the type rules:

$$A \vdash c : A(c) \qquad \text{(ChVar)}$$

$$\frac{A \vdash e : \tau \quad A \vdash e' : \tau}{A \vdash \texttt{commit}(X, e, e') : \tau} \qquad \text{(Commit)}$$

*Values* are expressions that do not contain any redexes outside the scope of $\lambda$-abstraction or $\Lambda$-abstraction:

$$v ::= \lambda x : \tau . e \mid \{l_1 = v_1, \ldots, l_n = v_n\} \mid [l = v] \mid c$$

Note that a value may contain free channel identifiers. An *evaluation context* is used to specify the next redex to reduce (if any) in an expression:

$$E ::= [\,] \mid (E\ e) \mid (v\ E) \mid \{l_1 = v_1, \ldots, l_i = E, \ldots, l_n = e_n\} \mid E.l \mid$$
$$[l = E] \mid \text{case } E \text{ of } l \Rightarrow e' \mid\, _- \Rightarrow e'' \mid \text{case } v \text{ of } l \Rightarrow E \mid\, _- \Rightarrow e \mid$$
$$\text{case } v \text{ of } l \Rightarrow v' \mid\, _- \Rightarrow E \mid \text{fork}(E) \mid \text{send}(E, e) \mid \text{send}(v, E) \mid$$
$$\text{receive}(E, e) \mid \text{receive}(v, E) \mid \text{commit}(X, e, E) \mid$$
$$\text{sendout}(E, e) \mid \text{sendout}(e, E)$$

The `commit` construct essentially saves a snapshot of the computation in the `receive` and `case` constructs. Evaluation is allowed inside the second argument expression, while the first argument expression represents the original context (from the `receive` or `case`) that is saved for use in rollback. Since there is no rollback in the stock semantics, this operation always commits.

The reduction semantics for expressions are provided in Fig. 3, while the reduction semantics for processes are provided in Fig. 4. The latter semantics are described using configurations of the form

$$(\mathcal{V},\ \mathcal{E},\ \mathcal{S},\ \mathcal{T})$$

where:

1. $\mathcal{V} \subseteq \text{TermVar} \cup \text{ChanVar} \cup \text{ProcVar}$ is a (finite) set of identifiers.
2. $\mathcal{E}$ is a (finite) mapping from process identifiers $p$ to expressions $e$. These are the processes in the current computation, each process identified by a pid.
3. $\mathcal{S}$ is a multiset of *atoms*, defined by:

$$S ::= \{\} \mid \text{send}(c, v) \mid S_1, S_2$$

This multiset is used to describe asynchronous message-passing with a blocking `receive` but a non-blocking `send`. The `send` operation places a `send` atom in $\mathcal{S}$, and this is then removed by the `receive` operation that specifies a matching channel identifier. We refer to $\mathcal{S}$ as the *store* of the configuration.

4. $\mathcal{T}$ is a mapping from process identifiers to *traces*.

Configurations satisfy the invariant that $\text{dom}(\mathcal{E}) = \text{dom}(\mathcal{T}) = \mathcal{V} \cap \text{ProcVar}$. A trace gives the history of a process; it is a sequence of "history atoms." A trace is described by:

$$T ::= \varepsilon \mid T_1, T_2 \mid \text{fork}(p) \mid \text{chan}_\tau(c) \mid \text{send}(c, v) \mid \text{sendout}(c, v) \mid$$
$$(v = \text{receive}(c)) \mid \text{spec}(X) \mid \text{commit}(X)$$

$\mathcal{T} \oplus (p, T)$ denotes the extension of the trace for process $p$ (writing an entry to the log):

$$\mathcal{T} \oplus (p, T) = \mathcal{T}[p \mapsto (\mathcal{T}(p), T)]$$

$(\mathcal{V}, (\mathcal{E}[p \mapsto E[\texttt{fork}(v)]]), S, T) \longrightarrow$

$\quad (\mathcal{V} \cup \{p'\}, (\mathcal{E}[p \mapsto E[\{\}]][p' \mapsto v()]), S, T \oplus (p, \texttt{fork}(p')))$ for some $p' \notin \mathcal{V}$

$(\mathcal{V}, (\mathcal{E}[p \mapsto E[\texttt{chan}_\tau()]]), S, T) \longrightarrow$

$\quad (\mathcal{V} \cup \{c\}, (\mathcal{E}[p \mapsto E[c]]), S, T \oplus (p, \texttt{chan}_\tau(c)))$ for some $c \notin \mathcal{V}$

$(\mathcal{V}, (\mathcal{E}[p \mapsto E[\texttt{send}(c, v)]]), S, T) \longrightarrow$

$\quad (\mathcal{V} \cup \{X\}, (\mathcal{E}[p \mapsto E[\{\}]]), (S, \texttt{send}(c, X), X = v), T \oplus (p, \texttt{send}(c, X)))$

$\quad$ for some $X \notin \mathcal{V}$

$(\mathcal{V}, (\mathcal{E}[p \mapsto E[\texttt{sendout}(c, v)]]), S, T) \longrightarrow$

$\quad (\mathcal{V} \cup \{X\}, (\mathcal{E}[p \mapsto E[\{\}]]), (S, \texttt{send}(c, X), X = v), T \oplus (p, \texttt{sendout}(c, X)))$

$\quad$ provided $Y$ is commitable, for all $\texttt{spec}(Y)$ in $T(p)$,

$\quad$ for some $X \notin \mathcal{V}$

$(\mathcal{V}, (\mathcal{E}[p \mapsto E[\texttt{receive}(c, v)]]), S, T) \longrightarrow$

$\quad (\mathcal{V} \cup \{Y\}, (\mathcal{E}[p \mapsto E[\texttt{commit}(Y, \texttt{receive}(c, v), v(Y))]]), (S, Y = \texttt{receive}(c)),$

$\quad\quad T \oplus (p, (\texttt{spec}(Y), Y = \texttt{receive}(c))))$ for some $Y \notin \mathcal{V}$

$(\mathcal{V}, (\mathcal{E}[p \mapsto E[\texttt{commit}(X, e, v)]]), S, T) \longrightarrow$

$\quad (\mathcal{V}, (\mathcal{E}[p \mapsto E[v]]), S, T \oplus (p, \texttt{commit}(X)))$

$\quad$ provided $X$ is committable in $S, T$

**Fig. 5.** Derivative Process Semantics

$(\mathcal{V}, (\mathcal{E}[p \mapsto E[X.l]]), S, T) \longrightarrow$

$\quad (\mathcal{V} \cup \{Y\}, (\mathcal{E}[p \mapsto E[Y]]), (S, Y = X.l, X \rightarrow Y), T)$ for some $Y \notin \mathcal{V}$

$(\mathcal{V}, (\mathcal{E}[p \mapsto E[X(v)]]), S, T) \longrightarrow$

$\quad (\mathcal{V} \cup \{Y\}, (\mathcal{E}[p \mapsto E[Y]]), (S, Y = X(v), X \rightarrow Y), T)$ for some $Y \notin \mathcal{V}$

$(\mathcal{V}, (\mathcal{E}[p \mapsto E[\texttt{case } X \texttt{ of } l \Rightarrow e' \mid \_ \Rightarrow e'']]), S, T) \longrightarrow$

$\quad (\mathcal{V} \cup \{Y\}, (\mathcal{E}[p \mapsto E[\texttt{commit}(Y, (\texttt{case } X \texttt{ of } l \Rightarrow e' \mid \_ \Rightarrow e''), e'(Y))]]),$

$\quad (S, X = [l = Y], X \rightarrow Y), (T \oplus (p, \texttt{spec}(Y)))$ for some $Y \notin \mathcal{V}$

$(\mathcal{V}, \mathcal{E}[p \mapsto E[X]], (S, X = v), T) \longrightarrow (\mathcal{V}, \mathcal{E}[p \mapsto E[v]], (S, X = v), T)$

**Fig. 6.** Speculation Semantics

## 4 Derivative Operational Semantics

In this section we give the optimistic derivative semantics. Configurations are still 4-tuples $(\mathcal{V}, \mathcal{E}, S, T)$, but some of the components change. Values may now contain free program variables:

$$v ::= \ldots \mid X$$

$(\mathcal{V}, \mathcal{E}, (S, \texttt{send}(c,X), Y = \texttt{receive}(c)), T) \longrightarrow (\mathcal{V}, \mathcal{E}, (S, Y = X), T)$
 provided $X$ does not causally depend on $Y$

$(\mathcal{V}, \mathcal{E}, (S, X = \{l_1 = v_1, \ldots, l_n = v_n\}, Y = X.l_i), T) \longrightarrow$
  $(\mathcal{V}, \mathcal{E}, (S, X = \{l_1 = v_1, \ldots, l_n = v_n\}, Y = v_i), T)$

$(\mathcal{V}, \mathcal{E}, (S, X = (\lambda x : \tau.e), Y = X(v)), T) \longrightarrow$
  $(\mathcal{V} \cup \{c, p\}, (\mathcal{E}[p \mapsto \texttt{send}(c, (\lambda x : \tau.e)v)]), (S, X = (\lambda x : \tau.e), Y = \texttt{receive}(c)), T)$
  for some $c, p \notin \mathcal{V}$

$(\mathcal{V}, \mathcal{E}, (S, X = [l = v], X = [l = Y]), T) \longrightarrow (\mathcal{V}, \mathcal{E}, (S, X = [l = v], Y = v), T)$

$(\mathcal{V}, \mathcal{E}, (S, X = Y, Y = v), T) \longrightarrow (\mathcal{V}, \mathcal{E}, (S, X = Y, Y = v, X = v), T)$

$(\mathcal{V}, \mathcal{E}, (S, X \to Y, Y \to Z), T) \longrightarrow (\mathcal{V}, \mathcal{E}, (S, X \to Y, Y \to Z, X \to Z), T)$

$(\mathcal{V}, \mathcal{E}, (S, (X = [l = v]), (X = [l' = v']), Y \to X), T[p \mapsto (T, \texttt{spec}(Y), T')]) \longrightarrow$
  $(\mathcal{V}, \mathcal{E}, (S, \neg\texttt{spec}(Y)), T[p \mapsto (T, \texttt{spec}(Y), T')]), \quad l \neq l'$

**Fig. 7.** Store Semantics

$(\mathcal{V}, \mathcal{E}, (S, \neg\texttt{send}(c,X), \texttt{send}(c,X)), T) \xrightarrow{rb} (\mathcal{V}, \mathcal{E}, S, T)$

$$\frac{T(p) = (T, Y = \texttt{receive}(c), T')}{(\mathcal{V}, \mathcal{E}, (S, (Y = X), \neg\texttt{send}(c,X)), T) \xrightarrow{rb} (\mathcal{V}, \mathcal{E}, (S, \neg\texttt{spec}(Y)), T[p \mapsto (T, T')])}$$

**Fig. 8.** Message Rollback

These variables are the derivatives in the operational semantics. They represent incomplete data values, about which speculative assertions may be made about the structure of the value.

The store (multiset of proposition atoms) $S$ is generalized to contain these speculative assertions:

$$S ::= \{\} \mid S_1, S_2 \mid \texttt{send}(c, X) \mid (Y = \texttt{receive}(c)) \mid$$
$$X = v \mid X = Y.l \mid X = Y(v) \mid X \to Y$$

The derivative process semantics are provided in Fig. 5. Once again the **send** operation places a **send** atom in the store. The value being transmitted is equated with a new variable $X$ that identifies the send event at the sending process. The variable $X$ is introduced to track dependencies between events in the traces. Now the **receive** operation does not block, but rather places a **receive** atom in the store. Again, for dependency tracking, a new variable $Y$ is introduced to denote the value that is received. $Y$ is the derivative. The **sendout** operation also places a **send** atom in the store; however it

$$(\mathcal{V}, \mathcal{E}, (S, \neg\texttt{spec}(X)), \; T[p \mapsto (T, \texttt{spec}(X), T', \texttt{fork}(p'))]) \xrightarrow{\text{rb}}$$
$$(\mathcal{V}, \mathcal{E}, (S, \neg\texttt{spec}(X), \neg\texttt{fork}(p')), \; T[p \mapsto (T, \texttt{spec}(X), T')])$$

$$(\mathcal{V}, \mathcal{E}, (S, \neg\texttt{spec}(X)), \; T[p \mapsto (T, \texttt{spec}(X), T', \texttt{chan}_\tau(c))]) \xrightarrow{\text{rb}}$$
$$(\mathcal{V}, \mathcal{E}, (S, \neg\texttt{spec}(X)), \; T[p \mapsto (T, \texttt{spec}(X), T')])$$

$$(\mathcal{V}, \mathcal{E}, (S, \neg\texttt{spec}(X)), \; T[p \mapsto (T, \texttt{spec}(X), T', \texttt{send}(c, Y))]) \xrightarrow{\text{rb}}$$
$$(\mathcal{V}, \mathcal{E}, (S, \neg\texttt{spec}(X), \neg\texttt{send}(c, Y)), \; T[p \mapsto (T, \texttt{spec}(X), T')])$$

$$(\mathcal{V}, \mathcal{E}, (S, \neg\texttt{spec}(X)), \; T[p \mapsto (T, \texttt{spec}(X), T', \texttt{sendout}(c, Y))]) \xrightarrow{\text{rb}}$$
$$(\mathcal{V}, \mathcal{E}, (S, \neg\texttt{spec}(X)), \; T[p \mapsto (T, \texttt{spec}(X), T')])$$

$$(\mathcal{V}, \mathcal{E}, (S, \neg\texttt{spec}(X), Y = Z), \; T[p \mapsto (T, \texttt{spec}(X), T', Y = \texttt{receive}(c'))]) \xrightarrow{\text{rb}}$$
$$(\mathcal{V}, \mathcal{E}, (S, \neg\texttt{spec}(X), \texttt{send}(c', Z)), \; T[p \mapsto (T, \texttt{spec}(X), T')])$$

$$(\mathcal{V}, \mathcal{E}, (S, \neg\texttt{spec}(X)), \; T[p \mapsto (T, \texttt{spec}(X), T', \texttt{spec}(Y))]) \xrightarrow{\text{rb}}$$
$$(\mathcal{V}, \mathcal{E}, (S, \neg\texttt{spec}(X)), \; T[p \mapsto (T, \texttt{spec}(X), T')])$$

$$(\mathcal{V}, \mathcal{E}, (S, \neg\texttt{spec}(X)), \; T[p \mapsto (T, \texttt{spec}(X), T', \texttt{commit}(Y))]) \xrightarrow{\text{rb}}$$
$$(\mathcal{V}, \mathcal{E}, (S, \neg\texttt{spec}(X)), \; T[p \mapsto (T, \texttt{spec}(X), T')])$$

$$(\mathcal{V}, \mathcal{E}[p \mapsto A[\texttt{commit}(X, e, e')], (S, \neg\texttt{spec}(X)), \; T[p \mapsto (T, \texttt{spec}(X))]) \xrightarrow{\text{rb}}$$
$$(\mathcal{V}, \mathcal{E}[p \mapsto A[e], S, \; T[p \mapsto T])$$

**Fig. 9.** Speculative Execution Rollback

first checks that all speculative assumptions made so far in this process are commitable; intuitively, if this process did nothing else, it could commit its changes and complete.

Fig. 6 provides the rules for making speculative assertions about the shape of data values. These rules add *dependency arrows* $X \to Y$, denoting that $Y$ has been introduced to denote some subterm of the term denoted by $X$.

The semantics of the store are provided in Fig. 7. The first rule provides the rendezvous between a send event and a corresponding receive event on the same channel. This rendezvous is only allowed provided the send event does not depend causally on the receive event. The next three rules replace speculative assertions about derivatives with information provided by a communicated value. The third rule creates a new process to evaluate the function application that was previously executed speculatively because the function itself was not known. The next two rules provide transitivity. The final rule detects an inconsistency in the store due to contradictory assertions about the value of a variable. This inconsistency causes the generation of a *negative atom* (as explained below) that causes rollback to some point at which a derivative was introduced that led eventually to this inconsistency.

Causal dependency is defined as follows. First we need to define the notion of the bound variables in a trace:

$$BV(\varepsilon) = \{\}$$

$$(\mathcal{V}, \mathcal{E}, (S, \neg\texttt{fork}(p)), T[p \mapsto (T, \texttt{fork}(p'))]) \xrightarrow{rb}$$
$$(\mathcal{V}, \mathcal{E}, (S, \neg\texttt{fork}(p), \neg\texttt{fork}(p')), T[p \mapsto T])$$

$$(\mathcal{V}, \mathcal{E}, (S, \neg\texttt{fork}(p)), T[p \mapsto (T, \texttt{chan}_\tau(c))]) \xrightarrow{rb}$$
$$(\mathcal{V}, \mathcal{E}, (S, \neg\texttt{fork}(p)), T[p \mapsto T])$$

$$(\mathcal{V}, \mathcal{E}, (S, \neg\texttt{fork}(p)), T[p \mapsto (T, \texttt{send}(c, X))]) \xrightarrow{rb}$$
$$(\mathcal{V}, \mathcal{E}, (S, \neg\texttt{fork}(p), \neg\texttt{send}(c, X)), T[p \mapsto T])$$

$$(\mathcal{V}, \mathcal{E}, (S, \neg\texttt{fork}(p)), T[p \mapsto (T, \texttt{sendout}(c, X))]) \xrightarrow{rb}$$
$$(\mathcal{V}, \mathcal{E}, (S, \neg\texttt{fork}(p)), T[p \mapsto T])$$

$$(\mathcal{V}, \mathcal{E}, (S, \neg\texttt{fork}(p), Y = X), T[p \mapsto (T, Y = \texttt{receive}(c))]) \xrightarrow{rb}$$
$$(\mathcal{V}, \mathcal{E}, (S, \neg\texttt{fork}(p), \texttt{send}(c, X)), T[p \mapsto T])$$

$$(\mathcal{V}, \mathcal{E}, (S, \neg\texttt{fork}(p)), T[p \mapsto (T, \texttt{commit}(X))]) \xrightarrow{rb}$$
$$(\mathcal{V}, \mathcal{E}, (S, \neg\texttt{fork}(p)), T[p \mapsto T])$$

$$(\mathcal{V}, \mathcal{E}, (S, \neg\texttt{fork}(p)), T[p \mapsto (T, \texttt{spec}(X))]) \xrightarrow{rb}$$
$$(\mathcal{V}, \mathcal{E}, (S, \neg\texttt{fork}(p)), T[p \mapsto T])$$

$$(\mathcal{V}, \mathcal{E}, (S, \neg\texttt{fork}(p)), T[p \mapsto ()]) \xrightarrow{rb} (\mathcal{V}, \mathcal{E}[p \mapsto ()], S, T[p \mapsto ()])$$

**Fig. 10.** Process Rollback

$$BV(T_1, T_2) = BV(T_1) \cup BV(T_2)$$
$$BV(\texttt{fork}(p)) = \{p\}$$
$$BV(\texttt{chan}_\tau(c)) = \{c\}$$
$$BV(\texttt{send}(c, X)) = \{X\}$$
$$BV(\texttt{sendout}(c, X)) = \{X\}$$
$$BV(Y = \texttt{receive}(c)) = \{Y\}$$
$$BV(\texttt{spec}(X)) = \{X\}$$
$$BV(\texttt{commit}(X)) = \{\}$$

**Definition 1.** Given a configuration $(\mathcal{V}, \mathcal{E}, S, T)$. Given $\alpha, \beta \in \textit{TermVar} \cup \textit{TrapVar} \cup \textit{ProcVar} \cup \textit{ChanVar}$, $\alpha$ is *causally dependent* on $\beta$ if one of the following holds:

**(Reflexive)** $\alpha = \beta$; or
**(Transitive)** $\alpha$ depends on $\gamma$ and $\gamma$ depends on $\beta$, for some $\gamma$; or
**(Sequential)** $T(p) = (T, T')$ and $\beta \in BV(T), \alpha \in BV(T')$; or
**(Rendezvous)** $\alpha = Y$ and $\beta = X$, and $(Y = X) \in S$; or
**(Speculate)** $\alpha = Y$ and $\beta = X$, and $(X \rightarrow Y) \in S$; or
**(Fork)** $\beta = p$, $T(p) = (T, \texttt{fork}(p'), T')$ and $\alpha \in BV(T(p'))$.

We also use this to define committability.

**Definition 2.** Given $S$ and $T$, given that $T(p) = (T, \text{spec}(X), T')$, the derivative $X$ is *committable* if:

1. for all receive events $(Y = \text{receive}(c))$ in $T$, there is a corresponding rendezvous $(Y = X)$ in the store; and
2. for all derivatives $Y$ such that $X$ is causally dependent on $Y$, one of the following holds:
   (a) $Y$ is committed $(T(p) = (T, \text{commit}(Y), T')$ for some $p$); or
   (b) there is some $\text{spec}(Z)$ in $T$, such that $Z$ is not committed and $Z$ is causally dependent on $Y$.

We also need to define rollback in this semantics. For this we add *negative atoms* to the store:

$$ S ::= \ldots \mid \neg\text{spec}(X) \mid \neg\text{send}(c, X) \mid \neg\text{fork}(p) $$

Rollback is performed by the rules for message rollback (Fig. 8), speculative execution rollback (Fig. 9) and process rollback (Fig. 10). Rollback is denoted by the reduction relation $\xrightarrow{rb}$. This rollback process is controlled by the negative atom $\neg\text{spec}(X)$ that is added to the store. Rollback uses the trace associated with the process that introduced the derivative $X$, to undo communications with other processes since that speculative guess was made.

The rules in Fig. 9 describe the rollback of the trace for process $p$ to the point at which it introduced the derivative $X$ (this point is denoted in the logs by the atom $\text{spec}(X)$). If the trace contains a fork event, a negative fork atom is added to the store, to cause the undoing of any communication with the process that was forked. If the trace contains a send event, then a negative send atom is added to the store. This is akin to an "anti-message" that is intended to cancel the message that was originally sent. If the trace contains a receive event, then the send atom that was consumed by rendezvous is regenerated in the store. Finally if the rollback reaches the spec event in the trace that introduced the derivative, the process itself is restored to the state it was at before evaluation inside this breakpoint began.

The rules in Fig. 10 describe the rollback of the trace for process $p$ all the way to the beginning of that process' trace, because of a negative fork atom in the store. These rules are basically similar to rolling back a process to the point of introduction of a derivative.

Fig. 8 provides the semantics for undoing messages, following the addition of an anti-message to the store. The first rule corresponds to removing a message that has not yet been delivered. The second rule corresponds to undoing a receive event (because the message that was received was never sent). This latter step requires backing up the receiving process to receive event.

## 5 Related Work and Conclusions

Derivatives are a first step towards investigating language-based support for programming in wide-area networks. The issue we are focused on for now is reducing latency and (temporarily at least) surviving disconnected operation using optimistic computation. Derivatives are related to, and we claim subsume, other approaches to reducing latency using futures, promises and most recently QRPC [6, 11, 8]. Optimistic computation for concurrency control is well-known [15, 7]. More recently optimistic computation for disconnected operation has been used in distributed file systems and distributed database systems [15, 10, 5]. Optimistic computation has also been used in the programming languages community, to reduce latency in communication in parallel and distributed applications [1, 2].

Cowan [3] provides a programming environment for supporting optimistic computation in applications, motivated by the desire to reduce latency in communication. The framework is provided as an abstract data type, assumption identifiers, with a boolean operation that guesses that an assumption is correct, an operation for affirming an assumption, and an operation for denying an assumption. Denial of an assumption causes computation to be rolled back to the point at which the assumption was guessed to be true. An operational semantics is defined in terms of execution of the primitives on an abstract machine. Cowan's framework can be seen as more general and more low-level approach than that of derivatives. A significant difference is our requirement that the `receive` and `case` constructs block on completion until the tentative computation at the synchronization point is confirmed. Cowan deliberately does not make this restriction, with the consequence that rollback is difficult and non-portable. It is not yet clear what such a requirement costs us in terms of expressiveness.

Speculatively choosing a path to execute, then backtracking on failure to a choice point, is a familiar idea from concurrent logic and concurrent constraint programming. We deliberately make a connection with this approach by using a store in the operational semantics, that contains atomic propositions constraining global variables. On the other hand our work is couched in the realm of conventional Algol-like languages (optionally with first-class closures); and we use language constructs to limit the scope of speculative computation for performance. Concurrent constraint (CC) languages either provide no mechanism for recovering from an inconsistent state, or backtrack on an inconsistent state, or use or-parallelism to speculatively investigate all possible execution paths. Our approach is related to the second option, though limiting the context of speculative computation.

Futures combined with abortive constructs (such as exceptions or continuations) introduce speculative computation. Evaluation of a MultiScheme [12] expression (`future` `e`) forks a thread to evaluate $e$, while the continuation executes speculatively with a placeholder for the value of this evaluation. If the evaluation of $e$ raises an exception or throws a continuation that causes control to escape the context of the `future` expression, then the speculative execution of the continuation must be undone. The correctness of futures is based on the original sequential execution of the program, therefore correctness of the combination of futures and continuations is based on isolating nonspeculative execution from the effects of speculative execution [9, 13].

We differ from this work in two respects. First, we want to consider making effects visible as soon as possible. This is the whole motivation for using optimistic computation to overcome latency problems in wide-area networks. We then need to use rollback of process state when a speculative execution is found to be unwarranted. Note that effects are "made visible" with messages that are transmitted to other processes; subsequent retraction of these messages may cause these other processes to roll back some of their executions.

Second, for portability and efficiency reasons, we want to be able to support optimistic computation on a stock run-time, in particular without using upward continuations to capture process state. Therefore we introduce constructs for delimiting the scope of optimistic computation, that allow a process' sequential execution to be backed up using standard exception-handling facilities. This approach appears more realistic than the use of continuations in a distributed environment. For example, MultiScheme relies on a garbage collector to reclaim process resources (when it is determined that a process can no longer be restarted).

Optimistic computation has been used in concurrency control for database systems, and on-line transaction processing includes notions of transaction rollback for failure recovery or for optimistic concurrency control. It is not clear if any of this database technology can be applied to our framework. There is no intrinsic notion of transactions or database update in our semantics, only notions of message-passing between concurrently executing processes. For example we do not require notions of serializability for correctness. Transactions are designed for short-lived sequences of update operations on shared databases, whereas derivatives are designed for long-lived (or even perpetual) processes executing in parallel. Database notions of correctness are wholly unsuited to this framework. Finally, part of the motivation for derivatives is to track application dependencies in the programming language; trying to shoehorn derivatives into transactions undermines this motivation. More recent extended transaction models such as sagas are more closely related to derivatives, and the connection between these deserves further investigation. However it should be noted that these extended transaction models still are based on the notion of a finite sequence of operations that must be completed wholly or not-at-all; they differ from traditional transaction models in that they allow the effects of uncommitted updates to be viewed, with visible undo operations performed if the updates must be undone. Furthermore rollback happens because of process failure or invalid optimistic assumptions about the concurrent execution of update operations. Although there are superficial analogies to be drawn between derivatives and extended transactions, it should be clear that the two are somewhat different. At this point it is not clear if an implementation of derivatives could leverage run-time support for extended transactions.

There are various safety properties of the semantics that can be verified. Distributed algorithms for rollback, and for determining commitability, are a necessary step for an implementation. A lower-level semantics, related to the semantics described here, may be a useful step in providing an implementation.

# Bibliography

[1] David F. Bacon and Robert E. Strom. Optimistic parallelization of communicating sequential processes. In *Symposium on Principles and Practice of Parallel Programming*, 1991.

[2] R. Bubenik and W. Zwaenepoel. Semantics of optimistic computation. In *International Conference on Distributed Computing Systems*, pages 20–27, 1990.

[3] Crispin Cowan and Hanan Lutfiyya. Formal semantics for expressing optimism. In *Proceedings of ACM Symposium on Principles of Distributed Computing*, 1995.

[4] Alessandro Giacalone, Prateek Mishra, and Sanjiva Prasad. Facile: A symmetric integration of concurrent and functional programming. *International Journal of Parallel Programming*, 18(2):121–160, 1989.

[5] J. Gray, P. Helland, P. O'Neil, and D. Shasha. The dangers of replication and a solution. In *Proceedings of the 1996 SIGMOD Conference*, 1996.

[6] Robert Halstead. Multilisp: A language for concurrent symbolic computation. *ACM Transactions on Programming Languages and Systems*, 7(4):501–538, 1985.

[7] David Jefferson. Virtual time. *ACM Transactions on Programming Languages and Systems*, 7(3):404–420, 1985.

[8] A. Joseph, A. F. deLespinasse, J. A. Tauber, D. K. Gifford, and F. Kaashoek. Rover: A toolkit for mobile information access. In *Symposium on Operating Systems Principles*, 1995.

[9] Morry Katz and Daniel Weise. Continuing into the future: On the interaction of futures and first-class continuations. In *Proceedings of ACM Symposium on Lisp and Functional Programming*, pages 176–184. ACM Press, 1990.

[10] J. J. Kistler and M. Satyanarayanan. Disconnected operation in the Coda file system. *ACM Transactions on Computer Systems*, 10:3–25, 1992.

[11] B. Liskov and L. Shrira. Promises: Linguistic support for efficient asynchronous procedure calls in distributed systems. In *Proceedings of ACM SIGPLAN Conference on Programming Language Design and Implementation*, 1988.

[12] James S. Miller. *MultiScheme: A Parallel Processing System Based on MIT Scheme*. PhD thesis, MIT, 1987.

[13] Luc Moreau. The semantics of Scheme with future. In *Proceedings of ACM International Conference on Functional Programming*, pages 146–156. ACM Press, 1996.

[14] Hanne Riis Nielson and Flemming Nielson. Higher-order concurrent programs with finite communication topology. In *Proceedings of ACM Symposium on Principles of Programming Languages*, pages 84–97. ACM Press, 1994.

[15] R. E. Strom and S. Yemini. Optimistic recovery in distributed systems. *ACM Transactions on Computer Systems*, 3(3):204–226, 1985.

# Network Programming Using PLAN

Michael Hicks, Pankaj Kakkar, Jonathan T. Moore,
Carl A. Gunter, and Scott Nettles *

Department of Computer and Information Science
University of Pennsylvania
200 South 33rd Street
Philadelphia, PA 19104-6389
{mwh,pankaj,jonm,gunter,nettles}@dsl.cis.upenn.edu

**Abstract.** We present here a methodology for programming active networks in the environment defined by our new language PLAN (Packet Language for Active Networks). This environment presumes a two-level architecture consisting of:

1. *active packets* carrying PLAN code; and
2. downloadable, node-resident *services* written in more general-purpose languages.

We present several examples which illustrate how these two features can be combined to implement various network functions.

## 1 Introduction

The Internet consists of separate networks of host computers that are interconnected by routers to form a homogeneous internetwork. General-purpose computation is done on hosts, possibly involving communication with other hosts in the internetwork, while routers are specialized to the task of moving packets between the networks. To do this, routers 'store and forward' packets to their 'next hop,' guided by information in the packet header, such as the destination address. An *active* network is one in which the routers go beyond this basic model and allow themselves to be programmed either by the packets passing through them or via some 'off-line' method. Such a network could have significant advantages if basic issues of security and performance are solved and a convenient programming model enables the creation of new or improved network services. Such services might be stored on the routers themselves, in the packets, or partly in the packet and partly on the router, and invoked when the packet is processed by the router. This enables entirely new ways of thinking about routing (for instance, a packet may not require an explicit destination address because its *evaluation* will determine its routing) and network protocols, which

---

* This work was supported by DARPA under Contract #N66001-96-C-852 and by the National Science Foundation CAREER Grant #CCR-9702107, with additional support from the Hewlett-Packard and Intel Corporations and the University of Pennsylvania Research Foundation.

can be supported by programming routers within the network on a per-user, per-connection, or per-packet basis.

We have developed a new Packet Language for Active Networks (PLAN) [12] whose programs are intended to be carried in packets and executed on routers (or hosts) through which the packets pass. PLAN is a simple scripting language that seeks to perform a number of functions in the active network:

1. Network management and configuration: customization of the use of network services by system administrators and applications.
2. Distributed communications: information exchange among applications and network elements.
3. Diagnostics: analysis of network status or behavior.

The natural question here is: why a new language? In short, PLAN was designed to fit within an architecture that makes solving the problems of security and performance more tractable. For instance, to protect the network while still making it available to all users, all PLAN programs must, by nature, terminate, and may not access information private to the router or other programs. PLAN was also designed so that its programs would be small enough to fit within network packets. No existing general purpose language meets these criteria while presenting a fundamentally distributed computational model. A more detailed analysis of this issue may be found in [12].

Because PLAN programs are limited in nature, they form only one part of our architecture. Additional functionality is available via calls to node-resident *services*, which may be written in general-purpose languages, such as Caml [6] or Java [8]. Some services may be available only to certain users and therefore may require authentication and authorization of the packets requesting their use. To provide full extensibility, service routines can be dynamically loaded into routers.

Together, PLAN packets and general-purpose services form a two-level active network architecture. Using this architecture, we have recently built an active internetwork called *PLANet* [14] in which all packets in the network contain PLAN programs. This paper illustrates how to program the network by giving examples of packet level and service level programs. We also illustrate an interesting active application which takes advantage of network programmability. We conclude by discussing future challenges and some related work.

## 2 Packet-Level Programming

PLAN programs are limited first in the amount of computation they can do on a router, and second in the number of routers on which the program can cause computation to occur. The programs are carried in packets and their evaluation may produce other packets, but this proliferation is controlled by the resource bound of the original packet, which must share its resource counter with its progeny. A PLAN program which only calls 'safe' services will evaluate on a given router in a predictable number of steps and then terminate without affecting the state of the router. PLAN packets do not communicate with one another directly at the PLAN level, although they can do so indirectly through application programs at endpoints or through service calls on routers, if such calls are permitted.

## Ping

PLAN 3.1, our current version and implementation, is a small script-like functional programming language with a syntax similar to Standard ML whose basic programming model is a form of remote evaluation. How this is used is perhaps best illustrated with a small sample program that performs an active ping.

```
fun ping (source:host, destination:host) : unit =
  if thisHostIs(destination) then
    OnRemote(|ack|(), source, getRB(), defaultRoute)
  else
    OnRemote(|ping|(source, destination), destination,
             getRB(), defaultRoute)
```

where ack is a simple acknowledgment function. The program is invoked with a destination to be pinged and a source to receive the acknowledgment. Remote evaluation occurs with the invocation of the OnRemote primitive. The result of an evaluating OnRemote is that a new packet is created which evaluates some code on a remote node. This primitive takes four arguments:

1. The name of the function to be evaluated remotely and the arguments to give it (evaluated locally). This construct is termed a *chunk*, and may be manipulated as data by PLAN programs. Chunk literals resemble regular function applications except that the function name is surrounded by |'s, indicating that the evaluation of the function itself is delayed.
2. The name of the site where the evaluation is to occur.
3. The amount of resource bound to give to the remote evaluation (we will explain this later).
4. A routing function name.

If we invoke ping with a specific source and destination on a machine that is not the destination, the call will evaluate

```
OnRemote (|ping|(source, destination), destination,
          getRB(), defaultRoute)
```

This means that ping(source, destination) should be invoked on destination. When this is done, the program will then evaluate:

```
OnRemote (|ack|(), source, getRB(), defaultRoute)
```

which indicates that the acknowledgment function should be invoked on source. The defaultRoute argument determines how the ping and acknowledgment packets reach their destinations; it names a function used to determine the 'next hop' on each intermediate node on the way to the destination. Note that defaultRoute, getRB, and thisHostIs are all node-resident service functions expected to be present on each node in the network.

PLAN programs are guaranteed to terminate locally because of the limited nature of the language. PLAN does not allow (direct) recursive function calls[1], and there are no general looping constructs with which to encode infinite loops. Of course, it is assumed that the service functions available to non-authenticated PLAN programs will also respect the termination property.

PLAN programs by nature will terminate globally as well. This is because each time a new computation is initiated with OnRemote, some amount of resource bound from the current computation must be provided to the new one. The current computation's resource bound can be obtained via the call getRB(). Once the resource bound of a packet reaches zero, no further hops or evaluations may take place. There is no function in PLAN for increasing the resource bound, and it is decreased on arrival to each router, so the computation is guaranteed to complete and will not migrate around the network forever. To see this in a stark example, consider the following program:

```
fun ping_pong(pingHost:host, pongHost:host) : unit =
    OnRemote (|ping_pong|(pongHost, pingHost),
              pongHost, getRB(), defaultRoute)
```

This program will globally terminate after hopping between pingHost and pongHost for long enough to exhaust the resource bound.

### Traceroute

The ping program is comparatively simple as network operations go and does not illustrate active networks especially well because its evaluation is on the endpoints of the ping. A more interesting function is traceroute, which is implemented in IP as a series of messages with increasing Time To Live (TTL) values. Each time the TTL value is exhausted (presumably one hop further away than the preceding message), an ICMP [16] packet is sent back to the source indicating the point of exhaustion. This algorithm has the characteristic that if the destination is unreachable due to a failure in the network, all of the nodes up to that point will be reported. Figure 1 is a PLAN analog, where ack prints the hop count and host reached.

The OnNeighbor primitive evaluates its first argument on the indicated dest, where that destination must be on the same physical network as the sender (i.e. it is one hop away). Therefore, the routing function argument is replaced by the name of the link layer device which accesses the shared network.

This implementation of traceroute is better than the way it must be implemented for the IP network: it will always provide information about a consistent route. The use of expiring TTLs to trace routers can provide information about

---

[1] In particular, a 'recursive' call like the call to ping within the body of its definition will result in a reduction in the resource bound by OnRemote.

```
fun traceroute (source:host, dest:host, count:int) : unit =

(* First send response back to source that we got this far *)
(OnRemote(|ack|(count,thisHost()), source, count, defaultRoute);

  (* If we're at the end, we're done *)
  if thisHostIs(dest) then ()

  (* Otherwise, proceed to the next hop *)
  else
    let val next:host*dev = defaultRoute(dest) in
      OnNeighbor (|traceroute|(source, dest, count+1),
                  fst next, getRB(), snd next)
    end
```

**Fig. 1.** Tracing a route in PLAN.

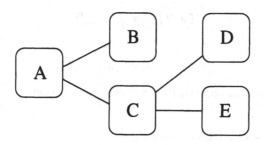

**Fig. 2.** A sample network topology

routers along more than one path between the source and destination if the routing topology changes mid-way.

## Multicast

So far, our examples have been of diagnostic functions, but PLAN is also able to express more general network computations, such as multicast. The idea behind multicast is to trade off computation for bandwidth, so it is in keeping with the goals of an active network. Consider the topology depicted in Figure 2. If a program at node $A$ were to send packets individually to nodes $B$, $C$, $D$ and $E$, a total of 6 transmissions would occur: $A \to B$, $A \to C$, $A \to C \to D$, and $A \to C \to E$. A multicast packet takes advantage of common prefixes among destination nodes, resulting in only 4 transmissions: $A \to B$, $A \to C$, $C \to D$, and $C \to E$. However, the reduction in messages is compensated for by additional computation as the multicast tree must be computed by the routers.

Figure 3 illustrates a PLAN program which multicasts a computation to a list of destinations. The way the program works is as follows. Each time `multicast` evaluates, the local function `find_hops` is called for each node in the destination list `addrs` by the primitive `foldl` (explained below). The result is a pair containing the list of next hops in the multicast tree and a list of the remaining destinations. `multicast` is then invoked remotely on each hop parameterized by the new list of destinations. Note that `find_hops` also evaluates the designated task when the function is evaluating at a destination. This is done via a call to `eval` on the *chunk* task. Recall that a chunk is an encapsulation for a function name and a list of values, and is supplied as the first argument to `OnRemote` or `OnNeighbor`. `eval` simply resolves the name present in the chunk with the current environment and then evaluates it, subtracting 1 from the resource bound, as with `OnRemote`.

`foldl` is based on the well-known functional programming construct `fold`. Since PLAN does not (currently) support language-level parametric polymorphism or higher-order functions[2] the list iterators are provided as language primitives, rather than as proper functions. The meaning of

$$\mathrm{foldl}(f, a, [b_1; \ldots; b_n])$$

is

$$f(f \ldots f(f(a, b_1), b_2) \ldots, b_n)$$

where $f$ is the name of either a PLAN or service function.

## 3   Service-Level Programming

In each of our example programs to this point, the majority of the functionality is expressed within the PLAN program. The calls to services have been relatively simple: determining the local host address with `thisHostIs`, querying the remaining resource bound with `getRB`, etc. However, it is inconvenient or impossible to do most network programming entirely at the packet level. More generally, we envision the packet language as a 'glue' language for calls to programs at the service level. An interesting question to network programmers using the PLAN system is how to partition the functionality of their protocol between the services and the packets. This is best explained by illustration, using a networking protocol that we implemented for address resolution in PLANet.

To support universal addressing, internetworks impose a uniform virtual addressing scheme on top of the varying addressing schemes provided by the underlying link layers. Sending data requires a link-layer address, and so internetworks need a mechanism to resolve network addresses into link layer ones. The process of obtaining such an address is called *address resolution*.

The Address Resolution Protocol (ARP [15]) works as follows. The sender, which has network address $n$ and link layer address $l$, knows the network address

---

[2] Some services, such as `print`, do support these features.

```
fun multicast(addrs:host list,task:chunk): unit =
  let

    (* This function has two purposes:
        - if this node is a destination, perform the task and remove
          the address from the destination list
        - calculate a list of next hops to take which form the tree *)
    fun find_hops(res:(host * dev) list * host list,dest:host):
      (host * dev) list * host list =
      let val hops: (host * dev) list = fst res
          val dests: host list = snd res in
        if thisHostIs(dest) then
          (eval(task); (hops,remove(dest,dests)))
        else
          let val hop_info:host*dev = defaultRoute(dest) in
            if member(hop_info,hops) then (hops,dests)
            else (hop_info::hops,dests)
          end
      end

    (* This function is called by fold for each hop to be taken.
       It sends the multicast packet to each hop *)
    fun send_packs(params:int*host list,hop:host*dev): int*host =
      (OnNeighbor(|multicast|(snd params,task),
                  fst hop,fst params,snd hop);
       params)

    (* The list of hops and pruned destinations *)
    val hops_dests:(host*dev) list * host list =
      foldl(find_hops,([],addrs),addrs)

    val hops: (host*dev) list = fst hops_dests
    val dests: host list = snd hops_dests
    val num_hops: int = length(hops) in

      (* If we haven't reached the end of the road, send out more
         packets, else quit *)
      if num_hops > 0 then
        foldl(send_packs,(getRB()/length(hops),dests),hops)
      else
        ()
  end
```

**Fig. 3.** Packet-directed multicast PLAN.

$m$ of some node on its local area network and desires to acquire the link layer address $k$ of $m$. It therefore *broadcasts* onto its LAN a packet which asks the question "$(n,l)$ is asking who out there has network address $m$?" The node with address $m$ responds with its link layer address $k$, which $n$ stores in its ARP table for future use. In addition, $m$ stores the binding $l$ for $n$ as contained in the packet. Beyond this basic exchange there is one additional bit of policy: every node other than $m$ which receives the broadcast request packet checks its own ARP table for the binding of the $n$ (the requester). If such a binding exists, then it is updated by the binding $l$ contained in the packet.

Clearly, some elements of this protocol cannot be expressed by PLAN alone. In particular, each node must store and retrieve network address to link layer address bindings from a table. The fact that this table is long-lived and must be accessible from PLAN programs prevents it from being itself expressed as a PLAN program.

A very basic implementation of this protocol would have $n$ broadcast the following PLAN program:[3]

```
fun ask(l:blob,n:host,m:host): unit =
  doARP(l,n,m)
```

In this implementation, all of the functionality of ARP is contained within the service call doARP: the check to see if the packet arrived at $m$, the sending of a response packet (itself a similar looking PLAN program), the storing of the binding for $n$, etc. In this implementation, PLAN packets are essentially being used as a vehicle for distributed communication. In fact, this function for PLAN programs is part of the advantage of the PLAN system—there is no need for special-purpose packet formats since the packet format is defined *implicitly* by the standard wire format of PLAN programs. In general, new network functionality may be provided entirely by the introduction of new service functions that are called from PLAN packets passing through the active routers. This is essentially the approach of ANTS [21].

Of course, implementing a protocol in this way does not take advantage of the programmability of PLAN packets. In particular, much of the policy of ARP can be encoded within PLAN rather than within a service. This allows the protocol implementor to present a more granular, flexible service interface which can then be used by PLAN programs implementing different policies. For example, we might imagine that some versions of ARP would not perform the binding of the requester on a node other than the destination.

As mentioned above, the only thing that really needs to be encoded as a service is the table itself. In our ARP implementation we provide the services:

$$bind : blob * host \rightarrow unit$$
$$retrieveBinding : host \rightarrow blob$$

---

[3] Note that since there is no specific type for link layer addresses, they are represented by the PLAN type blob which represents arbitrary data.

where `bind` adds a binding to the ARP table (raising the exception `BindFailed` if the table is full), and `retrieveBinding` looks up a binding (raising the exception `NoBinding` if the lookup fails). Given these services, the ARP packet is written as follows:

```
fun ask(l:blob,n:host,m:host): unit =
  try
    if thisHostIs(m) then
      (try
          bind(l,n)
        handle BindFailed => ();
        OnNeighbor(|bind|(retrieveBinding(m),m), n,
                   getRB(),getSrcDev()))
    else
      let val pa:blob = retrieveBinding(n) in
        bind(l,n)
      end
  handle NoBinding => ()
```

When broadcast by the requester, this function is invoked on each host on the local network. The program first checks to see if it is evaluating on $m$. If so, the program should report a binding back to the requester. This is done by retrieving the link layer address $k$ with `retrieveBinding` and remotely invoking `bind` on the requester $n$ via `OnNeighbor`.[4] If the program evaluates on a node other than $m$ (the `else` case), then it checks the ARP table for an entry for $n$. If a binding is present, it is replaced by the one in the packet; if no binding is present (as indicated by an exception being thrown) then no action is taken.

ARP is a simple example, but it illustrates well how functionality may be partitioned between PLAN and the services. Here, the reason for adding more functionality to the PLAN part is the enhanced overall flexibility. The drawback is that with added flexibility comes potentially increased risk. The solution here is to either mitigate the risk by requiring calls to services to be authorized (as is done in some versions of current Internet routing protocols), or by limiting their interface. Another drawback is the overhead of carrying the policy code in the packet. This is isn't a problem for ARP, but could be for packet flows in which the code is essentially constant and only the bindings change.

## 4  Active Applications

Thus far we have seen examples of network functionality which are all provided in some form by the current Internet. However, the PLAN programming language environment provides us with more flexibility than does IP; this section presents an example of a performance improvement made possible by this extra

---

[4] The service routine `getSrcDev` returns the link layer device through which the evaluating packet was received.

programmability. In particular, we will show how an application can adapt to network congestion by using active packets to route data packets intelligently.

Consider the network topology shown in Figure 4, and suppose we have an application trying to send data from a source $S$ to a destination $D$. Usual shortest-hop-count routing metrics, such as the one employed by RIP [10], would send traffic along the route $S \rightarrow R_1 \rightarrow R_2 \rightarrow D$. Now suppose, however, that the hosts $X$ and $Y$ begin communicating at a high rate, thus saturating the link $R_1 \rightarrow R_2$; the bandwidth from $S$ to $D$ will be severely reduced.

Notice, though, that there is another path $S \rightarrow R_3 \rightarrow R_4 \rightarrow R_5 \rightarrow D$ which is unused. Unfortunately, RIP-like protocols will not see this extra route, even though there may be more than enough spare bandwidth to satisfy the application running at $S$ and $D$. If the application could detect this alternate route and use it, however, the improvement to bandwidth would be well worthwhile.

PLAN's flexibility permits the application to make this adjustment by using a routing scheme called *flow-based adaptive routing*. The application periodically sends out "scout packets" which explore the network searching for good paths. These scout packets perform a distributed graph computation to find the best currently available route, and then adjust state at the routers to reflect the discovered route, thus establishing a *flow*. The application then simply needs to send regular transport packets along the flow, with scout packets periodically sprinkled in to keep the flow up-to-date.

Figure 5 shows the full PLAN code for a sample scout packet, but we will only highlight some of the key portions here. In this example, the scout packet and its descendents will perform a depth-first fanout to find the least congested path, which we roughly quantify as a combination of the length of the intermediate routers' input queues and their distance in hops from the source:[5]

```
fun computeMetric(lastMetric : int):int =
    lastMetric + (10 * getQueueLength()) + 1
```

The main workhorse of the algorithm is the dfs function. At each node, an incoming packet computes its metric to the current node with a call to computeMetric. It then atomically compares its metric with the best metric found so far to the current node by accessing some soft state that other packets may have left behind:

```
setLT("metric",session,newMetric,15)
```

(the 15 here indicates the number of seconds which should elapse before the soft state is reclaimed by the node). If the provided metric is less than the old one then the check succeeds and the old value is replaced with the new one; if the check fails, some other packet has been at the node previously with a better route, so the current packet terminates. On success, the depth-first search continues, with the current packet spawning calls to dfs on all the neighboring nodes by using the foldl construct:

---

[5] Note that the constant 10 here is somewhat arbitrarily tuned to be effective in our experiments.

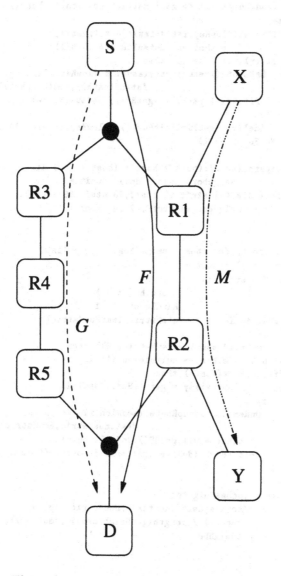

**Fig. 4.** A network topology with alternate paths

```
fun computeMetric(lastMetric : int):int =
  lastMetric + (10 * getQueueLength()) + 1

fun setupRoute(session:key, flowKey:key, path:(host * int) list,
               last:host, lastMet:int, finalMet:int) : unit =
   if (not(thisHostIs(fst(hd(path))))) then ()
   else
     try
        if (snd(hd(path)) <> get("metric",session)) then ()
        else
          (flowSet(flowKey,fst(defaultRoute(last)),
                  lastMet,snd(defaultRoute(last)));
            if (tl(path) <> []) then
              OnRemote(|setupRoute|(session,flowKey,tl(path),
                                   fst(hd(path)),snd(hd(path)),finalMet),
                fst(hd(tl(path))), getRB(), defaultRoute)
            else
              (deliver(getImplicitPort(),(flowKey,finalMet))))
        handle NotFound => ()

fun processNeighbor(stuff:(host * host * (host * int) list * int * key),
                    neighbor: host * dev) : unit =
   (OnNeighbor(|dfs|(#1 stuff,#2 stuff,#3 stuff,#5 stuff),
               #1 neighbor,#4 stuff,#2 neighbor);
     stuff)

fun dfs(source:host, dest:host, path:(host * int) list,
        session:key) : unit =
  let val lastHopMetric:int = try
                                snd(hd(path))
                              handle Hd => ~1
      val newMetric:int = computeMetric(lastHopMetric)
  in
    if (setLT("metric",session,newMetric,15)) then
      let val hostname:host = hd(thisHost()) in
        if (thisHostIs(dest)) then
          let val flowKey:key = genKeyHost(dest) in
            try
              OnRemote(|setupRoute|(session,flowKey,path,
                                   dest,newMetric,newMetric),
                fst(hd(path)),getRB(),defaultRoute)
            handle Hd => (deliver(getImplicitPort(),(flowKey,newMetric)))
          end
        else
          foldl(processNeighbor,
                ((source,dest,(hostname,newMetric)::path,
                  getRB() / length(getNeighbors()),session)),
                getNeighbors())
      end
    else ()
  end
```

**Fig. 5.** PLAN code for a scout packet

```
foldl(processNeighbor,
        ((source, dest, (hostname,newMetric)::path,
          getRB() / length(getNeighbors()), session)),
        getNeighbors())
```

where `processNeighbor` creates a packet with `OnNeighbor` to do a recursive call to `dfs` on a single neighboring node. Note that the resource bound of the current packet, retrieved with the call to `getRB`, is divided equally among the child packets.

Finally, we reach the case where a packet arrives at the destination with the best metric. In this case, the packet is responsible for establishing the flow for the later transport packets to follow. This is done by creating a globally unique key and then calling `setupRoute` to work backwards. At each node on the way back, the packet adjusts the routing table:

```
flowSet(flowKey, dest, lastMet, nextHop)
```

Thus, given a transport packet with a flow identifier `flowKey` and destination `dest`, the router will forward the packet on to `nextHop`, after decrementing its resource bound. The final step of the protocol occurs when the setup packet reaches the source: it reports the new `flowKey` to the controlling application via the `deliver` construct. The application may then begin sending transport packets with the new flow identifier.

Using this approach in our experimental testbed we achieved two favorable ends. First, the bandwidth between $S$ and $D$ was raised to the application's desired level. Second, the overall utilization of the network increased: where originally path $G$ was idle and paths $F$ and $M$ were congested, we transitioned to $G$ and $M$ both being utilized at the desired levels. Details are presented in [14].

This approach provides a "free market" style to quality of service in a best-effort network. Of course, there is nothing to prevent vendors from writing router software which implements this particular adaptation. However, note that it is easy to change the metric which determines the best route: one can simply redefine the `computeMetric` function in an appropriate way. Different metrics do not require new router software, so long as the nodes present appropriate diagnostic information through services such as `getQueueLength`, and even these can be straightforwardly added by downloading new service implementations. Furthermore, applications may set metrics which are *individually* appropriate, rather than having the infrastructure impose a "one size fits all" routing topology. As the Internet evolves and more and more different types of applications come into use, this style of flexibility will be invaluable.

## 5   Related Work

There are a number of active network projects, each of which provides its own programming model:

- The *Active Bridge* [5] is part of the SwitchWare Project [19] at the University of Pennsylvania, and provides a study of the kinds of services that PLAN is meant to provide glue for. It is an extensible software bridge where OCaml [6] services can be added to provide new functionality, including dynamic service cutover between different network topology standards. Work on the Active Bridge evolved into ALIEN [1]. In ALIEN, packets can be programmed in a general-purpose programming language (Caml). This requires more heavy-weight security (based on SANE [4]) on a per-packet basis than PLAN, as reported in [2].
- *Sprocket* is a language from the Smart Packets project at BBN [17]. It uses a byte-code language and is similar to PLAN in sharing a design goal to provide flexible network diagnostics. It differs from PLAN in that it targets a fixed set of service routines, and is designed with maximum compactness in mind.
- *ANTS* [21] is a toolkit for deploying Java protocols on active nodes. Packets carry hash values that refer to a service. Services are demand loaded if they are not present on the node. This model provides much less flexibility at the packet programming level than PLAN.
- *PLAN-P* [20] is a modification of PLAN to support programming services rather than packets. The PLAN-P work focuses on studying the use of optimization techniques based on partial evaluation to provide fast implementations of these service routines.
- *JRes* [7] is a system that concerns itself with resource bounding in Java. While it is not aimed at active networking directly, it is likely that some of its resource bounding techniques will be applicable in this domain.

There are a variety of projects related to networks, distributed computing, and operating systems that are related to PLAN's philosophy of active networks. Other related projects include Liquid Software [9] and Netscript [22]. The reader is referred to the SwitchWare architecture paper [3] for more details.

## 6    From the Internet to PLANet

PLAN was developed to replace the inflexible network-layer of the current Internet. However, there is something to be said for the real problem of upgrading an inactive network to an active one. A hybrid approach is feasible: PLAN programs can be used to customize the operations of a traditional network. This is suggested by our example in Section 4; active programs are used to discover and establish custom routes that may be traversed by inactive packets. A generalization of this idea is that of a Active Router Controller [18] in which active nodes are used to administer the control-plane (i.e., for routing, configuration, etc.) while switches are used for packet-forwarding. As fast-path operations can be made more efficient in an active context, more functionality may be made fully programmable.

There are still many areas in our current architecture that require more study. These roughly fall into the categories of security, scalability, and performance.

*Security.* While it is true that all PLAN programs terminate both locally and globally, such a guarantee may not be enough. In particular, one can write PLAN programs that execute in time and space exponential in their size. With some loss of *a priori* reasoning, we can strengthen this bound to be linear, using some straightforward alterations to the language, including one presented in [12]. We are currently researching the effects of such alterations and whether they are, in fact, enough, or whether further restriction is necessary. Additional security mechanisms for PLANet are considered in [11] and [13].

*Scalability.* So far, we have only experimented with small topologies, thus far avoiding problems of scalability. One area of needed improvement is in the lack of organization of service namespaces. Currently, all services exist in a flat namespace with the effect that newly installed services shadow older ones with the same name. While this is a useful property, since changes in technology or circumstance might necessitate upgrades of the service library, namespace organization is essential to make this process less *ad hoc*. Namespaces may also be used as a source of security, as described in [13]. Abstractions like Java packages or ML modules present possible solutions to this problem. It should also be noted that while the services suffer from this problem, PLAN programs themselves do not, as they are self-contained and may not interfere with each other.

*Performance.* Our performance experiments, as reported in [14], are promising: running in user-mode with an implementation written in byte-code-interpreted OCaml, we are able to switch active packets at around 5000 packets per second, up to a rate of 48 Mbps. This constitutes just over half of the useful bandwidth of our 100 Mbps Ethernet. However, as reported in that paper, there is much room for improvement. In particular, our scheduling strategy, wire representation, and evaluation strategy drastically affect performance. On the other hand, we have found that by designing PLAN to be authentication-free we can prevent costly cryptographic operations [2]. Furthermore, by including support for routing in the language (through the use of routing functions, like `defaultRoute`), we can avoid costly evaluations on every hop. Together, these optimizations represent up to a four-fold increase in performance.

*For More Information.* We invite readers to browse the PLAN home page:

`http://www.cis.upenn.edu/~switchware/PLAN`

The site provides downloadable software for both Java 1.1 and OCaml, detailed documentation, and a number of technical papers covering the issues presented here in greater length.

# References

1. D. S. Alexander. *ALIEN: A Generalized Computing Model of Active Networks.* PhD thesis, University of Pennsylvania, September 1998.

2. D. S. Alexander, Kostas G. Anagnostakis, W. A. Arbaugh an d A. D. Keromytis, and J. M. Smith. The Price of Safety in an Active Network. Technical Report MS-CIS-99-02, University of Pennsylvania, January 1999.
3. D. Scott Alexander, William A. Arbaugh, Michael Hicks, Pankaj Kakkar, Angelos Keromytis, Jonathan T. Moore, Carl A. Gunter, Scott M. Nettles, and Jonathan M. Smith. The SwitchWare Active Network Architecture. *IEEE Network Magazine*, 12(3):29–36, 1998. Special issue on Active and Controllable Networks.
4. D. Scott Alexander, William A. Arbaugh, Angelos D. Keromytis, and Jonathan M. Smith. A Secure Active Network Architecture: Realization in SwitchWare. *IEEE Network Special Issue on Active and Controllable Networks*, 12(3):37–45, May/June 1998.
5. D. Scott Alexander, Marianne Shaw, Scott M. Nettles, and Jonathan M. Smith. Active Bridging. In *Proceedings, 1997 SIGCOMM Conference*. ACM, 1997.
6. Caml home page. http://pauillac.inria.fr/caml/index-eng.html.
7. Grzegorz Czajkowski and Thorsten von Eicken. JRes: A Resource Accounting Interface for Java. In *Proceedings of 1998 ACM OOPSLA Conference*, 1998.
8. James Gosling, Bill Joy, and Guy Steele. *The Java Language Specification*. Addison Wesley, 1996.
9. John Hartman, Udi Manber, Larry Peterson, and Todd Proebsting. Liquid Software: A New Paradigm for Networked Systems. Technical report, Department of Computer Science, University of Arizona, June 1996. http://www.cs.arizona.edu/ liquid.
10. C. Hedrick. Routing Information Protocol. RFC 1058, June 1988.
11. Michael Hicks. PLAN System Security. Technical Report MS-CIS-98-25, Department of Computer and Information Science, University of Pennsylvania, April 1998.
12. Michael Hicks, Pankaj Kakkar, Jonathan T. Moore, Carl A. Gunter, and Scott Nettles. PLAN: A Packet Language for Active Networks. In *Proceedings of the Third ACM SIGPLAN International Conference on Functional Programming Languages*, pages 86–93. ACM, 1998. Available at http://www.cis.upenn.edu/ ~switchware/ papers/ plan.ps.
13. Michael Hicks and Angelos D. Keromytis. A Secure PLAN. In *International Workshop on Active Networks*, 1999. Submitted; available at http://www.cis.upenn.edu/ ~switchware/ papers/ secureplan.ps.
14. Michael Hicks, Jonathan T. Moore, D. Scott Alexander, Carl A. Gunter, and Scott Nettles. PLANet: An Active Internetwork. In *Proceedings of the Eighteenth IEEE Computer and Communication Society INFOCOM Conference*. IEEE, 1999. To appear; Available at http://www.cis.upenn.edu/ ~switchware/ papers/ plan.ps.
15. David C. Plummer. An Ethernet Address Resolution Protocol. Technical report, IETF RFC 826, 1982.
16. J. Postel. Internet Control Message Protocol. Technical report, IETF RFC 792, September 1981.
17. B. Schwartz, A. Jackson, T. Strayer, W. Zhou, R. Rockwell, and C. Partridge. Smart Packets for Active Networks. In *IEEE OPENARCH*, New York, New York, March 1999.
18. J. M. Smith, D. S. Alexander, W. S. Marcus, M. Segal, and W. D. Sincoskie. Towards an Active Internet. Available at http://www.cis.upenn.edu/~switchware/ papers/arc.ps, July 1998.
19. SwitchWare project home page. http://www.cis.upenn.edu/ ~switchware.
20. Scott Thibault, Charles Consel, and Gilles Muller. Safe and Efficient Active Network Programming. In *17th IEEE Symposium on Reliable Distributed Systems*, 1998.

21. David J. Wetherall, John Guttag, and David L. Tennenhouse. ANTS: A Toolkit for Building and Dynamically Deploying Network Protocols. In *IEEE OPENARCH*, April 1998.

22. Y. Yemini and S. da Silva. Towards Programmable Networks. In *IFIP/IEEE International Workshop on Distributed Systems: Operations and Management*, L'Aquila, Italy, October 1996.

# Lecture Notes in Computer Science

For information about Vols. 1–1640
please contact your bookseller or Springer-Verlag

Vol. 1641: D. Hutter, W. Stephan, P. Traverso, M. Ullmann (Eds.), Applied Formal Methods – FM-Trends 98. Proceedings, 1998. XI, 377 pages. 1999.

Vol. 1642: D.J. Hand, J.N. Kok, M.R. Berthold (Eds.), Advances in Intelligent Data Analysis. Proceedings, 1999. XII, 538 pages. 1999.

Vol. 1643: J. Nešetřil (Ed.), Algorithms – ESA '99. Proceedings, 1999. XII, 552 pages. 1999.

Vol. 1644: J. Wiedermann, P. van Emde Boas, M. Nielsen (Eds.), Automata, Languages, and Programming. Proceedings, 1999. XIV, 720 pages. 1999.

Vol. 1645: M. Crochemore, M. Paterson (Eds.), Combinatorial Pattern Matching. Proceedings, 1999. VIII, 295 pages. 1999.

Vol. 1647: F.J. Garijo, M. Boman (Eds.), Multi-Agent System Engineering. Proceedings, 1999. X, 233 pages. 1999. (Subseries LNAI).

Vol. 1648: M. Franklin (Ed.), Financial Cryptography. Proceedings, 1999. VIII, 269 pages. 1999.

Vol. 1649: R.Y. Pinter, S. Tsur (Eds.), Next Generation Information Technologies and Systems. Proceedings, 1999. IX, 327 pages. 1999.

Vol. 1650: K.-D. Althoff, R. Bergmann, L.K. Branting (Eds.), Case-Based Reasoning Research and Development. Proceedings, 1999. XII, 598 pages. 1999. (Subseries LNAI).

Vol. 1651: R.H. Güting, D. Papadias, F. Lochovsky (Eds.), Advances in Spatial Databases. Proceedings, 1999. XI, 371 pages. 1999.

Vol. 1652: M. Klusch, O.M. Shehory, G. Weiss (Eds.), Cooperative Information Agents III. Proceedings, 1999. XI, 404 pages. 1999. (Subseries LNAI).

Vol. 1653: S. Covaci (Ed.), Active Networks. Proceedings, 1999. XIII, 346 pages. 1999.

Vol. 1654: E.R. Hancock, M. Pelillo (Eds.), Energy Minimization Methods in Computer Vision and Pattern Recognition. Proceedings, 1999. IX, 331 pages. 1999.

Vol. 1655: S.-W. Lee, Y. Nakano (Eds.), Document Analysis Systems: Theory and Practice. Proceedings, 1998. XI, 377 pages. 1999.

Vol. 1656: S. Chatterjee, J.F. Prins, L. Carter, J. Ferrante, Z. Li, D. Sehr, P.-C. Yew (Eds.), Languages and Compilers for Parallel Computing. Proceedings, 1998. XI, 384 pages. 1999.

Vol. 1657: T. Altenkirch, W. Naraschewski, B. Reus (Eds.), Types for Proofs and Programs. Proceedings, 1998. VIII, 207 pages. 1999.

Vol. 1659: D.G. Feitelson, L. Rudolph (Eds.), Job Scheduling Strategies for Parallel Processing. Proceedings, 1999. VII, 237 pages. 1999.

Vol. 1660: J.-M. Champarnaud, D. Maurel, D. Ziadi (Eds.), Automata Implementation. Proceedings, 1998. X, 245 pages. 1999.

Vol. 1661: C. Freksa, D.M. Mark (Eds.), Spatial Information Theory. Proceedings, 1999. XIII, 477 pages. 1999.

Vol. 1662: V. Malyshkin (Ed.), Parallel Computing Technologies. Proceedings, 1999. XIX, 510 pages. 1999.

Vol. 1663: F. Dehne, A. Gupta. J.-R. Sack, R. Tamassia (Eds.), Algorithms and Data Structures. Proceedings, 1999. IX, 366 pages. 1999.

Vol. 1664: J.C.M. Baeten, S. Mauw (Eds.), CONCUR'99. Concurrency Theory. Proceedings, 1999. XI, 573 pages. 1999.

Vol. 1666: M. Wiener (Ed.), Advances in Cryptology – CRYPTO '99. Proceedings, 1999. XII, 639 pages. 1999.

Vol. 1667: J. Hlavička, E. Maehle, A. Pataricza (Eds.), Dependable Computing – EDCC-3. Proceedings, 1999. XVIII, 455 pages. 1999.

Vol. 1668: J.S. Vitter, C.D. Zaroliagis (Eds.), Algorithm Engineering. Proceedings, 1999. VIII, 361 pages. 1999.

Vol. 1669: X.-S. Gao, D. Wang, L. Yang (Eds.), Automated Deduction in Geometry. Proceedings, 1998. VII, 287 pages. 1999. (Subseries LNAI).

Vol. 1670: N.A. Streitz, J. Siegel, V. Hartkopf, S. Konomi (Eds.), Cooperative Buildings. Proceedings, 1999. X, 229 pages. 1999.

Vol. 1671: D. Hochbaum, K. Jansen, J.D.P. Rolim, A. Sinclair (Eds.), Randomization, Approximation, and Combinatorial Optimization. Proceedings, 1999. IX, 289 pages. 1999.

Vol. 1672: M. Kutylowski, L. Pacholski, T. Wierzbicki (Eds.), Mathematical Foundations of Computer Science 1999. Proceedings, 1999. XII, 455 pages. 1999.

Vol. 1673: P. Lysaght, J. Irvine, R. Hartenstein (Eds.), Field Programmable Logic and Applications. Proceedings, 1999. XI, 541 pages. 1999.

Vol. 1674: D. Floreano, J.-D. Nicoud, F. Mondada (Eds.), Advances in Artificial Life. Proceedings, 1999. XVI, 737 pages. 1999. (Subseries LNAI).

Vol. 1675: J. Estublier (Ed.), System Configuration Management. Proceedings, 1999. VIII, 255 pages. 1999.

Vol. 1976: M. Mohania, A M. Tjoa (Eds.), Data Warehousing and Knowledge Discovery. Proceedings, 1999. XII, 400 pages. 1999.

Vol. 1677: T. Bench-Capon, G. Soda, A M. Tjoa (Eds.), Database and Expert Systems Applications. Proceedings, 1999. XVIII, 1105 pages. 1999.

Vol. 1678: M.H. Böhlen, C.S. Jensen, M.O. Scholl (Eds.), Spatio-Temporal Database Management. Proceedings, 1999. X, 243 pages. 1999.

Vol. 1679: C. Taylor, A. Colchester (Eds.), Medical Image Computing and Computer-Assisted Intervention – MICCAI'99. Proceedings, 1999. XXI, 1240 pages. 1999.

Vol. 1680: D. Dams, R. Gerth, S. Leue, M. Massink (Eds.), Theoretical and Practical Aspects of SPIN Model Checking. Proceedings, 1999. X, 277 pages. 1999.

Vol. 1682: M. Nielsen, P. Johansen, O.F. Olsen, J. Weickert (Eds.), Scale-Space Theories in Computer Vision. Proceedings, 1999. XII, 532 pages. 1999.

Vol. 1683: J. Flum, M. Rodríguez-Artalejo (Eds.), Computer Science Logic. Proceedings, 1999. XI, 580 pages. 1999.

Vol. 1684: G. Ciobanu, G. Păun (Eds.), Fundamentals of Computation Theory. Proceedings, 1999. XI, 570 pages. 1999.

Vol. 1685: P. Amestoy, P. Berger, M. Daydé, I. Duff, V. Frayssé, L. Giraud, D. Ruiz (Eds.), Euro-Par'99. Parallel Processing. Proceedings, 1999. XXXII, 1503 pages. 1999.

Vol. 1686: H.E. Bal, B. Belkhouche, L. Cardelli (Eds.), Internet Programming Languages. Proceedings, 1998. IX, 143 pages. 1999.

Vol. 1687: O. Nierstrasz, M. Lemoine (Eds.), Software Engineering – ESEC/FSE '99. Proceedings, 1999. XII, 529 pages. 1999.

Vol. 1688: P. Bouquet, L. Serafini, P. Brézillon, M. Benerecetti, F. Castellani (Eds.), Modeling and Using Context. Proceedings, 1999. XII, 528 pages. 1999. (Subseries LNAI).

Vol. 1689: F. Solina, A. Leonardis (Eds.), Computer Analysis of Images and Patterns. Proceedings, 1999. XIV, 650 pages. 1999.

Vol. 1690: Y. Bertot, G. Dowek, A. Hirschowitz, C. Paulin, L. Théry (Eds.), Theorem Proving in Higher Order Logics. Proceedings, 1999. VIII, 359 pages. 1999.

Vol. 1691: J. Eder, I. Rozman, T. Welzer (Eds.), Advances in Databases and Information Systems. Proceedings, 1999. XIII, 383 pages. 1999.

Vol. 1692: V. Matoušek, P. Mautner, J. Ocelíková, P. Sojka (Eds.), Text, Speech and Dialogue. Proceedings, 1999. XI, 396 pages. 1999. (Subseries LNAI).

Vol. 1693: P. Jayanti (Ed.), Distributed Computing. Proceedings, 1999. X, 357 pages. 1999.

Vol. 1694: A. Cortesi, G. Filé (Eds.), Static Analysis. Proceedings, 1999. VIII, 357 pages. 1999.

Vol. 1695: P. Barahona, J.J. Alferes (Eds.), Progress in Artificial Intelligence. Proceedings, 1999. XI, 385 pages. 1999. (Subseries LNAI).

Vol. 1696: S. Abiteboul, A.-M. Vercoustre (Eds.), Research and Advanced Technology for Digital Libraries. Proceedings, 1999. XII, 497 pages. 1999.

Vol. 1697: J. Dongarra, E. Luque, T. Margalef (Eds.), Recent Advances in Parallel Virtual Machine and Message Passing Interface. Proceedings, 1999. XVII, 551 pages. 1999.

Vol. 1698: M. Felici, K. Kanoun, A. Pasquini (Eds.), Computer Safety, Reliability and Security. Proceedings, 1999. XVIII, 482 pages. 1999.

Vol. 1699: S. Albayrak (Ed.), Intelligent Agents for Telecommunication Applications. Proceedings, 1999. IX, 191 pages. 1999. (Subseries LNAI).

Vol. 1700: R. Stadler, B. Stiller (Eds.), Active Technologies for Network and Service Management. Proceedings, 1999. XII, 299 pages. 1999.

Vol. 1701: W. Burgard, T. Christaller, A.B. Cremers (Eds.), KI-99: Advances in Artificial Intelligence. Proceedings, 1999. XI, 311 pages. 1999. (Subseries LNAI).

Vol. 1702: G. Nadathur (Ed.), Principles and Practice of Declarative Programming. Proceedings, 1999. X, 434 pages. 1999.

Vol. 1703: L. Pierre, T. Kropf (Eds.), Correct Hardware Design and Verification Methods. Proceedings, 1999. XI, 366 pages. 1999.

Vol. 1704: Jan M. Żytkow, J. Rauch (Eds.), Principles of Data Mining and Knowledge Discovery. Proceedings, 1999. XIV, 593 pages. 1999. (Subseries LNAI).

Vol. 1705: H. Ganzinger, D. McAllester, A. Voronkov (Eds.), Logic for Programming and Automated Reasoning. Proceedings, 1999. XII, 397 pages. 1999. (Subseries LNAI).

Vol. 1707: H.-W. Gellersen (Ed.), Handheld and Ubiquitous Computing. Proceedings, 1999. XII, 390 pages. 1999.

Vol. 1708: J.M. Wing, J. Woodcock, J. Davies (Eds.), FM'99 – Formal Methods. Proceedings Vol. I, 1999. XVIII, 937 pages. 1999.

Vol. 1709: J.M. Wing, J. Woodcock, J. Davies (Eds.), FM'99 – Formal Methods. Proceedings Vol. II, 1999. XVIII, 937 pages. 1999.

Vol. 1710: E.-R. Olderog, B. Steffen (Eds.), Correct System Design. XIV, 417 pages. 1999.

Vol. 1711: N. Zhong, A. Skowron, S. Ohsuga (Eds.), New Directions in Rough Sets, Data Mining, and Granular-Soft Computing. Proceedings, 1999. XIV, 558 pages. 1999. (Subseries LNAI).

Vol. 1712: H. Boley, A Tight, Practical Integration of Relations and Functions. XI, 169 pages. 1999. (Subseries LNAI).

Vol. 1713: J. Jaffar (Ed.), Principles and Practice of Constraint Programming – CP'99. Proceedings, 1999. XII, 493 pages. 1999.

Vol. 1714: M.T. Pazienza (Eds.), Information Extraction. IX, 165 pages. 1999. (Subseries LNAI).

Vol. 1715: P. Perner, M. Petrou (Eds.), Machine Learning and Data Mining in Pattern Recognition. Proceedings, 1999. VIII, 217 pages. 1999. (Subseries LNAI).

Vol. 1716: K.Y. Lam, E. Okamoto, C. Xing (Eds.), Advances in Cryptology – ASIACRYPT'99. Proceedings, 1999. XI, 414 pages. 1999.

Vol. 1717: Ç. K. Koç, C. Paar (Eds.), Cryptographic Hardware and Embedded Systems. Proceedings, 1999. XI, 353 pages. 1999.

Vol. 1718: M. Diaz, P. Owezarski, P. Sénac (Eds.), Interactive Distributed Multimedia Systems and Telecommunication Services. Proceedings, 1999. XI, 386 pages. 1999.

Vol. 1727: P.P. Chen, D.W. Embley, J. Kouloumdjian, S.W. Liddle, J.F. Roddick (Eds.), Advances in Conceptual Modeling. Proceedings, 1999. XI, 389 pages. 1999.

Vol. 1728: J. Akoka, M. Bouzeghoub, I. Comyn-Wattiau, E. Métais (Eds.), Conceptual Modeling – ER '99. Proceedings, 1999. XV, 539 pages. 1999.